About Island Press

Island Press is the only nonprofit organization in the United States whose principal purpose is the publication of books on environmental issues and natural resource management. We provide solutions-oriented information to professionals, public officials, business and community leaders, and concerned citizens who are shaping responses to environmental problems.

In 2001, Island Press celebrates its seventeenth anniversary as the leading provider of timely and practical books that take a multidisciplinary approach to critical environmental concerns. Our growing list of titles reflects our commitment to bringing the best of an expanding body of literature to the environmental community throughout North America and the world.

Support for Island Press is provided by The Bullitt Foundation, The Mary Flagler Cary Charitable Trust, The Nathan Cummings Foundation, Geraldine R. Dodge Foundation, Doris Duke Charitable Foundation, The Charles Engelhard Foundation, The Ford Foundation, The George Gund Foundation, The Vira I. Heinz Endowment, The William and Flora Hewlett Foundation, W. Alton Jones Foundation, The John D. and Catherine T. MacArthur Foundation, The Andrew W. Mellon Foundation, The Charles Stewart Mott Foundation, The Curtis and Edith Munson Foundation, National Fish and Wildlife Foundation, The New-Land Foundation, Oak Foundation, The Overbrook Foundation, The David and Lucile Packard Foundation, The Pew Charitable Trusts, Rockefeller Brothers Fund, The Winslow Foundation, and other generous donors.

PERVERSE
SUBSIDIES

PERVERSE SUBSIDIES

How Tax Dollars Can Undercut the Environment and the Economy

*Norman Myers
and Jennifer Kent*

This book is published in cooperation with the
International Institute for Sustainable Development.

ISLAND PRESS
Washington • Covelo • London

Perverse Subsidies was originally published in 1997 by the International Institute for Sustainable Development, Winnipeg, Manitoba, Canada.

Library of Congress Cataloging-in-Publication Data

Myers, Norman.
  Perverse subsidies : how tax dollars can undercut the environment and the economy / Norman Myers and Jennifer Kent.
    p.   cm.
Includes bibliographical references and index.
  ISBN 1-55963-834-6 (cloth : alk. paper) — ISBN 1-55963-835-4 (pbk. : alk. paper)
  1. Subsidies—United States. 2. Environmental degradation—United States. I. Kent, Jennifer. II. Title.
  HC110.S9 M94 2001
  338.973'02—dc21
                                                    00-012384

British Library Cataloguing in Publication Data available.

Printed on recycled, acid-free paper ✺

Manufactured in the United States of America
10 9 8 7 6 5 4 3 2 1

Contents

PART II. Sectoral Analyses

PART III. Policy

List of Tables, Figures, and Boxes

Tables

Figures

Boxes

Preface

Our initial report on perverse subsidies was published in mid-1998 by the International Institute for Sustainable Development in Winnipeg, Manitoba, Canada. The timing was favorable. In May of that year, the annual G8 meeting, a gathering of presidents and prime ministers from the eight biggest economies in the world, was to meet in Birmingham, England. What a splendid opportunity, we thought: our text would show those heavyweights how they could do more to boost their economies through phasing out perverse subsidies than through any other single measure. They could cancel their budget deficits at a stroke, they could offer huge tax cuts, they could reorient their fiscal priorities by supplying large increases to front-rank sectors such as education and health, and they could do lots of other things, with enough left over to throw nationwide parties. At the same time, they could go far to reduce the grand-scale degradation of their environments and repairing past damage. We duly ensured that copies of the report were put into the hands of leading advisers of each president and prime minister.

Alas for our hopes. Not a single word from on high was breathed with regard to perverse subsidies. Nor has there been any mention of perverse subsidies in other topflight gatherings of political leaders, except at the World Bank. There is a long way to go before these subsidies take their rightful place in the center of the radar screens of those who shape our future.

Because of the issue's importance and the lack of attention given to it, I decided to revise the original report and present a more detailed assessment of the problem. Hence this book, the preparation of which was kindly supported by Island Press and its senior editor, Todd Baldwin, together with the International Institute for Sustainable Development and Stephan Barg. As a result of fine-grain analysis, our calculation of the subsidies total was bumped up from $1.9 trillion to $2.5 trillion per year. I am convinced that were the issue to be given an even more in-depth treatment, the total would turn out to be larger still. An assessment of the United States by Paul Hawken[1] found that one-third of the country's economy serves no worthwhile human purpose, and much of the waste is fostered by those (expletive deleted) subsidies. Worldwide, Hawken believes, the waste could amount to $10 trillion.

Fortunately, there has been a scattering of initial efforts to cut perverse subsidies in countries west, east, north, and south. These efforts are a start: nothing more, and also nothing less. "Nothing more": it is a curious circumstance that greater attention, or much attention at all, is not directed at such a prominent phenomenon of our daily lives. Of course, there should always be room for constructive subsidies: they help our world to go around better. But many other subsidies are "perverse" in that they are damaging to our environments and economies alike. The perverse ones total around $2 trillion, within a global economy of $35 trillion; hence, they are highly distortional and damaging. Were they to be phased out, huge sums would be released to pursue the Holy Grail of sustainable development. The 1992 Rio Earth Summit offered a budget for sustainable development, with a total of $600 billion per year—which was dismissed by governments as quite unavailable. Yet perverse subsidies, which by definition are superb supports of *un*sustainable development, could supply funds three times larger than the Rio proposal. This surely presents an insurmountable opportunity.

Key question: why has the issue not attracted more attention from professional analysts, policy makers, political leaders, and the general public? Still more to the point, why has it remained a black hole for research? Primarily, I think, because it is such a murky subject. Data are hard to track down or are simply not available, which is understandable when most governments do not keep even minimal track of subsidies overall. Then there is the age-old problem of what constitutes a subsidy, let alone a perverse subsidy.

As a result, this was the most complex and challenging of all the fifteen "big-picture" research projects I have undertaken during the past quarter century. The issues are manifold, the sectors are wide ranging, and the information base is extraordinarily deficient. So I was far more dependent than usual on support from a host of friends and colleagues around the world. Many sent or directed me to papers and reports; over 2,000 have been collated in all—a total so large that we cannot thank all these helpful individuals by name here. Certain others supplied analytic insights, and anyone who has tackled an intractable research issue such as this one will understand that "idea people" contribute much more than they are often aware. In the front rank of these are Stephan Barg, Jane Corbett, André de Moor, Peter Gleick, Arthur J. Hanson, Rick Heede, Douglas Koplow, Todd Litman, Jim MacNeill, Mara Myers, David Pimentel, Sandra Postel, David Roodman, and Ronald Steenblik.

In particular, I want to express hefty thanks to those people who took great amounts of time to read chapters and send back detailed critiques: Dennis Anderson, Bill Barclay, Stephan Barg, Chris Barr, John Browder, Tom Burke, Peter Dauvergne, Tom Downing, Malin Falkenmark, Chris Flavin, Fred Gale, Robert Gale, Peter Gleick, the late David Hall, Arthur J. Hanson, Rick Heede, William Hyde, David Kaimowitz, Douglas Koplow, Ann Platt McGinn, Randal O'Toole, David Pimentel, Sandra Postel, Andrew Rajkumar, David Roodman, Carl Safina, Douglas Southgate, Ronald Steenblik, Michael Strauss, Michael Sutton, Michael Weber, and Peter Weber.

Of course, the original research project would not have got to the starting line if it were not for the generous financial support of The John D. and Catherine T. MacArthur Foundation in Chicago. Special thanks go to Dan Martin, director of the Program on Global Security and Sustainability. I much appreciated Dan's believing in my seemingly way-out idea in the first place.

Thanks also to Arthur J. Hanson, former president, and Stephan Barg, senior program advisor, of the International Institute for Sustainable Development in Winnipeg, who agreed to publish my original report in 1998. They have continued to highlight perverse subsidies by setting up a World Wide Web site with regular listings of subsidies news from around the world. The 1998 report subsequently caught the eye of Todd Baldwin, senior editor of Island Press in Washington, D.C. He suggested that I engage in a full-bore revision of the earlier report with a view to commercial publication, and the result is what you, the reader, now hold in your hands. I warmly welcomed Todd's enthusiasm for the beefing-up exercise and his steady support while I and my research associate sweated away with mountains of statistics and analyses. The result is a much more comprehensive assessment. The book now includes forests as a sixth sector, and it features many more fine-grain evaluations of what's what. It is not a "Son of *Perverse Subsidies*"; it is more like a "Father and Mother Account of *Perverse Subsidies*." As the reader will note at numerous points in the book, this latest estimate of perverse subsidies—$2 trillion per year—is surely more of an underestimate of the real-world situation than was the first-time assessment.

I also want to recognize the support of my literary agent, Virginia Barber of New York. As with most of my sixteen books, she handled the contract negotiations with her customary acumen, and she remained enthusiastic about the venture at those times when I felt underwhelming interest in giving it another whirl. Hefty thanks to you, Ginger: you contribute more than you know.

Finally and foremost, I conducted the project from start to finish with the super-est support of my research associate, Jennifer Kent. Self-trained, she has become far more of a statistical guru than I am. At the same time, she has researched, chased down references, dug out endless streams of nitty-gritty detail, re-rechecked a hundred this's and a thousand that's, and spent huge amounts of time clarifying the entire manuscript (often working at it until nearer dawn than dusk). This was a monumental task for her, and she did it monumentally well. I can best express my thanks to Jennie by saying that it long since became plain that her name belongs on the title page as coauthor—and in certain respects, her name should come first.

To reiterate the central point: perverse subsidies remain little known. Precisely because we are generally unaware of them, they are free to work away cancer-like in our body politic. This book not only sees them as problems but also views them as opportunities—surely insurmountable opportunities. Governments of the world: go for it!

NORMAN MYERS

Part I

BACKGROUND

Chapter 1

INTRODUCTION: WHAT ARE SUBSIDIES?

Subsidies: the term sounds like the ultimate bore. But subsidies are a prime feature of our economic landscape. That much is well understood; we can live with the idea. But who has heard of—or who cares about—"perverse" subsidies? What have they ever done for us, or, rather, against us? Well, they affect us at every turn of our daily lives, and their harmful effect detracts from the pleasure and fulfillment we gain from every one of those daily lives. We can consider them to be subsidies that exert adverse effects on our economies and our environments alike. Hardly any other factor has such a downside influence on us.

Here we go, then, with a book that aims to document the problem of perverse subsidies in six main sectors: agriculture, fossil fuels and nuclear energy, road transportation, water, fisheries, and forestry. Total subsidies (perverse or not) in these sectors and a few others have long been thought to be around $2 trillion worldwide per year,[1] but they have remained almost entirely undocumented. This means that subsidies play a prime role in the functioning of the global economy. Suppose too that perverse subsidies amount to a sizeable proportion of subsidies overall. Then they exert a significantly distortional effect on the global economy.

As was argued a decade and a half ago in the Brundtland Report,[2] many subsidies are detrimental to the environment. Subsidies for agriculture can foster overloading of croplands, leading to erosion and compaction of topsoil, pollution from synthetic fertilizers and pesticides, denitrification of soils, and release of greenhouse gases, among other adverse effects. Subsidies for fossil fuels aggravate pollution effects such as acid rain, urban smog, and global warming, while subsidies for nuclear energy generate exceptionally toxic waste with an exceptionally long half-life. Subsidies for road transportation lead to overloading of road networks, a problem that is aggravated as much as relieved by the building of new roads when further subsidies promote overuse of cars; the sector also generates severe pollution of several sorts. Subsidies for water encourage misuse and overuse of water supplies that are increasingly scarce in many lands. Subsidies for fisheries foster overharvesting of already depleted fish stocks. Subsidies for forestry encourage overexploitation at a time when many forests have been reduced by excessive logging, acid rain, and agricultural encroachment. Hence, the environmental consequences of perverse subsidies can be widespread and profound.

This is not to say that subsidies per se cannot serve many positive purposes. They can overcome deficiencies of the marketplace. They can promote environmentally friendly technologies. They can support disadvantaged segments of society. Subsidies can do many other fine things. The key question is, Which subsidies, of what sorts, of what scope, and with what impacts, can be viewed as perverse, that is, adverse to society's overall and long-term interests? What is their total scale worldwide? Clearly, this is a question of major import, yet it has scarcely been identified as a salient issue of our times, let alone documented and analyzed.[3] This book aims to establish the significance of perverse subsidies worldwide and to examine the nature and scale of the problem.[4]

Plainly, we cannot determine what perverse subsidies are without an intellectual lock on what constitutes a subsidy at all. This is a complex issue; hence, it warrants an extended examination here. There are many sorts and conditions of subsidies, and they come in all shapes and sizes. Not surprisingly, they have become a prime instrument of public policy. How, and in what sectors, do they arise? What do they cost? Whom do they benefit? Does anybody "disbenefit"? What is their influence on the economy at both macro and micro levels? Are there better ways to achieve their purposes?

Definition

A subsidy is a form of government support extended to an economic sector (or institution, business, or individual), generally with the aim of promoting an activity that the government considers beneficial to the economy overall and to society at large. Indeed, this is one of the main roles that governments are created to perform: to encourage activities that, if left solely to markets, would occur in unfavorable— or, to use the economists' phrase, less than socially optimal— amounts. A subsidy can be supplied in the form of a monetary payment or other transfer or through relief of an opportunity cost.[5]

There are other definitions, a trifle more technical. For instance, a subsidy amounts to any government expenditure that makes a resource such as energy or water cheaper to produce than its full economic cost, or that makes a product, notably food or education, cheaper for consumers. Energy can be made to look cheaper than it really is if subsidies pay some of its cost. Many developing countries offer "lifeline rates" for electricity, that is, subsidized discounts on the first increment of electricity bought each month, thus constituting an implicit expenditure. These subsidies are directed at the poor, and the electricity is made cheaper on the grounds that all citizens, no matter how impoverished, should be able to enjoy a modicum of convenient energy. People who cannot be reached by electricity are often given a kerosene subsidy instead. In developing countries, most energy subsidies assist consumers, whereas in developed countries they usually support producers.

The subsidies just described are all direct subsidies (there can be indirect subsidies too). Consider road transportation in the United States, where direct subsidies for roads, related infrastructure, and so forth total around $150 billion. If the value of free employee parking—largely stimulated in the first place by the car culture, dependent in turn on direct subsidies for road transportation—is included, the figure rises to roughly $300 billion, while some economists would add the costs of traffic congestion, estimated to be at least $100 billion.

All six sectoral chapters in this book deal with natural resources. In this particular field, subsidies are so diverse that they can include the following: financing or below-market pricing of natural resources such as agricultural lands, fossil fuels, water, forests, and fisheries, plus associated infrastructure; commodity price programs; below-market supply of exploration rights for oil, coal, and natural gas, together with tax preferences for extraction of these resources; and a lengthy list of minor supports such as tax preferences for private-vehicle travel relative to other modes of transportation. Subsidies can also be taken to include unpaid costs, notably environmental costs, that have not been internalized through government policies; by their very nature, they rank as implicit subsidies.

In addition, government costs of environmental protection can be regarded as a subsidy, since these are costs that in a perfect market would be internal to market transactions. There are further subsidy-style incentives to support the environment. In the United States, these include deductibility or direct tax credits for enhanced energy measures (use of nonpolluting and renewable energy sources, energy efficiency, and conservation); agricultural set-aside programs; funding of forest replanting costs; tax incentives for preserving open spaces; and government sharing of costs for biodiversity protection.[6]

For a look at three main types of subsidies, see Box 1.1; for a fur-

---

Box 1.1. THREE MAIN TYPES OF SUBSIDY

First are subsidies that provide preferential treatment for a particular sector of society. Education, for example, is widely subsidized to ensure that children receive enough schooling to enable them to make the most of their lives and to contribute to society through their work. This means that education ranks as both a private and a public good: it benefits not only the individual but also society.[*]

Second are subsidies that encourage a certain activity or process that otherwise would not be undertaken at a sufficient level. Lead-free gasoline is subsidized in certain countries to encourage motorists to use it rather than leaded gasoline. Similarly, wind power, photovoltaics, and other new forms of energy deserve to be subsidized because they are renewable and do not pollute. Recycling schemes and equipment are often subsidized to encourage the reuse of waste.[†]

Third are subsidies that ensure the survival and stability of certain industries of strategic importance, such as defense and agriculture. In addition, both sunrise and sunset industries are frequently subsidized on the grounds that such industries would not otherwise survive.

[*] J. Keppler, *Public Goods, Infrastructure, Externalities, and Subsidies* (Paris: Organization for Economic Cooperation and Development, 1995).

[†] For a host of illustrations, see R. J. P. Gale and S. R. Barg, "The Greening of Budgets: The Choice of Governing Instrument," in R. J. P. Gale, S. R. Barg, and A. Gillis, eds., *Green Budget Reform: An International Casebook of Leading Practices* (London: Earthscan, 1995), 1–29.

Box 1.2. SUBSIDIES BROAD AND NARROW

Subsidies can be both broad and narrow. The conventional or text-book definition of subsidies covers the narrow sense. The broad sense applies when the cost of an activity is borne not entirely by the source of the activity but by some other agent who may not directly and unequivocally benefit from the activity. Scandinavia, for example, can be said to be subsidizing Britain's electricity generation by bearing the cost of the acid rain that falls on it as a result of British sulfur diox-ide emissions. This is a way of bringing externalities into the debate—and just as subsidies are a case of government intervention, external-ities are a case of what happens when governments do not intervene.[*]

Whereas narrow subsidies include only monetary transfers, broad subsidies include transfers both monetary and nonmonetary. Precisely because of their "broadness," broad subsidies are often difficult, if not impossible, to quantify. Nor is it always clear who or what is the origin of a broad subsidy. For instance, the cost of air pollution caused by automobile use is not easily attributable to any particular agent, since many parties are involved. In any case, motorists do not intend that the pollution-absorbing environment should subsidize their driving. By contrast, a narrow subsidy—for example, a payment to farmers—is easily attributable to governments, and its intent is clear.

[*] P. H. Templet, "Grazing the Commons: An Empirical Analysis of Externalities, Subsidies, and Sustainability," *Ecological Economics* 12 (1995): 141–159.

---

ther division into subsidies broad and narrow, see Box 1.2. See also Table 1.1.

Precisely because of their varied manifestations, it is not easy to compare subsidies, even though that is required for this book. Too often, we run into the problem of apples and oranges. An agricul-tural subsidy of one dollar in the United States is very different from a similar sum in India. For present purposes, however, it is consid-ered acceptable to view subsidies as essentially of one type, bearing in mind their highly differentiated nature. The goal here is not to determine that some perverse subsidies should be reduced or elimi-nated while others should be left alone. The aim is to rid ourselves of all perverse subsidies—not on the grounds that they are subsidies but on the grounds that they are perverse. So we should not be overly concerned with multiple manifestations of subsidies. Nor should we

Table 1.1. Types of Subsidy

A. ESTABLISHED CLASSIFICATION

Types of Subsidy	Examples
Direct transfers	Direct grants or payments to consumers or producers; provision of inputs at below-market prices
Changing market prices	Reducing market prices to consumers; increasing prices received by producers; import tariffs or barriers
Preferential tax policies	Tax credits, exemptions, deferrals, exclusions, and deductions
Reducing input costs	Preferential loans and loan or liability guarantees; indirect expenditures such as research and development
Reducing cost of complementary goods	Provision of infrastructure goods

Source: H. Putman and I. Bartlett. *Studying the Environmental Implications of Supports to the Energy Sector* (Paris: OECD, 1993).

B. RECENT CLASSIFICATION

Types of Subsidy	Examples

Transfers to producers	1. Market price support
	2. Payments to producers, e.g., deficiency payments
	3. Payments to factors of production based on:
	  a. Use of variable input, e.g., water at below-market prices, fuel rebates, etc.
	  b. Use of a service, e.g., extension services, state-provided pest control
	  c. On-site investment, e.g., capital grants, interest concessions
	  d. Constraints on factor use, e.g., the U.S. Conservation Reserve Program.
	4. Direct payments to producers, based on:
	  a. Past support, e.g., the U.S. Production Flexibility Contract (PFC) payments
	  b. Past income, e.g., income tax concessions, disaster payments
	  c. Established minimum income, i.e., welfare payments

Transfers to consumers, other transfers	General services, research and development, training and education, marketing and promotion, public stockholding

Sources: Organisation for Economic Co-operation and Development. *Agricultural Policies in OECD Countries: Monitoring and Evaluation* (Paris: OECD, 1997); R. Steenblik, "A Note on the Concept of 'Subsidy,'" *Energy Policy* 23 (1995): 483–484.

bother too much about pinning down their precise sizes and values, despite the apples-and-oranges dilemma. There is little need to calculate our precise speed if we are heading over the cliff.

Equity Concerns

Subsidy support for one activity causes countervailing effects for other activities. This is a built-in factor. A subsidy is like a cake of limited size: if one person enjoys a larger slice, other persons have to make do with smaller slices. If everybody receives a subsidy, nobody does. By their very nature, then, subsidies have a marked distributional effect. This means in turn that subsidies carry all manner of equity implications, as would occur in any situation in which a group receives financial assistance from the government. Similarly, subsidies can be supplied for social rather than economic reasons, for example, to relieve unemployment, to offset disease (notably black lung disease in miners), or to correct regional disparities, as in the notable cases of Canada and the European Union.

It is these equity concerns that make subsidies a politically contentious issue. Whom should governments try to assist through subsidies: the poor, the unemployed, the socially disadvantaged, rural residents, entrepreneurs in general and innovators in particular, both sunrise and sunset industries? The list can be long. Should the government target many or few? Future equity questions are equally important. Do we owe anything to our descendants in terms of securing their livelihoods, especially at the expense of our own?

Regrettably, experience shows that in virtually all societies, it is often the powerful who obtain subsidies by causing weaker groups to shoulder some of the costs of their activities: "To him that hath shall be given." In the case of U.S. agriculture, huge subsidies go to a few so-called farmers who are actually millionaire industrialists and rarely set foot on a farm. In Colombia, the largest 1 percent of farmers receive 50 percent of public credits, while the smallest 50 percent of farmers receive little more than 4 percent.[7] In Indonesia, kerosene subsidies are supposed to help the poorest people, yet nine-tenths go to richer people.[8] In an international context, each American farmer receives annual subsidies worth 100 times the income of a corn farmer in the Philippines,[9] while annual subsidies for a dairy cow in the United States exceed the per capita income of half the world's population.[10]

Despite their distortional effects, there is nothing necessarily bad about subsidies. Sometimes we need a bit of positive distortion. Subsidies make the postal system cost the same everywhere; otherwise a letter sent to the remote parts of Alaska would cost fifty times more than a letter sent within New York City. The same is true for water, electricity, gas, and telephone service, wherein urban communities subsidize rural ones. Without subsidies, we might never get as much as we want of, for example, nonpolluting and renewable sources of energy, with their manifold benefits—economic, environmental, political, security, social, and ethical benefits. True, these energy sources should be able to make their way in the open marketplace once they become established—but without help in their opening phase, they might never become established at all because of competition from entrenched energy sources. The same applies to recycling, dematerialization, agricultural set-asides, and a host of other subsidies beneficial to the environment.[11] In addition, certain subsidies should be established simply because they are a good thing. In Chapter 5, on road transportation, we shall see that this sector generates huge spillover costs such as traffic pollution, accidents and injuries, and even military supports. These adverse effects could be countered by subsidies for alternatives to private cars, notably buses and trains. It seems altogether justifiable from economic and social standpoints that there should be sizeable subsidies for, say, rapid transit systems in San Francisco and Washington, D.C., even though these two are among the higher-income cities in the United States.

Why Subsidies Are Often Unpopular

Despite their many positive features, subsidies often receive bad press. For one thing, they have grown to be enormously costly for governments. The government of India, for example, has been spending $40 billion per year on subsidies, a whopping 14 percent of the country's gross domestic product (GDP).[12] In the United States, direct subsidies for agriculture, water, forestry, fossil fuels/nuclear energy, and road transportation amount to $275 billion, or 16 percent of the federal budget. The European Union's Common Agricultural Policy costs the average citizen $380. If governments were to reduce their spending on subsidies, they would take a solid step toward better balancing of their budgets.

> *India has been spending $40 billion a year on subsidies—14 percent of the country's GDP.*

A second and still more significant problem with subsidies is that through their potential featherbedding effect, they encourage inefficiency and waste of all sorts. As concerns environmental resources in particular (farmlands, forests, water, fisheries, etc.), they foster misuse and overuse of the resources. They perpetuate the status quo in production processes by making it cheaper to continue with existing methods than to adopt costly new technologies. Irrigation subsidies encourage farmers in

> *In the United States, direct subsidies for agriculture, water, forestry, fossil fuels/nuclear energy, and road transportation amount to $275 billion—16 percent of the federal budget.*

developed and developing countries alike to persist with inefficient but cheap flooding methods rather than moving on to more expensive but more efficient trickle-drip techniques.

In short, certain subsidies can promote greater economic efficiency and productivity, as in the case of the New Deal's agricultural subsidies. Or they can foster social equity, as in the case of subsidized transportation for poorer sectors of society. But they can become overabundant, unnecessary, and distortional. In an extreme instance, water subsidies in Saudi Arabia (of all countries) are so high that farmers can afford to shower their cows to keep them cool.

For more on the pros and cons of subsidies, see Box 1.3.

Box 1.3. PROS AND CONS OF SUBSIDIES

There has been a great expansion in subsidies since the beginning of the twentieth century, stemming in part from the two world wars and the Great Depression. These events served to generate subsidies of many new sorts, sometimes with multibillion-dollar budgets and often with beneficial purposes. For instance, food subsidies in developing countries improve nutrition among the poor, ensure markets for farmers, and help foster socioeconomic equality across income groups. Trouble arises when subsidies are retained long after they have exceeded their useful life—by which time they may also have expanded far beyond what was originally envisaged. Regrettably, institutional inertia often prevents them from being reduced, let alone eliminated. In any case, ditching them is often perceived to be a vote-loser for governments. In fact, subsidies are often used to appease large and politically powerful groups whose support is of special value to the government. Farmers in many countries lobby for agricultural subsidies, and governments are reluctant to disenchant a group that wields exceptional political muscle.

(continues)

Box 1.3. CONTINUED

In the United States in particular, special-interest groups are adept at penetrating the political process and using their electoral influence to secure subsidies. In Washington, D.C., there are tens of thousands of lobbyists, plus lawyers for backup, swarming around Capitol Hill, several dozen for every member of the U.S. Congress. Between 1993 and mid-1996, American oil and gas companies gave $10.3 million to political campaigns and received tax breaks worth $4 billion.[*]

Many subsidies benefit more people than those who are directly involved. If these side benefits or externalities are not paid for, the subsidized activities may not take place at all or may take place on a scale smaller than is socially desirable. People who travel by bus or train, for instance, benefit those who travel by car because they leave the roads less congested and create less pollution than would be the case if everyone used cars. Unless the car users subsidize bus and train riders in order to pay for the clearer roads, fewer people will use buses and trains than is optimal. To this extent, subsidies make the free market work better. They should be anathema to neither politicians nor voters.

But many subsidies make the market work less well, especially in the long run. Because the amount of a subsidized activity will most likely increase, the result tends to be inefficiencies, waste, pollution, and other ills economic or environmental, often both.

[*] E. Drew. *The Corruption of American Politics: What Went Wrong and Why* (Secaucus, N.J.: Birch Lane Press, 1999). D. M. Roodman, *Paying the Piper: Subsidies, Politics, and the Environment* (Washington, D.C.: Worldwatch Institute, 1996).

The Scale of Subsidies

Now for a quick look at the scale of the subsidies covered in this book. How do they stack up against other outlays by governments?

- Subsidies for agriculture in countries that are members of the Organization for Economic Cooperation and Development (OECD) (or the "rich-nations club") total $362 billion per year; over one-quarter of them are in the United States. Compare this with the estimated cost of upgrading developing-world agriculture, $40 billion per year, and the current inadequate funding of the international network of research centers for agriculture, a mere $235 million per year.

Subsidies for agriculture in OECD countries total $362 billion a year—over one-fourth in the United States.

- Subsidies for fossil fuels and nuclear power in just the United States are around $21 billion per year. This is equivalent to 75 percent of the annual spending of the World Bank.
- Subsidies for road transportation in OECD countries total $1.1 trillion; almost two-thirds of them are in the United States.
- Subsidies for water total $247 billion. This is to be compared with the $60 billion per year investments required in developing countries over the next decade. This sum would go far to overcome the many water-related diseases that cause 80 percent of developing-country sickness and that largely lead to several million child deaths per year.
- Subsidies for marine fisheries total $25 billion per year, or 31 percent of the value of the catch.
- Conventional subsidies for forestry total only $14 billion per year worldwide, but the externalities are so significant that they outweigh the formal subsidies almost sixfold.

Note too that many subsidies generate ripple effects. The energy subsector of oil forms the economic mainstay of several Middle East countries, plus large segments of the economies of Russia, Britain, Norway, Mexico, Venezuela, Indonesia, and Nigeria. Oil subsidies reverberate through associated sectors such as transportation and agriculture, as well as banking interests and many others.

Environmental Externalities

We have looked briefly at certain indirect subsidies. These make up a good share of conventional subsidies, as one would expect. Not so well recognized are certain other indirect subsidies that deserve a category of their own: the implicit and otherwise "hidden" subsidies of environmental externalities (or spillover costs). When I drive my car and pollute everyone's atmosphere without compensating everyone, I effectively gain a freebie opportunity at everyone's expense. Much the same applies when farmers spray their crops with pesticides, the toxic effects of which extend into everyone's ecosystems. Or when industrialists fail to clean up and recycle water taken from everyone's water supplies, which are becoming increasingly scarce in many lands. Or when loggers overexploit forests and deplete the habitats of everyone's wildlife. However little it is acknowledged, these activities with their uncompensated costs amount to implicit subsidies in both spirit and substance, even though they are not dispensed by a government department with appropriate paperwork. They are as economically distorting and environmentally damaging (as well as socially unfair) as any financial subsidy.[13]

They are also sizeable, and they occur in all walks of life. Consider too some externality costs imposed on society by certain corporations in the United States. The health consequences of cigarettes cost the public an estimated $54 billion per year. American society also bears costs through workers who suffer injuries and accidents in unsafe workplaces, $142 billion, or die from workplace cancer, $275 billion. Estimates from a number of studies reveal a conservative total figure of $2.6 trillion per year, roughly five times as much as corporate profits.[14] On top of this is the severe and sometimes permanent depletion or destruction of the productive capital of society in the form of environmental resources, as will be demonstrated at several points in this book.

As this book will also show, environmental subsidies—or externalities, to give them their technical label—are widespread and significant, and growing fast. The current level of environmental injury is ample evidence that they should be included in a comprehensive assessment of subsidies. In Costa Rica, for instance, the depletion of soils, forests, and fisheries results in a 25–30 percent reduction in potential economic growth.[15] As we shall see in Chapter 3, on agriculture, soil erosion worldwide levies unintended costs on society of around $150 billion per year, while pesticides harm society's interests to the extent of $100 billion per year. This means that these implicit subsidies are 65 percent as large as the conventional subsidies in agriculture. In Chapter 6, on water, we shall see that conventional subsidies of $67 billion per year are widely exceeded by environmental externalities of $180 billion. We shall come across similar instances in the other four sectoral chapters. These implicit subsidies are environmentally adverse by definition, and their societal costs make them economically adverse too.

> Soil erosion levies unintended costs on society of around $150 billion per year, while pesticides harm society's interests to the extent of $100 billion per year.

To make our economies work with greater benefit, we need to correct certain deficiencies. First off, we should devise a more accurate measure of total economic output than gross national product (GNP). This indicator is simplistic with a vengeance. For instance, the Exxon oil spill off Alaska cost $3 billion in cleanup activities. According to the undiscriminating calculus of GNP, these activities boosted society's welfare just as much as growing a field of wheat or educating a child, even though they were merely restoring society to its level of welfare before the oil spill occurred. Instead of being added on to GNP as a "good," the costs should have been subtracted as a "bad."

GNP reflects all expenditures, including many corrective measures such as policing, prisons, hospital services, homeless shelters, lawsuits, and every form of pollution and waste. According to the innovative analyst Paul Hawken,[16] as much as one-third of the U.S. economy does nothing to enhance Americans' lifestyles. The onwards-and-upwards rise of GNP presumes that the more people spend, the better their lives must become. But GNP makes no distinction between desirables and undesirables; it only distinguishes more from less.[17] The citizen much beloved of GNP devotees is someone who has recently been through a costly divorce, has been badly burglarized, has just emerged from a stupendous car smash, and has been diagnosed with long-term cancer. A Japanese economist has calculated that the Kobe earthquake left the national economy slightly ahead of the game in light of the massive reconstruction activities it generated. To cite Paul Hawken again, "Where economic growth is concerned the government uses a calculator with no minus sign," ignoring the "difference between the supposed wealth of nations and the true welfare of people."

Rising output means rising incomes, but not necessarily rising living standards. GNP measures quantity of livelihood but ignores quality of life. While one-third of Americans are overweight, the U.S. GNP includes both the billions of dollars they spend on food they wish they did not eat and the $33 billion they spend on diet and weight-loss schemes to take off the resulting fat. GNP also adds on the $118 billion spent on obesity-related health problems.

Plainly GNP should be replaced with a measurement of a Net National Product as a truer indicator of how we are doing. Even better would be a genuine progress indicator (GPI). The United States' per-capita GNP registered an increase of 38 percent during the period 1980–1998, yet a decline in GPI of 25 percent.[18]

We shall take a longer look in Chapter 2 at environmental values and how they are being depleted—and how far that gives rise to lots of implicit subsidies. Note that these should rank as subsidies in and of themselves. They are not dependent on the "up-front" subsidies in the form of financial and other transfers from governments, so we need not ask what proportion of the annual $150 billion "subsidy" from soil erosion is due to conventional subsidy payments to farm-

> The United States' per-capita GNP registered an increase of 38 percent between 1980 and 1998, yet the "Genuine Progress" indicator registered a decline of 25 percent.

ers. All environmental externalities are regarded in this book as 100 percent perverse.

At the same time, we should note a salient difference from subsidies as generally understood. Formal subsidies raise problems because of what governments do, while environmental subsidies raise problems because of what governments do not do. Obviously, this has major implications for policy.

Research Methodology

The research for this book was exceptionally difficult. We have undertaken other big-picture surveys in the past, dealing with such amorphous issues as species extinctions, tropical deforestation, and environmental security, and none has turned out to be a fraction so taxing because of problems in obtaining adequate data. Such information as is available tends to be unusually incomplete, imprecise, and inconsistent. Working with the voluminous literature and trying to pin down the essential information has been like putting one's foot on a dozen jellyfishes.

Understandably, perhaps, governments are reluctant to admit that they hand out subsidies of myriad sorts in munificent amounts. Still less do they want to concede that some of these subsidies could be ill conceived, out of date, politically dubious, or otherwise off target. In many instances, moreover, governments simply do not compile consistent and comprehensive records on an issue as contentious as subsidies; even in a country with advanced accounting systems, such as Canada, there are "serious problems" in obtaining "reliable estimates of subsidies."[19] The consequence for this book is that the authors have come up with sometimes patchy sets of statistics that nonetheless tell a distinctive tale.

As shown by the more than 800 references in this book, there is a huge literature on the subsidies issue—on their nature and extent, their positive and negative features, their costs and benefits, and the lengthy like, all as applied to the six major sectors dealt with in this book and as manifested in countries around the world. Given this abundance of background material, then, it is surprising that there has been no clear, concise agreement on just what subsidies amount to. Every standard definition seems to have several qualifiers, and each of those has its own string of qualifiers. Still less are there specific accounts of just how many subsidies apply in each sector, at least on the part of the principal countries involved.

Even in the case of the United States, there are only partial, and conflicting, data for road transportation, notwithstanding that this sector accounts for direct subsidies totaling $150 billion per year. As for specific and precise data by subsector, statistical information is still more difficult to track down. When the authors asked American economists and other analysts why this should be so, they were told that there are so many covert and indirect subsidies, plus overlapping and otherwise cross-related subsidies (apart from the fact that there is limited consensus on what is a subsidy anyway), that most professionals believe that the task of assembling all relevant data would simply be too time-consuming.

True, the situation is better for the United States with respect to agriculture and fisheries. But as concerns water, the information is even more fragmentary than in fossil fuels and nuclear energy, even though water subsidies in the United States appear to total "only" $5 billion per year, meaning that this smaller figure could perhaps be expected to be more accurate and precise. There seems little prospect of arriving at a credibly comprehensive figure for just the main subsidies in the water sector, whether within the United States or worldwide, without a great deal more background research. This book presents water findings that are far from complete, so the statistical conclusions reflect only part of the subsidies picture in that sector. It is not that more research would alter the prime conclusion with respect to water: subsidies of multiple kinds exert widespread and significant adverse effects. Even in a research project with several times the scope of that underpinning this book, it would be difficult to track down the full array of subsidies in each of the six sectors. This is all the more regrettable in that a main reason why perverse subsidies persist is that few people have a clear idea of how many subsidies are at work, let alone whether they work for good or ill.

The situation is epitomized by the forestry sector. Research has generated volumes of documentation and analysis, but little of that is comprehensive and conclusive. The best research effort over a whole year produced a total for formal subsidies worldwide of only $14 billion per year, though this is a very partial estimate because of sheer lack of data from several major forestry countries and only limited data from the rest. Environmental externalities have likewise been assessed at no more than $78 billion per year, even though there is much circumstantial evidence to suggest they could be many times more. Note the $30 billion of damages arising from the 1998 flooding in China. The flooding was exacerbated by deforestation in the Yangtze Basin, which has lost 85 percent of its tree cover.

To this considerable extent, the findings presented here are to be viewed as conservative and cautious. The holes in the database mean that many subsidies are only partially assessed or are overlooked altogether, which means in turn that many estimates are surely underestimates. For illustrations of the uncertainties, ambiguities, and inconsistencies that seem endemic to data on subsidies, see Box 1.4.

Moreover, the subsidies picture is constantly shifting. In recent

---

Box 1.4. INCONCLUSIVE STATISTICS

Some of the most important subsidy issues are subject to remarkably variable documentation. For instance, there is doubt about the cost to the United States of defending oil shipping lanes, primarily in the Persian Gulf (an implicit and concealed subsidy to oil users, especially car drivers). Estimates range from the Department of Defense's $1 billion per year to the Cato Institute's $70 billion per year. The range reflects the problems of assessing defense spending in particular regions and widely differing assumptions about the potential fall in military expenditures were oil protection no longer needed. There is even confusion about the cost to the United States of fighting the Persian Gulf War, estimated to have been anywhere from $12 billion to $30 billion.

Equally surprising are the divergent estimates of energy subsidies in the United States, ranging from $5 billion to $80 billion per year in the early 1990s.* The Department of Energy cannot make up its mind between less than $5 billion and more than $14 billion per year, while the Alliance to Save Energy puts the figure at somewhere between $21 billion and $36 billion. In the latter case, the wide variation reflects different definitions. Should subsidies include, for instance, government-funded research and development and government compensation for past occupational diseases, such as black lung disease among former miners? A more remarkable review cites estimates ranging from as little as $5 billion in the entire economy to as much as $174 billion in the transportation sector alone, with only part of the divergence stemming from differences in definition.[†]

* M. Toman, *Analyzing the Environmental Impacts of Subsidies: Issues and Research Directions* (Washington, D.C.: Resources for the Future, 1995).

† M. Shelby et al., *The Climate Change Implications of Eliminating U.S. Energy and Related Subsidies* (Washington, D.C.: Environmental Protection Agency, 1995).

years, New Zealand has gone far to eliminate agricultural subsidies, while Russia, India, and China have undertaken a parallel effort with their fossil fuel subsidies. At the same time, subsidies for agriculture, electricity, and water in many developing countries seem to be expanding. So the authors often found themselves aiming at a moving target. Worse: while a sudden reduction of subsidies (in New Zealand, Russia, etc.) is usually well documented if only because it is a remarkable occurrence, a steady rise in subsidies is more likely to go unnoticed among the "background noise" of ongoing economics and politics. In addition, certain sets of subsidy figures, notably those for tropical forestry, were well established for the mid-1980s but have been somewhat neglected in the professional literature since then. As it happens, a set of increases in forestry subsidies in one tropical country has often been balanced out by a parallel set of decreases in another tropical country. So the mid-1980s figures for forestry subsidies in tropical countries may not have become much different today, except for a moderate increase to reflect factors such as increased exploitation.

In the upshot, the authors decided to sidestep the problem often associated with ultra-complex topics, that is to say, the problem of analysis paralysis. They chose to go with the best and most recent set of data available for each of the six sectors. This means that they were not able to come up with an assembly of overall findings for a year as recent as 1999 (though most data are of post-1994 vintage). To that extent, they often found themselves comparing likes with unlikes. But then, a similar problem arises with respect to many aspects of this book. A $1,000 subsidy for commercial logging in Alaska is far different from a $1,000 subsidy for cattle ranching in Amazonia.

Some observers might think that a single composite figure for perverse subsidies in all six sectors and for all parts of the world is simplistic. Nonetheless, the authors believed it worthwhile to come up with such a figure (set around with numerous qualifications) on the grounds that political leaders, policy makers, and the general public should be apprised of the overall scale of these perverse subsidies— and hence of their adverse impact on both our economies and our environments.

In summary, while it has been difficult to pin down the scale of subsidies in general, it has been still more difficult to do as much for perverse subsidies. The book's findings should be viewed as more than indicative but less than comprehensive (let alone conclusive). The purpose of the research is limited to demonstrating how far there is indeed a problem of perverse subsidies. The reader may judge for himself or herself whether the case has been made. When the authors began their research project in 1996, they had reason to suppose that the total might well be somewhere between $400 billion and $800 billion per year (if they had not suspected that the total would be in that significant order, they would not have taken on the project). Were the total to have worked out in fact to be somewhere near the median of $600 billion, it would ironically have matched the budget figure proposed for Agenda 21 at the 1992 Rio Earth Summit, a figure calculated as the amount needed to fund programs in support of sustainable development—whereas perverse subsidies, by definition, foster unsustainable development.

Key Caveat

Herein lies the biggest caveat of all. While it is not overwhelmingly difficult to document the scale of subsidies, it is much more difficult to come up with substantive estimates for perverse subsidies. Hardly any of the 2,000-plus papers that we consulted tackle the question of how many subsidies are perverse. In the face of this virtual wall-to-wall lack of data and analysis, we had to depend on our own best-judgment assessments, based on such information and illumination as were available. Our conclusions may seem rough and ready to many readers, particularly by comparison with the precise findings presented in most reports reviewing major sectors of public policy, whether as concerns the economy or the environment. To some readers, the figures may even appear arbitrary, and some may appear simply off target. We consider that the exercise was worth doing, however preliminary, approximate, and exploratory the outcome.

We take this stance because of (1) the size of the problem and (2) the asymmetry of evaluation. If the perverse subsidies total were not the $600 billion postulated earlier but $400 billion (let alone $800 billion), it would still be larger than the GNP of most countries. At this order of magnitude, it is a powerfully distortional factor at the heart of most economies around the world. Were these perverse subsidies to be reduced or phased out, that would correct a factor that grossly depletes economies and environments alike and would release enormous funds for more productive forms of fiscal management. The measure would also open up the six sectors to marketplace discipline, making them, it is hoped, more productive and efficient.

On the grounds of their sheer scale, then, perverse subsidies need to be documented and appraised as far as possible. This leads to the second reason for tackling this unusually "mushy" issue. As long as the issue of perverse subsidies remains untackled, there tends to be an implicit presumption that their total must effectively be zero: there is the asymmetry of evaluation at distortional work. Of course, this is not what is intended. But as long as a problem is not accorded adequate attention, it is implicitly viewed as if it is not a problem at all. It becomes obfuscated by institutional inertia and relegated to the remotest of back burners. It is out of sight, out of mind, with a bureaucratic vengeance—whereupon it can readily become an even greater problem with covert, cancer-like growth.

These are the twin rationales for attempting to come up with a quantified assessment of perverse subsidies and their magnitude. Again: the estimates of the percentage shares of subsidies "enjoyed" by perverse subsidies, together with the dollar estimates of their values, are strictly best-judgment affairs—no more *and* no less. Future research will no doubt come up with more accurate and precise estimates, and the authors hope this will be both speedy and bountiful. To date, we must make do with whatever is available—and resist the temptation to say we simply cannot appraise perverse subsidies in quantified fashion at all. The reader is asked to attach this qualifier to any quantified assessment he or she comes across in this book. For more on the central question of scientific uncertainty and how to deal with it in the policy domain, see the next chapter.

◆ ◆ ◆

Now that we have determined what, in general, subsidies are, we shall go on in Chapter 2 to take a conceptual crack at the character and extent of perverse subsidies. Thereafter, we shall review the six main categories of sectoral subsidies in the course of Chapters 3–8. In Chapter 9, we shall consider an assessment of perverse subsidies overall, before going on in Chapter 10 to appraise the scope for policy responses and other ameliorative measures.

Chapter 2

WHEN DO SUBSIDIES
BECOME PERVERSE?

How shall we define a perverse subsidy—that is, when does a subsidy become detrimental to both the environment and the economy in the long run? Many subsidies that cause environmental harm may nonetheless meet economic needs, for example, by providing jobs in rural areas where there are few other work opportunities or by lowering prices for staple foods in developing countries. The opposite applies to subsidies that are environmentally supportive but economically costly, such as financial support to save those threatened species that have no perceived economic value. Some subsidies may be positive in one field and merely neutral in the other. In this book, for a subsidy to qualify as perverse, *it must exert effects that are demonstrably and significantly adverse in both fields.*

Many subsidies have been constructive at the time of their introduction but have later become perverse. They have completed their original purpose but have not been eliminated afterward. The American West was settled partly in response to a host of subsidies established by the U.S. government in the late 1800s. The aim of these subsidies was to encourage settlers to exploit the West's resources as rapidly and widely as possible, which was an eminently desirable goal at the time. Today, however, the West's settlement frontier has long since closed, and its resources are more commonly viewed as a public trust to be carefully managed for all Americans both now and in the future. Resource exploitation has often degenerated into over-logging of forests, overgrazing of grasslands, depletion of water-sheds, overpumping of aquifers, decline of biodiversity, and mining-related pollution of water and air, sometimes with toxic wastes. Yet many of the original pro-exploitation subsidies remain in place, even though they are now harmful to both the environment and the economy at large over the long term.

The same applies to a host of government subsidies around the world. Indeed, certain subsidies have become so extensive and entrenched and are so environmentally harmful that subsidy policies may unwittingly represent a prime statement of a government's environmental policy.[1] True, governments are becoming alerted to the virtues of the environmental cause, and many are taking safeguard measures. But what they supply with an environmentally supportive right hand is often taken away by half a dozen left hands wielding subsidies.[2]

Consider, for instance, the central function of commercial energy in virtually every economy around the world and, hence, the pivotal role played by energy subsidies. These subsidies can harm the environment not only directly but also indirectly by increasing the environmental degradation associated with key sectors such as agriculture, industry, and transportation.[3] Artificially cheap energy is the basis of the U.S. agricultural system, ostensibly the most productive in the world. When measured by output per unit of labor input, this may be true, but when reckoned by energy input per food energy output, it is one of the world's least efficient, using nine calories of fossil-fuel energy to produce one calorie of food energy.[4] In addition, energy subsidies for fossil fuels (the main target for such subsidies) rig the market against renewable and nonpolluting forms of energy.[5] In all these ways, many energy subsidies run counter to the interests of both the economy and the environment.

When a perverse subsidy is threatened with removal, however, a host of vested interests are likely to protest that the step will cause profound harm to the economy. These protesters should consider the case of New Zealand, where the government set about eliminating virtually all agricultural subsidies in the mid-1980s. This was a momentous step for a country deeply dependent on agriculture. In the upshot, there have been abundant benefits for both the economy

Box 2.1. WHEREIN LIES PERVERSITY?

In general, subsidies are *economically perverse* when they do the following:

- Maintain production processes that would otherwise be non-starters. Examples include growing rice and alfalfa in California desertlands and continuing to overexploit fish stocks that are already so depleted that they should be relieved of further exploitation forthwith.
- Reduce costs so far that natural resources are overexploited or wasted. Examples include overloading of cropland soils, misuse of water stocks, and overlogging of forests.
- Deter efforts at sustainable exploitation, use of cost-saving technologies, and improved management. For instance, the harvesting of natural forests (such as those in the Pacific Northwest of the United States, Canada's British Columbia, southeastern Australia, and Borneo) militates against a shift toward plantation forestry.
- While attempting to benefit one economic area, harm others to the extent that their net impact is negative. For instance, many subsidy costs are eventually passed on to consumers (the people who, as taxpayers, provide the subsidy in the first place). Agricultural subsidies, especially in the form of protection of domestic agricultural markets, can make food products more expensive. In the United States, citizens pay an average of an extra $360 per year for agricultural subsidies and for food that is priced higher than it would be without subsidies. In the countries of the European Union, the increased cost is $380 per citizen per year. However, in New Zealand, a country that has virtually abolished agricultural subsidies, the extra cost is just $26 per person.

Subsidies are *environmentally perverse* when they do the following:

- Foster activities that result in environmental harm, whether at the site in question (e.g., overlogging of a forest or waterlogging of a rice paddy) or farther afield (downstream siltation, acid rain), and whether immediately (urban smog) or later (global warming).
- In the agricultural sector in particular, stimulate practices that degrade the natural resources underpinning agriculture, notably soils and water; that encourage overuse of agrochemicals such as synthetic fertilizers and pesticides; and that reduce biodiversity, especially the natural enemies of insect pests and weeds, and reduce the genetic variability that enhances crop productivity and helps crops resist new diseases.
- Encourage inefficient, if not profligate, use of fossil fuels, with their many polluting effects, and stimulate development of nuclear energy, with its many problems of environmental risk and toxic waste.

- Foster grand-scale expansion of the car culture, especially at a time when the many externalities (environmental, economic, and social) of road transportation indicate that we should emphasize public transportation instead.
- Promote inefficient and wasteful use of water, especially now that water is becoming scarce in many regions.
- Lead to overexploitation of fisheries and forests, eventually causing stocks to fall away to commercial if not biological extinction.
- Generate gross pollution that results in acid rain, ozone-layer depletion, and global warming, among other climatic dislocations.

and the environment, and hardly any long-term problems for the agricultural sector[6] (for further details, see Box 3.2 in Chapter 3). This indicates that all the subsidies eliminated could be construed as having been perverse.

For a short taxonomy of subsidies that are perverse for either economic or environmental reasons, see Box 2.1.

U.S. citizens on average pay an extra $360 per year for agricultural subsidies and for food priced higher than it would be without subsidies.

Environmental and Economic Values

Are economic and environmental values separate and distinct, and can they can be traded off against each other? Or should they be seen as complementary and mutually supportive for the most part?[7] That the second alternative is more likely is demonstrated by the extent to which national economies are set back through restorative measures required due to environmental problems such as pollution, overuse of natural resources, and the lengthy like. In Japan, 2 percent of GDP is being lost to these problems,[8] and the same is true in Australia.[9] In the United States, the United Kingdom, and Germany, the amount is 4 percent; in most countries of Eastern Europe and the former Soviet Union, 6–10 percent; and in many developing countries, 10–18 percent.[10] In China, where the economy is reputed to be expanding by 7–10 percent per year, the loss to environmental problems is put at 8–15 percent of GDP.[11] None of these estimates takes account of global warming, so they are all underestimates, possibly severely so. They show clearly that environmental problems can levy sizeable economic costs—and hence that the fortunes of the economy and of the environment are strongly interrelated. To quote a leading analyst, Jim MacNeill, "All economic decisions have an environmental consequence, just as all environmental decisions have economic consequences."[12]

So the costs involved should properly be considered as both economic and environmental costs combined. True, there is an operational difference. While economic costs are revealed through the marketplace with many sensitive and accurate signals, environmental costs do not generally enjoy such detailed manifestation, since environmental services (e.g., a watershed function) and resource goods (e.g., a species) are simply not marketed for the most part. This does not mean, of course, that depletion of a service or good is to be regarded as without cost; rather, the cost is not recorded in conventional and easily quantified fashion. But nonmarket values are still values. It seems unduly theoretical, then, to say that economic costs are intrinsically different from environmental costs. They are all costs, and in this book they are viewed that way.

Environmental and Economic Costs

Fortunately, a good number of environmental costs in question can be shadow priced or otherwise estimated. Since the environmental values at stake are often large, let us look first at a few instances as an indication of implicit subsidies arising:

> *Water shortages,* due in part to wasteful use of water by farmers who practice irrigation, industrial users, and municipal consumers, all of whom tend to use heavily subsidized water. The shortages problem is particularly acute in developing countries, where 80 percent of all disease incidence is related to water shortage. The economic cost of just work time lost to disease is estimated to be $125 billion per year.[13] In addition, many people (particularly women) have to compensate for water shortages by spending hours each day transporting water from distant collecting points. The opportunity costs of their lost time, which otherwise might have been spent on, for example, farm work, are put at $40 billion per year.[14]

> *Degradation of irrigation systems.* As much as 20 percent of the world's irrigated croplands are salinized.[15] This leads to a sizeable loss of crops. Again, the problem derives primarily from subsidies that encourage careless and prodigal use of seemingly plentiful water supplies.

Desertification, which affects one-third of habitable lands and levies costs merely through agricultural output forgone to the tune of $42 billion per year.[16] In countries as diverse as the United States, Australia, Spain, Turkey, Mexico, Botswana, and Namibia, also parts of the Sahel, the problem lies largely with subsidies that encourage overgrazing by domestic stock and cultivation of inappropriate crops.

Soil erosion, which is widespread around the world and affects parts of Indiana as much as parts of India. Damages can be measured by the cost of replacing lost water and nutrients on eroded agricultural lands: some $250 billion worldwide per year. In addition, there are off-site damages to human health, private property, navigation, recreation, and so on, worth at least $150 billion per year. Thus, total costs are in the order of $400 billion per year.[17] In the United States, the two sets of costs amount to some $44 billion per year, whereas control measures would amount to little over $8 billion per year.[18] Despite these large costs, soil erosion is increasing faster than ever in

> *Plant-derived anticancer drugs now save 30,000 lives in the United States each year, with annual economic benefits amounting to $400 billion.*

many parts of the world. Much of the problem is due to subsidies fostering overuse of cropland and pastureland.

Mass extinction of species, which deprives humankind of resource stocks for industrial raw materials; new sources of energy; improved forms of present crops and potential future crops; new drugs, medicines, and other pharmaceuticals, among many other goods; and a host of environmental services. Plant-derived anticancer drugs now save 30,000 lives in the United States each year, with annual economic benefits amounting to $400 billion per year. When we consider all developed countries, the benefits double.[19] Tropical-forest plants in particular offer many potential sources of potent drugs, and their net present worth is estimated variously at $147 billion,[20] $420 billion,[21] and $900 billion.[22] Suppose that thirty plant species with pharmaceutical or medicinal potential are eliminated by 2050; the cumulative retail-market loss from each such extinction would amount to $12 billion for the United States alone.[23] The total value of goods and services from biodiversity worldwide is conservatively estimated to be in the order of $2.9 trillion, or roughly 10 percent of global GNP.[24] Many habitats rich in biodiversity are being depleted through subsidies that foster overexploitation.

Tropical deforestation leads to a loss of soil cover, which otherwise offers on-site benefits that, for example, in India are worth $5–$12 billion per year.[25] Indian forests also help regulate river flows and contain floods, a service that is roughly assessed at $72 billion per year.[26] Tropical forests are declining faster than ever, with loss of many environmental outputs, and much deforestation is due to subsidies (see Chapter 8). These forests also provide fuelwood for at least 500 million people in developing countries, who, because of deforestation, spend an average of one and one-half hours per day roaming far and wide to find supplies.[27] With an opportunity cost of lost time that could be spent on, for example, tilling crop fields, if worth roughly $0.10 per hour, the cost to them would amount to almost $28 billion per year.[28] Tropical forests supply a still larger benefit in the form of "carbon sinks" that mitigate potential damage from global warming. The economic value of this function can be roughly estimated at $600–$4,400 per hectare per year.[29] To replace the carbon-storage service of tropical forests could cost as much as $3.7 trillion.[30]

Environmental Externalities Revisited

Thus far, we have looked only at environmental costs that can for the most part be directly and demonstrably attributed to specific subsidies. But as briefly noted in Chapter 1, many forms of environmental degradation are not immediately and directly linked to subsidies but arise in a world where a host of exploitative activities entail environmental costs that spill over onto society at large. Many of these environmental externalities cannot be readily attributed to subsidies, but any externality, being an uncompensated cost, is effectively a subsidy paid by society. Let us remain aware, however, of a distinctive difference: a formal subsidy can cause problems because of what a government *does,* whereas an implicit subsidy in the form of an environmental externality causes problems because of what a government *does not do.* This has profound implications for the government's policy responses when it seeks to correct subsidy problems.

Since the externalities in question are exceptionally large, let us look at a few illustrative examples of environmental and economic values at stake and hence of what could be some concealed costs when the environmental resources are degraded or destroyed:

Freshwater systems enable us to dilute pollutants. The value of this in-stream service, as measured by the cost of removing all con-

taminants and nutrients from municipal wastewater by techno-
logical means, can be estimated at $150 billion worldwide per
year (the estimate does not cover removal of pesticides, nitrates,
and other pollutants from agricultural drainage waters). Freshwater bodies also offer benefits by supplying transportation services
that generate revenues in the United States of $360 billion per year
and in Western Europe of $169 billion per year (lower-bound esti-
mates). In addition, again, we can count the freshwater opportunity for sportfishing, worth $46 billion per year in the United
States alone. The total global value of fish, waterfowl, and other
goods extracted from freshwater systems amounts to at least $100
billion per year, possibly several times as much.[31]

Agricultural pests cause the loss of over 40 percent of all food
grown.[32] Only a very small number of all insect species—perhaps
9,000, or 0.1 percent of all such species—rank as pests today, but
many more potential pests are currently kept under control by
natural enemies in the form of predators and parasites.[33] These
pest control services are variously estimated to be worth at least
$54 billion per year[34] and possibly as much as $417 billion per
year.[35] A good number of these natural enemies are likely to be
preferentially eliminated as the mass extinction of species gathers
momentum.

Pollination services are also supplied by insects. At least forty
crops in the United States are completely dependent on insect pollinators, with a marketplace value of $30 billion.[36] Worldwide,
one-third of food production depends on insect pollination. Such
services are reckoned to be worth between $117 billion per year[37]
and $200 billion per year.[38] As pollinating insects are eliminated
as part of the species extinction spasm, their services will decline
accordingly, with significant economic costs. Already, certain
American farmers are finding it necessary to rent domestic bees
for pollination.

These estimates, like those given earlier under the heading "Environmental and Economic Costs," err on the side of caution, primarily because the lack of data precludes a comprehensive assessment
of what we gain overall from environmental resources—and what we
lose when they are degraded and depleted. In any case, there can be
no doubt that environmental externalities constitute sizeable subsidies, however covert. As we shall see in the six sectoral chapters that
follow, these implicit externalities are sometimes greater in economic

Box 2.2. THE PLANETARY ECOSYSTEM AND THE GLOBAL ECONOMY

Environmental values can be unusually significant—and the same goes for costs when environments are depleted. Recall the environmental goods and services considered in this chapter under the headings "Environmental and Economic Costs" and "Environmental Externalities Revisited." Let us now expand our analytic purview and consider the planetary ecosystem at large. According to a recent analysis, all of the earth's environmental outputs together could be worth some $33 trillion (range $16–$54 trillion) per year, almost as much as the world's economic output (both of these estimates are in mid-1990s dollars). Just over half of this, $17.1 trillion, is made up of nutrient cycling. Waste treatment, including pollution control and detoxification, is reckoned to be worth $2.3 trillion; disturbance regulation, such as flood control, storm protection, and drought recovery, $1.8 trillion; water supply, $1.7 trillion; food production, such as hunting, gathering, and subsistence farming, $1.4 trillion; control of soil erosion, $576 billion; pollination, $117 billion; and biological control, $417 billion.[*]

We can also assess environmental values by reflecting on the Biosphere II experiment, with $200 million of technological underpinnings over two years for eight people enclosed in an artificial ecosystem that nonetheless failed on several counts of vital environmental services. The cost worked out at $25 million per person. Were we ever to try to replicate such environmental services for the 6.1 billion people now on the earth, the cost would theoretically be $153,000 trillion. Just the annual growth in the world's population would require $2,000 trillion, or fifty-seven times more than the world's present GNP.

Or consider the environmental value of a fifty-year-old tree. Over its lifetime, it will have contributed environmental services worth $200,000 at today's values (or an average of $4,000 per year), including nutrient recycling, moisture regulation, air pollution control, oxygen generation, biodiversity habitat, and soil protection. The value of the tree in marketplace price is probably no more than its value as commercial timber, and that price is what the consumer pays. But when the tree is eliminated, society pays for its loss, including the loss of its myriad services.[†]

[*] R. Costanza et al., "The Value of the World's Ecosystem Services and Natural Capital," *Nature* 387 (1997): 253–260.

[†] T. Hermach, *Trees Restore the Earth* (Eugene, Oreg.: Native Forest Council, 1996).

terms than are the overt subsidies. Meantime, note that a recent research effort[39] concludes that all environmental benefits are worth some $33 trillion, almost equal to the world's GNP. This further demonstrates the scope for externalities to grow to exceptional scale when environmental outputs are depleted. For details, see Box 2.2.

> *All of the Earth's environmental benefits could be worth $33 trillion.*

A corollary of this section is that elimination of a perverse subsidy should yield a "double dividend" through benefits for both the economy and the environment. For instance, if there were a reduction in subsidies for road transportation, there would be environmental benefits in the form of less pollution and economic benefits in the form of less road congestion and hence more efficient travel.

The Question of Uncertainty

As has been repeatedly emphasized, there is often uncertainty about how big the costs of subsidies can be, whether direct or indirect subsidies or externality subsidies. Similarly, there is not always a clear idea of where the costs originate or where they have their greatest effects. Hence, there can sometimes be doubt about whether a subsidy should qualify as perverse. Gray areas abound. But this should not be seen as an insurmountable roadblock for policy responses. After all, we confront uncertainty every day in the policy sphere. What, for instance, are to be the ultimate and overall economic returns on today's investments in health, education, and defense?

The uncertainty question is so central to this book that it is worth reviewing a little further. What is "legitimate scientific caution" in the face of uncertainty, *especially when uncertainty can cut both ways*? Some observers consider that in the absence of conclusive evidence and assessment, it is better to stick with low estimates of subsidies on the grounds that such estimates are more "responsible." But note the asymmetry of evaluation at work. A low estimate, ostensibly "safe" because it takes a conservative view of such limited evidence as is to hand in documented detail, may fail to reflect the real situation just as much as does an "unduly" high estimate that is more of a best-judgment affair based on all available evidence with various degrees of demonstrable validity. A minimalist calculation with apparently greater precision may in fact amount to spurious accuracy. In a situation of uncertainty in which not all factors can be quantified to conventional satisfaction, let us not become preoccupied with what can be precisely counted if that is to the detriment of what ultimately counts.

This applies especially to issues with policy implications of exceptional scope, as in the case of perverse subsidies. Suppose a policy maker hears scientists stating that they cannot legitimately offer final guidance about a problem because they have not yet completed their research with conventionally conclusive analysis in all respects. Or suppose the scientists simply refrain from going public about the problem because they believe, in accordance with certain traditional canons of science, that they cannot validly say anything much before they can say all. In these circumstances, the policy maker may well assume there is little to worry about for the time being: absence of evidence about a problem implies evidence of absence of a problem. By consequence, the policy maker may decide to do nothing—and to do nothing in a world of unprecedentedly rapid change can be to do a great deal. In these circumstances, undue caution on the part of scientists can become undue recklessness in terms of the policy fallout: their silence can send a resounding message, however unintentionally. As in other situations beset with uncertainty, it will be better for us to find that we have been roughly right than to find that we have been precisely wrong.

In the case of perverse subsidies, and by sheer force of circumstance, both economic and environmental—a force that is becoming ever more forceful—it is appropriate to appraise the problem with as much (or as little) information as is available. This is all the more pertinent when dealing with an issue of exceptional import and urgency. The reader should bear this in mind while reading this book. What follows is a realistic reflection of the problem as it is understood today, less than complete as our knowledge may be in many respects. Where uncertainty has arisen, the authors have sought to describe the situation with as much "precise imprecision" as possible.

The six sectoral chapters in Part II all require that an estimate be made of how big the perverse subsidies are, that is, what proportion they make up of total subsidies. This is an exceedingly vexing question, and in the upshot the authors have often been obliged to come up with an informed guesstimate, proposing somewhere between one-half and three-quarters of the total (except for environmental externalities, which are counted as 100 percent perverse). These could well be on the low side. When the authors sent the chapters to established experts for assessment, the experts almost all proposed that the proportion be estimated at 100 percent.

Global Warming

The most prominent instance of uncertainty lies with global warming, partly because of the current lack of scientific understanding and partly because global warming is the biggest environmental problem foreseeable.[40] It could constitute the number one externality cost to be considered as an implicit subsidy from society to those sectors that are the main sources of greenhouse gases, namely, fossil fuels and road transportation. However, for the purposes of this book, with its emphasis on cautious and conservative estimates, global-warming calculations thus far must be viewed as too limited to warrant inclusion of the phenomenon as an environmental externality. We shall look at it here in a little further detail for what it reveals about uncertainty and how it can be handled in policy terms.

There have been various economic estimates[41] of the eventual costs of global warming. These estimates generally propose that the costs may be modest in relation to global GDP, just a few percentage points of it at most. Even so, a 2 percent reduction of global GDP, expressed as a present value discounted over 100 years, would amount to $800 billion.

In the view of many ecologists,[42] virtually all such estimates thus far fail to capture the many disruptive discontinuities and synergisms likely to attend global warming; hence, they are severe underestimates. The authors strongly agree with this viewpoint.[43]

As a preliminary and partial proxy of possible costs, note some recent comments by the insurance industry in response to freak weather phenomena such as floods, droughts, and windstorms. These phenomena, widely viewed as portents of global warming, cost insurers $20 billion in the single year of 1999, compared with $24 billion during the entire 1980s (though some of the increase was probably due to greater economic activity at risk).[44] Leaders of the insurance industry—which is worth $1.5 trillion per year, just ahead of the fossil-fuel industry, at $1.4 trillion—are perturbed. According to the head of the Reinsurance Association of America, Frank Nutter, were recent weather trends to persist, the industry could eventually face global collapse. Total damages, including uninsured damages, amounted to $67 billion in 1999, and a total of $430 billion in the 1990s—more than five times the total for the 1980s.[45]

> *Freak weather cost insurers $20 billion in 1999, compared with $24 billion during the entire 1980s.*

These statistics give an opening idea of the scale of possible costs involved in a single dimension of global warming as understood at a time when we are probably experiencing only the first signs of global warming. Almost entirely disregarded until just a few years ago, they should give pause to those who assert we know enough about global warming to reckon that the ultimate all-around costs will be no more than marginal.

According to a recent study,[46] which dealt extensively with multiple uncertainties, market damages of global warming can be estimated to range from zero to 10 percent of world GDP. When we include nonmarket damages, however, the additional costs could rise to as high as 30 percent of GDP. Moreover, when we include modest risk factors, potential surprises, and equity issues, the total could soar to 40 percent or even 50 percent of world GDP, and "it is not unimaginable for impacts to exceed 60 percent of GDP."[47]

Note too that valuations of global-warming effects, especially monetary valuations, have an uncertainty range corresponding to at least a factor of twenty. Thus, the "true" value may lie between 5 percent and 2,000 percent of a given estimate.[48]

In terms of policy responses, there need be little uncertainty thanks to the "no regrets" option. As has been pithily pointed out by energy expert Amory Lovins,[49] protecting the climate need not be costly and in fact can be profitable because saving fuel is generally cheaper than buying it (neglecting any further benefits from not burning it):

> With market failures corrected, such as the $300 billion of potential annual energy savings in the United States unrealized, huge energy savings can be speedily purchased at current prices. In this context, uncertainties about climate become irrelevant: we should buy energy efficiency merely to save money. The debate then shifts from prices and pain to markets, enterprise, innovation, competitive advantage, and economic opportunity. . . . Those theoretical economists who wouldn't pick up a banknote from the street (if it were real, someone would have done so already) will not capture these profits. Alert executives will.[50]

Summation and Conclusion

This book carries the issue of perverse subsidies one step beyond the treatment given it in two recent publications by American analyst David Roodman[51] and Dutch economist André de Moor.[52] Both review the subsidies phenomenon overall, though from standpoints more restricted than that used here (and de Moor does not deal with forestry or fisheries). Both present admirable accounts of the subsidies problem writ large, and both assert that a good share of these subsidies can be characterized as perverse. But neither attempts a substantive or firm estimate of how large a share this might be (de Moor suggests it could be anywhere from 35 percent to almost 80 percent). By contrast, this book seeks to come up with a substantive estimate of the share, albeit in exploratory terms.

How exploratory? As we shall see, there is a solid figure for perverse subsidies in fisheries, backed by authoritative documentation. There are sometimes good figures, sometimes no figures, for agriculture and for fossil fuels and nuclear energy. There are widely disparate estimates of subsidies for road transportation in the United States, a land where the car is king and where one would expect there to be lots of consistent documentation. There are sound detailed accounts for several other developed countries, but not all of them. In still other countries with large numbers of cars, data are all but nonexistent. The situation in forestry is confused and uncertain.

In the water sector, there are all too few data for subsidies in many countries, let alone those subsidies that should rank as perverse. In this instance, the authors had to limit themselves to a best-judgment estimate, drawing on such limited evidence as can be found. By comparison with the fisheries estimate, it is no more than a "halfway" estimate, and the authors readily recognize the shortcoming in this sector. To refrain from offering a water estimate of any kind, however, would have made it possible for certain observers to infer that perverse subsidies are negligible—quite the opposite of what seems to be the real-world situation. To reiterate a key point: uncertainty can cut both ways. The authors believe that it accords with the intent and spirit of this book to offer a preliminary and exploratory estimate, even a semi-estimate, rather than to let the water sector remain unexamined on an issue of major moment. In any case, wherever there is an acute lack of documentation, the assessment tends perforce toward an underestimate.

To this significant extent, the authors consider the estimates for perverse subsidies in the six sectors to be valid for present purposes, however uneven their databases. They represent an informed appraisal (see the 800-plus references) of the current understanding of perverse subsidies. The rationale is that an exploratory exercise is justified in light of the pivotal part played by perverse subsidies in the way our world works.

Part II

SECTORAL ANALYSES

Chapter 3

AGRICULTURE

There is nothing more important than getting supper on the table. Well might agriculture affect one-third of the earth's land surface, more than any other human enterprise. It also affects the entire planetary ecosystem through the recent intensification of farming practices. Higher harvests have been achieved by means of more irrigation, pesticides, and chemical fertilizers, among other methods of modernized farming, and these measures have been widely fostered by subsidies. Many, if not most, and possibly all such subsidies appear to be costly to the economy and are often harmful to the environment, especially the natural-resource base that underpins agriculture. For instance, pesticides and chemical fertilizers severely contaminate water supplies; short-rotation cropping and reduced fallows exacerbate soil erosion; high-yielding monocultures cause genetic wipe-out among old varieties of food plants; land clearing for agriculture is the largest single cause of deforestation; and many agricultural activities release greenhouse gases.[1]

What is the rationale for agricultural subsidies? Why should farmers need a helping hand at all from the government? There are several arguments. First is that governments consider it a prime responsibility to keep their citizens fed, so they feel duty bound to support farmers. Second, farmers worldwide have often been among the poorer segments of society, so they have been thought to deserve "a little extra." This applies especially in developing countries, where farmers generally form the majority of the population and governments are keen to keep them in favor. Third, and again in developing countries, many subsidies have been justified in times past as vital foundations of the Green Revolution; they enabled the one-third expansion of irrigated lands and the tripling of fertilizer use, thus helping to double crop yields. Overall, subsidies aim to guarantee food supplies, to keep farm prices stable, to maintain farming as a vibrant economic sector, and to support rural communities.

For all these reasons, financial support of agriculture has become an ancient and entrenched tradition in countries around the world. Farmers have become extremely powerful politically, leaving governments with the impression that to reduce agricultural subsidies would be to forfeit a pivotal part of the electorate. Remarkably enough, New Zealand, which is more dependent on agriculture than any other developed country, has grasped the nettle, with success for the government, farmers, the economy, and the environment (see the discussion later in this chapter).

Agricultural subsidies come in many shapes and sizes. As well as the obvious practice of encouraging farmers to use more inputs (fertilizers, pesticides, irrigation, machinery, etc.), subsidies can simply boost farm income by means of price supports. Less directly, they can facilitate marketing of crops by enhancing transportation networks. They can relieve weather problems and other risks by providing insurance. They can foster credit flows. They can stimulate conversion of wetlands to agriculture. Governments North and South do much to subsidize artificial pesticides and fertilizers. In developed countries, governments typically guarantee minimum prices for crops at levels above the market; in developing countries, governments primarily suppress farm prices in order to keep city communities supplied with cheap food.

This last indicates the technical differentiation between producer and consumer subsidies. The Organisation for Economic Co-operation and Development (OECD) defines the first in terms of producer support estimates (PSEs), being "an indicator of the annual monetary value of gross transfers from consumers and taxpayers to agricultural producers, measured at the farm gate, arising from policy measures which support agriculture."[2] These PSEs totaled $274 billion in OECD countries in 1998, or $210 per hectare of agricultural land (Figure 3.1).[3]

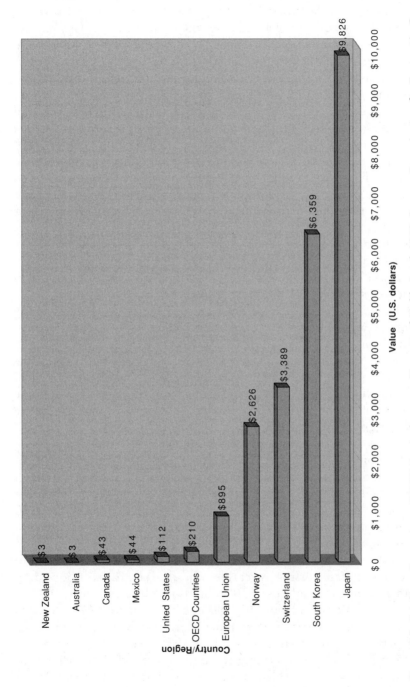

Figure 3.1. Producer Supports to OECD Agriculture per Hectare of Arable Land, 1998. Source: Organisation for Economic Co-operation and Development (OECD), Agricultural Policies in OECD Countries: Monitoring and Evaluation, 1999 (Paris: OECD, 1999).

Certain of these subsidies are well and good within particular perspectives. Not so justifiable are subsidies fostering crops grown in regions that would not have grown them at all had a free market existed. Notable examples are ultra-thirsty crops such as alfalfa and rice in California's desertlands. Also irrational are those many subsidies that may have made sense when they were first established but have since become obsolete or bloated, or both. In the European Union countries, for instance, excess production has led to milk and wine lakes and butter and beef mountains (not to mention a manure mountain in the Netherlands). In early 1993, cereal surpluses of 30 million tonnes (metric tons) would have been enough to provide an Italian-style diet to 75 million people for one year.[4] Taxpayers footed the bill to supply the subsidies that boosted these crops in the first place, and then they paid again to store or even dispose of the excess stockpiles. Much the same has applied to extravagant food surpluses in the United States, where in a typical year of the early 1990s, the Department of Agriculture obliged farmers to squander 1 billion oranges, 500 million lemons, 100,000 tonnes of raisins, and 30,000 tonnes (metric tons) of almonds.

Subsidies generate absurd outcomes in other ways too. Many countries pay their farmers to leave land fallow, whereupon they subsidize them to engage in directly conflicting activities, for example, to plant crops and practice fallowing simultaneously. Or consider the travels, if not the travails, of materials needed to make the daily 150 grams of yogurt beloved by many German consumers. To reach one of the main distribution outlets in southern Germany, ingredients are transported from all around the country and even from the Netherlands and Poland. To do the job, a theoretical truck must travel 3,500 kilometers.[5] It is enabled to do so in part by bountiful subsidies from the European Union's Common Agricultural Policy.[6] Much more efficient in both economic and environmental terms would be for yogurt producers to utilize local ingredients, but they have no incentive to do so as long as subsidized supplies can apparently do the job more cheaply.

In still more extreme fashion, four airports in Japan have been dedicated to transporting vegetables and flowers, to be followed by another five costing almost $30 million in subsidies. To fly 1 kilogram of green onions from Ono, on northeastern Kyūshū Island, to Tokyo costs nearly six times as much as to transport them by road. The airports, paid for entirely by taxpayers, have been built ostensibly to integrate isolated farming communities into the Japanese agro-economy—and, more realistically, they have served as a sop to the farming lobby after it made concessions to the Japanese government's negotiations for the 1993 Uruguay Round on world trade.

Numerous countries feature inappropriate subsidies for grains, beef, mutton and lamb, pork, poultry, milk and other dairy products, fruits, vegetables, cotton, oilseed, and tobacco, among a host of other agricultural products. So large and widespread are these subsidies that, as we shall see in detail later in the chapter, agriculture has become one of the most distorted and distortional sectors of the global economy.

In addition to economic dislocations, subsidies cause much environmental injury. Pesticides under conventional application regimes cause well-known hazards to human health even as they undermine their own usefulness. Excessive applications of nitrogenous fertilizers lead to washed-off nitrates contaminating drinking water supplies, with threats to human health. Intensified farming with heavy machinery aggravates soil erosion, as does the decline of crop rotation. Irrigation agriculture is far and away the largest user of water worldwide, and subsidies encourage farmers to misuse and overuse water on a grand scale, despite the growing evidence of sizeable water shortages impending, as examined in more detail in Chapter 6. Many agricultural activities contribute to global warming through emissions of carbon dioxide from use of fossil fuels, methane from ruminant livestock and rice paddies, and nitrous oxides from disturbed soils. These environmental externalities are widespread and unusually significant, and they merit detailed examination later in this chapter.

The Subsidies Phenomenon

In 1998, net financial transfers to agriculture in OECD countries amounted to $362 billion per year, rather higher than in 1996–1997.[7] These subsidies exerted a profound influence not only on the agriculture sector but also on the economy at large. They equated to 1.4 percent of the collective GDPs of twenty-nine OECD countries; 1.4 percent of the European Union's GDP; 1.5 percent of Japan's; 1.9 percent of Norway's; 2 percent or more of Switzerland's and Poland's; 5.4 percent of South Korea's; and 10.7 percent of Turkey's (Table 3.1).

Roughly $275 billion, over three-quarters of the subsidies, were producer supports.[8] These producer supports were sizeable for individual farmers. In 1998, the OECD average was around $11,000; in the United States and the European Union, $19,000; in Japan, $21,000; and in Switzerland, $33,000 (though in New Zealand, the

Table 3.1. Total Supports to OECD Agriculture, 1998

Country/Region	Subsidies ($ Billion)	Subsidies as Percentage of GDP
European Union (15 countries)	142	1.4
United States	97	1.2
Japan	57	1.5
Turkey	23	10.7
South Korea	16	5.4
Switzerland	6	2.4
Mexico	6	1.4
Canada	4	0.7
Poland	4	2.8
Norway	3	1.9
Australia	2	0.5
New Zealand	0.1	0.2
OECD (29 countries)	362	1.4

Source: Organisation for Economic Co-operation and Development (OECD), *Agricultural Policies in OECD Countries: Monitoring and Evaluation, 1999* (Paris: OECD, 1999).

figure was less than $1,000, for reasons explained later in the chapter). For details of supports in all leading OECD countries, see Figure 3.2. The payments amounted to 24 percent of farmers' revenues in the United States, 17 percent in Canada, 55 percent in the European Union, 67 percent in Japan, and 112 percent in Norway, with an average of 42 percent in OECD countries as a whole (though only 7 percent in Australia and 0.8 percent in New Zealand).[9] They were sizeable too for consumers because of increased food prices as well as taxes. In the United States, the burden of total support to agriculture amounted to $363 per citizen; in the European Union, $381; in Norway, $641; in Switzerland, $879; and in Japan, $449 (contrast this with Australia, at only $92, and New Zealand, at $26, both of these countries having eliminated most of their subsidies).[10] For further details, see Tables 3.1 and 3.2 and Figure 3.2.

Later in this chapter, we shall look at how many of these agricultural subsidies can be considered perverse. As an interim example of subsidies that are plainly bad news for both the economy and the environment, see Box 3.1, on sugar subsidies in Florida.

United States

The United States is the foremost food producer in the world. Each year, the country exports one-third of its agricultural products, for

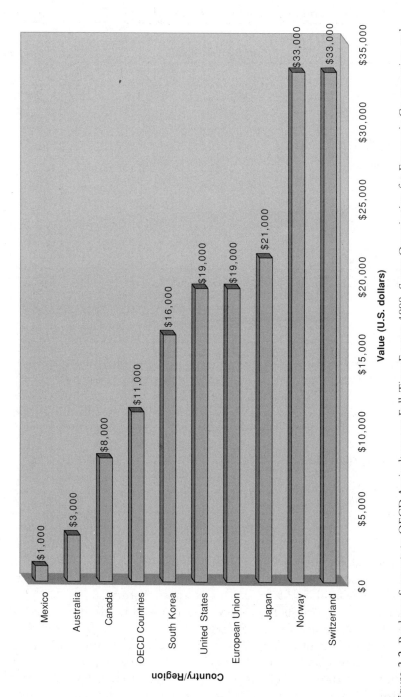

Figure 3.2. Producer Supports to OECD Agriculture per Full–Time Farmer, 1998. *Source:* Organisation for Economic Co-operation and Development (OECD), *Agricultural Policies in OECD Countries: Monitoring and Evaluation, 1999* (Paris: OECD, 1999).

Table 3.2. The Subsidies Burden for Consumers and Taxpayers, 1998

Country/ Region	Transfers from Taxpayers ($ billion)	Transfers from Consumers ($ billion)	Transfers per Capita
European Union (15 countries)	65	77	$381
United States	74	25	$363
Japan	11	71	$449
Turkey	12	12	$352
South Korea	4	12	$344
Switzerland	2.5	4	$879
Mexico	3	3	$63
Canada	2	2	$140
Poland	0.7	3.6	$109
Norway	1.4	1.4	$641
Australia	1.4	0.4	$92
New Zealand	0.07	0.03	$26
OECD (29 countries)	179	213	$249

Source: Organisation for Economic Co-operation and Development (OECD), *Agricultural Policies in OECD Countries: Monitoring and Evaluation, 1999* (Paris: OECD, 1999).

revenues of more than $55 billion (which help it pay for its $60 billion worth of oil imports).[11] But there is a price to pay for this vibrant activity: in 1998, American taxpayers underpinned agriculture to the tune of $74 billion in subsidies, and American consumers contributed $25 billion through higher food prices.[12] Per farmer and per farm hectare, U.S. agriculture is among the most strongly supported in the world, surpassed only by such super-supportive countries as Japan, Norway, and Switzerland. Or, rather, U.S. agriculture receives some of the strongest supports in the world; whether that is supportive of the agriculture sector and the U.S. economy overall or of the environmental underpinnings of agriculture is another story.

> In 1998, American taxpayers underpinned agriculture to the tune of $74 billion in subsidies, and American consumers contributed $25 billion through higher food prices.

As mentioned, production supports amounted to about one-quarter of farm revenues, or an average of $19,000 per farmer.[13] The main purposes of these subsidies are to ensure acceptable and stable prices for crops and other produce and to safeguard the farming community in the United States, especially the family farms and their workforces. These two sets of values seemed to be at exceptional risk during the Great Depression, whereupon the New Deal legislation of

Box 3.1. U.S. Sugar Growers

There could hardly be a more extreme case of perverse agricultural subsidies than the U.S. sugar sector. Especially during the past thirty-five years, the U.S. government has protected domestic sugar from competition by imports by supplying hefty price supports to sugar growers. This enrichment of a small number of such growers causes American consumers to pay sugar prices at least twice the world level. (It also prompts candy manufacturers to move to Canada, where they can purchase sugar on international markets.) Sugar growing is concentrated in southern Florida, where it drains water that would otherwise flow into the Everglades and returns it with fertilizer that causes eutrophication.

The subsidy program costs American consumers $1.4 billion a year. Transferring each $1.00 of subsidy to sugar producers costs the consumer $2.60 and the economy $0.70. Each sugar grower receives subsidies worth twice as much as the country's average family income.[*]

[*] A. Bonanno et al., *From Columbus to ConAgra: The Globalization of Agriculture and Food* (Lawrence: University Press of Kansas, 1994); Center for Responsive Politics, *The Politics of Sugar* (Washington, D.C.: Center for Responsive Politics, 1995); A. O. Krueger, *The Political Economy of Control: American Sugar: Program in International Political Economy* (Durham, N.C.: Duke University Press, 1988).

the early 1930s saw to it that "no sector of the economy received more systematic federal attention than agriculture; and none received more subsidy for research and development, more technical assistance, more public investment in education, in electrification and in infrastructure, more price stabilization, more export promotion, more credit, and more mortgage relief."[14]

In any case, farming had traditionally been seen as a risky enterprise. Crops could be destroyed by insect pests, diseases, and bad weather, and prices were subject to marketplace swings and demand changes. All the more reason, then, for prices to be supported and stabilized by government subsidies—thereby shifting a lot of the risk from the farmer to the taxpayer. When risk was reduced, however, food production was stimulated, usually leading to bulging food surpluses, which in turn caused prices to drop, leading to the need for further price supports. And so on and so repetitiously forth. The basic principles have not changed much today.

In practice, however, things have worked out differently. Whereas the early 1930s saw rural incomes 60 percent below urban incomes, today's full-time farmer (often a millionaire) may have a net worth more than ten times that of the average American household. But the modern farmer is far from the family farmer of tradition. Although there are still 350,000 American farms receiving federal farm hand-outs, almost 30 percent of subsidies go to the top 2 percent, and over four-fifths go to the top 30 percent (5 percent of subsidies go to farmers with annual incomes of over $1 million).[15] Ironically, if the U.S. government were to shift its target from the top 30 percent to the bottom 70 percent of farmers, it could save at least $8 billion a year while supplying a competitive boost to lower-income farms.[16] As it is, the small-scale farmer has long been under the squeeze. At the start of the twentieth century, the farm population made up 43 percent of the U.S. population, and in 1950 its share was 12 percent, but today it has slumped to well under 2 percent. Because farm payments are based on the production of crops and livestock rather than on the means of production, most subsidies are paid to a few top-bracket farmers. So the decline in numbers of farmers reflects the tendency for subsidies to support crops rather than farmers.[17]

Increasingly, U.S. agriculture has become the province of bigger and more efficient farmers, who no longer run farms but now operate agribusinesses. Farmland ownership has become highly concentrated: just 124,000 owners hold half of all farmlands, and 86 percent of farms are now small or part-time operations, earning less than 5 percent of all net farm income. At the other extreme, 5 percent of all farms enjoy sales of more than $200,000 per year, pulling in 84 percent of net farm income.[18]

U.S. farm subsidies should have been cut back somewhat in recent years following implementation of the 1996 Farm Bill, but in 1998 total supports were still higher than in the late 1980s, and they can still be viewed as public policy headed down a blind alley. Although intended to stimulate the production of food in general, they induce farmers to plant too much of what is subsidized and too little of the rest. Overproduction of subsidized items drives down prices, whereupon more subsidies are required to compensate farmers. Raised prices undermine farm exports, whereupon exports too have to be subsidized. There is a further whammy: the consumers hardest hit are the poorest people, the ones who spend proportionally the most on food.

Many farmers protest that without subsidies, they would have to quit. This brings us to the next vexing question, that of farm jobs— and another focus of subsidies insofar as they are supposed to safeguard jobs. Today, it is efficiency rather than subsidies that determines whether farm jobs go. As in other OECD countries where subsidies are overly generous, that is to say, Japan, Norway, and those in the European Union, it is the least efficient American farms that are losing the most jobs. By contrast, reduced subsidies and farming efficiency in New Zealand have done much to keep farmers down on the farm.

Subsidies are bad news not only for the U.S. economy but also for the U.S. environment (and even the planetary ecosystem via global warming).[19] Again, this is due to the overwhelming emphasis on ever more production. (By contrast, subsidies ignore or even discourage low-input and organic farming, which are more environmentally benign.) Subsidies encourage farmers to apply excessive amounts of synthetic pesticides and fertilizers, with widespread pollution of water stocks; indeed, this is one of the main forms of non-point-source water pollution (taxpayers then pay to clean up the rivers and lakes). Water stocks, and especially groundwater supplies such as the Ogallala Aquifer, are also being grossly depleted by intensified agriculture: farmers and ranchers account for two-fifths of all water withdrawals in the United States.[20] Subsidies contribute to a reduction in wildland habitat and therefore in biodiversity. Nitrogenous fertilizers and flatulent cattle release greenhouse gases.[21]

Perhaps most important of all, subsidy regulations serve to reduce if not eliminate crop rotations. Crop-support programs have locked farmers into planting the same crops on the same land year after year. If soil fertility declines, that can be overcome by adding more subsidized fertilizer. This stimulates soil erosion to the extent that it offsets all soil conservation programs put together. Soil erosion is aggravated too by the trend toward bigger farms with fewer shelterbelts and increased use of heavy machinery. One-third of original topsoil in the United States has already been eroded away, and another 4.5 billion tonnes are lost every year (albeit only 6 percent and perhaps as little as 2 percent of the global erosion total, lost from 11 percent of the world's agricultural lands). On-site costs comprise loss of plant nutrients, moisture, and soil depth, whereas off-site costs consist mostly of siltation of downstream water bodies, plus associated flooding. Both sets of costs together amount to $44 billion per year, increasing production costs by about 25 percent.[22]

Most of the above applies to arable crops, but some of it relates to livestock as well, especially on federal lands in the eleven western states, which make up one-third of "the West." Over 20 million beef cattle roam 2 million square kilometers, with 100,000 ranches producing less than one-fifth of the country's beef. Yet ranchers using federal lands have long paid less than one-third of the average private-land rate. American taxpayers have been subsidizing ranchers to overgraze these rangelands at a charge of just $1.61 per cow per month, less than it costs to feed a cat. Comparable private lands bring in an average grazing fee of $10 per cow per month. These low grazing fees cost the U.S. treasury over $50 million a year—and the entire federal grazing program, including taxpayer-funded predator control, emergency feed, and cheap water, costs Americans at least $500 million a year (without counting the cost of degraded grasslands, eroded soil, muddied streams, trampled vegetation, and runoff of scarce water). Overgrazing has caused as much as 85 percent of public rangelands to lose their productivity, thanks to "socialized ranching" on the part of welfare cowboys. Overall, the cost of federal grazing permits is some $4 billion.[23]

On top of economic inefficiency, there is social inequity. Many of the biggest ranches are financially marginal sideline investments by wealthy enterprises. Half of the rangelands are utilized by just 2 percent of all permit holders, these being grand-scale operators who make a fortune from the taxpayer. They include four billionaires, several oil companies, an insurance company, a California utility, and a major brewery.[24]

Subsidies are also bad news for people's health. The American Public Health Association has estimated that Americans could slash their medical costs by $17 billion a year if they were all to cut their daily intake of fat by just 8 grams, the amount in half a cup of premium ice cream. The U.S. food industry spends $30 billion a year on advertising to persuade consumers to eat more, whereupon the same consumers spend $33 billion trying to rid themselves of the inevitable

Americans could slash their medical costs by $17 billion a year if they were to cut their daily intake of fat by just 8 grams—the amount in half a cup of premium ice cream.

effects.[25] There were some 400,000 liposuctions in the United States in 1998, at a cost of at least $2,000 apiece.[26]

In summary of U.S. subsidies, note a recent critique:

> The government subsidizes agricultural production and agricultural non-production alike, also agricultural destruction and agricultural restoration. [It] subsidizes cattle grazing on western rangelands while it also pays for soil conservation. The government subsidizes energy costs so that farmers can deplete aquifers to grow alfalfa to feed cows that make milk that is stored in warehouses as surplus cheese that does not feed the hungry.[27]

All OECD Countries

In addition to the United States's subsidies of $97 billion in 1998, there were $142 billion on the part of the European Union, $57 billion by Japan, and $66 billion by other OECD countries.[28] This makes a total of $362 billion, say $360 billion. For details, see Table 3.1.

Non-OECD Countries

Subsidies are pervasive in non-OECD countries too, though not nearly on the same scale. As in OECD countries, they include both producer and consumer subsidies, generally with emphasis on the latter. In fact, agriculture is often taxed to keep consumers, and especially urban consumers, content by, for example, fixing retail food prices or imposing ceilings on producer prices. Price interventions include direct regulation; state trading; tariffs, both fixed and variable; and restrictions such as discretionary import and export licenses.

As for producer subsidies, governments often support farm credit programs and salient agricultural inputs such as fertilizer. Fertilizer use worldwide and particularly in developing countries increased by 40 percent per unit of farmland between the mid-1970s and the late 1980s. In Indonesia, for instance, fertilizer subsidies constituted 2.0 percent of government spending in 1989 (though greatly reduced today), and in India, 3.6 percent.[29] Producer subsidies also protect farmers through restrictions or tariffs on imported food. The net effect has generally been a huge income transfer out of agriculture.[30]

Consider the experience of India. Increasingly, subsidies have been allocated to inputs such as water, irrigation, fertilizers, pesticides, farm credit, and electricity (mainly for irrigation pumps). By contrast, relatively few subsidies go to non-input factors such as agronomic research, extension services, rural roads, and soil conservation. The share of input subsidies in public expenditures increased from 44 percent in the early 1980s to 83 percent by 1990. As a measure of the expected deceleration in productivity due to declining support for research and rural infrastructure, plus lack of attention to problems such as soil erosion, salinization and waterlogging, and loss of organic nutrients, the demand for cereals is projected to exceed production by 23 million tonnes by 2020, double the largest gap to date.[31] Of course, the gap will be primarily due to the increase in both human numbers and human demands, the latter arising as newly affluent people eat higher on the food chain. Yet despite heavy input subsidies, Indian agriculture is effectively taxed through artifi-

cially low prices and high foreign exchange rates. If these basic policies were corrected, there would be next to no need for subsidies at
all—as is the case in many other developing countries.[32]

Consumer and producer subsidies together in developing countries
accounted for almost 5 percent of annual government spending during
the past twenty-five years—a large slice indeed. In Zambia, for
instance, they soared to 17 percent of the government budget in the late
1980s.[33] Overall, however, subsidies are small compared with those in
the OECD countries. A recent estimate proposed a figure of $10 billion
per year.[34] This is not so much a cautious and conservative estimate as
a gross underestimate.[35] India subsidized fertilizer alone to the tune of
$2.9 billion in 1999/2000.[36] For want of anything better, the authors
posit a minimalist total for non-OECD countries of $25 billion but
believe that a more realistic guesstimate would be at least $50 billion.

The Environmental Resource Base

The environmental resource base underpinning agriculture is being
widely degraded by a variety of farming practices.[37] Much of this
degradation can be ascribed in part, at least, to agricultural subsidies
that foster overexploitative agriculture.[38]

Consider soil erosion. During the past twenty years, some 500 billion tonnes of topsoil have been eroded away, an amount roughly
equivalent to all the topsoil in India's croplands. Currently, between
25 billion tonnes[39] and 75 billion tonnes[40] of topsoil are lost each
year, two-thirds of it from agricultural lands. During the past forty
years, at least 4.3 million square kilometers of croplands were abandoned because of soil loss, an expanse equivalent to 30 percent of
today's croplands.[41] Without better soil-conservation practices,
between 1.4 million and 2.0 million square kilometers (the smaller
expanse is equal to Alaska) will lose most of their good-quality soil
over the next two decades—and this will apply in parts of Indiana
and India alike.[42] If soil erosion is allowed to continue virtually
unchecked, it could well cause a decline of 19–29 percent in food
production from rain-fed croplands during the twenty-five-year
period 1985–2010.[43]

The on-site costs of soil erosion are borne by farmers themselves,
so they are not considered to be a cost pushed off onto society and
hence a hidden subsidy. Of course, the loss of cropland productivity
results in higher food costs for consumers, so to that extent society
eventually pays part of the on-farm cost. In the longer run, moreover,
soil erosion will impose much bigger costs on society if, without

enough topsoil, the world finds itself unable to grow enough food: that would be an externality indeed. Let us limit the calculation, however, to costs borne by off-farm society, these being costs that sooner or later must be picked up by the public at large. Upshot: soil erosion costs are an implicit subsidy from society to farmers. According to recent research,[44] the off-farm costs worldwide can be put at $150 billion per year, just under two-fifths of total costs.

There are other societal costs of intensified agriculture, and these too can be considered as implicit subsidies from society to farmers. They include health hazards from runoff of nitrogenous fertilizer polluting public water supplies.[45] In China, for instance, nitrogenous fertilizer is applied to croplands at rates as high as 1.9 tonnes per hectare per year, and the amount of fertilizer actually taken up by plants is only about 40 percent. As a result of fertilizer washoff, more than half of local groundwater stocks are contaminated above the tolerance level. The same fertilizers cause much eutrophication of water bodies such as lakes and rivers.[46] The costs in China remain unquantified economically, but in the United States, runoff of agricultural chemicals causes an annual $9 billion worth of damage to surface waters.[47]

Another chemical additive, pesticides, can be considered as a final environmental externality. The annual average for global sales of pesticides in the mid-1990s was $30 billion.[48] Many governments, especially in the developing world, which accounts for one-third of all pesticide use, give outsize subsidies for pesticides. The average is 50 percent, within a range of 15–90 percent.[49]

Apart from direct subsidies for pesticides, there is a host of indirect subsidies, including below-market interest rates for loans from state-controlled banks, reduced prices for imported chemicals due to overvalued exchange rates, and tax advantages to agrochemical companies for the import and sale of pesticides.[50] These too remain economically unquantified for the most part.

The United States, which has used pesticides longer than developing countries, now applies ten times more insecticides than in 1945; meanwhile, crop losses to insects have almost doubled due a host of factors, including the pesticide-induced demise of pests' natural enemies and the capacity of insect pests to adapt evolutionarily to pesticides ("every pesticide selects for its own failure"). Since 1965, the number of species resistant to common pesticides has risen from 182 to more than 900.[51] (Figure 3.3). Pests now destroy 40 percent of crops worldwide, a proportion that is probably higher than before pesticides were widely introduced, in the late 1940s.[52]

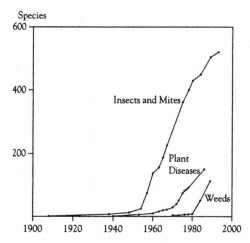

Figure 3.3. Pesticide-Resistant Species since 1908. Source: G. Gardner, "Preserving Agricultural Resources," in L. R. Brown et al., State of the World, 1996 (New York: Norton, 1996): 78–94.

Farmers find themselves on a chemical treadmill. Insect pests become resistant to pesticides, so next year's pesticides must be still more lethal, despite the ever greater cost to farmers' finances—and to human health. By definition, these synthetic chemicals are highly toxic, and every year some 3 million people in developing countries are affected to some degree by pesticide poisoning, of which 700,000 people suffer long-term effects and 220,000 die.[53] Unfortunately, there is no estimate available of this sizeable cost to society and hence of the implicit subsidy from society to pesticide-using farmers.

> Since 1965, the number of species resistant to common pesticides has risen from 182 to more than 900.

Nor are there good comprehensive data for other externality costs from pesticides. In the United States, however, it has been minimally estimated[54] that the environmental and social costs from pesticides, including groundwater contamination, wildlife and fishery losses, and public health impacts, total at least $8.3 billion per year. American farmers pay $3.2 billion of this cost through on-farm problems arising from the destruction of natural pest enemies and pesticide resistance, meaning that U.S. society pays the rest: $5.1 billion per year, say $5 billion. On top of the externality costs listed are many unrecorded losses from destruction of soil invertebrates, microfauna, and microflora. So the $5 billion estimate is cautious.

American farmers use pesticides worth $6 billion per year, one-fifth of the global total of some $30 billion. The same share arises with respect to volume: 0.5 billion kilograms versus 2.5 billion kilograms. But externality costs in the rest of the world are surely far higher by proportion, if only because of the ratio of pesticide deaths among humans: 20–25 in the United States per year versus 220,000 worldwide. Indeed, externality costs overall can be estimated at $100 billion per year, constituting a concealed subsidy from society to agriculture—and even this last figure can be confidently regarded as a severe underestimate.[55]

Agriculture also contributes significantly to what is likely to prove the biggest environmental problem of all, global warming. Both crops and livestock produce carbon dioxide, methane, and nitrous oxide. Regrettably, there is still no authoritative economic evaluation of the potential adverse effects of global warming (except for a few minimalist efforts), so the case here must go by default.

In summary of environmental externalities as covert subsidies from agriculture to society, they amount to $150 billion per year for soil erosion and $100 billion for pesticides. Total, $250 billion per year. If there were data for broad-scale pollution by nitrogenous fertilizers, as well as biodiversity decline leading to loss of pollination services and natural pest controls, that would raise the total for these implicit subsidies all the more. Recall, for instance, the $9 billion per year in just the United States for damage to surface waters from agrochemical runoff.

Subsidies Worldwide

According to the foregoing calculations, conventional or formal subsidies to agriculture now amount to $360 billion per year in OECD countries and $25 billion in non-OECD countries, for a total of $385 billion per year. In addition, there are the environmental externalities, at $250 billion per year. This makes for a grand total of $635 billion per year.

How many of these subsidies shall we consider to be perverse? Certain subsidies have sometimes been beneficial in certain local and short-term respects, but many subsidies reveal scope to exert long-term injury on both economies and environments writ large. The documentation in this chapter makes plain that there are many unfortunate repercussions of agricultural subsidies. As can be seen in Box 3.2, New Zealand has eliminated virtually all its subsidies, and the country's economy and environment alike are better off, as is

Box 3.2. THE CASE OF NEW ZEALAND

In the early 1980s, New Zealand took the momentous step of phasing out its agricultural subsidies (followed in 1988 by the removal of irrigation subsidies). This was all the more remarkable in a country with an economy more dependent on agriculture and food exports than virtually any other in the developed world (it features 4 million people and 65 million sheep). By 1995, primary agriculture accounted for 5.2 percent of GDP and related industries bumped up the total to 15.4 percent, while agricultural products accounted for 51 percent of the country's merchandised exports (excluding forestry).[*]

During the brief period 1979–1984, supports for agriculture increased from 15 percent to 40 percent of farmers' gross income and farm subsidies rose until they were equivalent to 14 percent of the government's budget and 6 percent of GNP.[†] The government decided that these amounts were far too high and started to eliminate subsidies as part of overall measures to deregulate key sectors of the economy. It canceled a wide range of support measures, including minimum prices for wool, beef, mutton, and dairy products, and it phased out land-development loans, fertilizer and irrigation subsidies, and subsidized credit.

As a result, farmland prices dropped at first by 60 percent and fertilizer use declined by 50 percent. By 1995, however, farmland prices had recovered to 86 percent of their 1982 value in real terms and fertilizer prices had returned nearly to prereform levels. Although the value of farm output initially declined, it increased again by the late 1980s. There was a halt to land clearing and overstocking, which in the past had been the principal causes of widespread soil erosion. Whereas stock raising had been encouraged by subsidies to encroach onto erodible hills, it has now intensified on better lands, and the hills have been planted with trees, leading to a 50 percent increase in the plantations' expanse. The number of farms today, 80,000, is slightly higher than in 1983, as is the number of full-time farmworkers. The meat industry has moved from being the least efficient in the world to being the second most efficient. Farming has become more diversified and competitive in the international marketplace.[‡]

Although there were seven difficult years as farmers adjusted, few of them want to return to subsidies. They prefer the marketplace, even with its risks, believing it is the only sustainable long-term option. Their country's experience could eventually lead other governments to follow suit to some extent, at least, however much the reforms may have been long viewed by certain communities as practically unworkable and politically unacceptable.[§]

[*]   B. Chamberlin, *Farming and Subsidies: Debunking the Myths* (Wellington, New Zealand: Government Printer, 1996); New Zealand Ministry of Agriculture and Fisheries, *Situation and Outlook for New Zealand Agriculture* (Wellington: New Zealand Ministry of Agriculture and Fisheries, 1996).

[†]   A. Bollard, *New Zealand: Economic Reforms, 1984–1991* (San Francisco: International Center for Economic Growth, 1992).

[‡]   Bollard, *New Zealand*; A. A. Shepherd, *New Zealand: The Environmental Effects of Removing Agricultural Subsidies* (Paris: Organisation for Economic Co-operation and Development, 1996).

[§]   B. L. Gardner, "Liberalization in New Zealand Agriculture," *American Journal of Agricultural Economics* 76 (1994): 1053–1054; F. Spinelli, *Farming Without Subsidies in New Zealand* (Washington, D.C.: U.S. Department of Agriculture, 1994); A. Walker and B. Bell, *Aspects of New Zealand's Experience in Agricultural Reform Since 1984* (Wellington: New Zealand Ministry of Agriculture and Fisheries, 1994).

agreed on all sides. To this limited extent, we could reasonably assume that virtually all subsidies in agriculture anywhere are perverse. This would perhaps be pushing the point too far. For the purposes of this book and because of the need to come up with some concluding figure, however far from conclusive, a total for perverse subsidies is proposed that is around two-thirds of the formal subsidies total, namely $256 billion, say $260 billion, per year. This is a somewhat arbitrary reckoning, and it is applied to a sector of unusually large financial size. But it is considered a realistic reckoning, and it reflects consultations on this point with established agricultural experts in various parts of the world. The true proportion could be 15 percent higher or lower, which postulates a range of $220–$300 billion per year. The authors believe it is unlikely to lie outside this range—unless better-judgment assessments can demonstrate otherwise.

On top of this are the environmental externalities described earlier and considered to be hidden subsidies from society to agriculture. Just the two instances documented amount to $250 billion per year. Since they are adverse for the environment by definition and adverse for the economy through their quantified costs, they are all viewed as perverse subsidies.

So the grand total of perverse subsidies is here estimated to be

Table 3.3. Agriculture Subsidies Worldwide, 1998

	Conventional Subsidies ($ billion)	Externalities ($ billion)	Total Subsidies ($ billion)	Perverse Subsidies ($ billion)
OECD	360		360	
Non-OECD	25		25	
TOTAL	385		385	260
Worldwide		250	250	250
TOTAL	385	250	635	510
				(range 470–550)

Source: Organisation for Economic Co-operation and Development (OECD), *Agricultural Policies in OECD Countries: Monitoring and Evaluation, 1999* (Paris: OECD, 1999).

$510 billion per year, within a range of $470 billion to $550 billion (Table 3.3).

Within a broader economic context, these figures must clearly rank as a low estimate. Consider some further indirect costs. Agricultural subsidies do much to distort trade patterns and even to heighten political tensions among the international community, especially as concerns North–South relationships.[56] Subsidies in developed countries make it unduly hard for developing countries to compete in international markets, thus reinforcing the inefficiency of their agriculture.[57] Modest liberalization of agricultural trade would be worth $150 billion to the global economy by 2002, most of it due to cutbacks in farm protection; full liberalization would be worth almost $400 billion a year (1991 values). European GDP would be 2.5 percent higher, and some Asian economies could benefit by 8 percent; the United States's balance of trade would be $42 billion better off.[58]

These ripple effects of international trade deserve a further look. Subsidized exports have undermined developing-country livelihoods by flooding local markets with cheap imported food, as witnessed in the impact of European Union beef dumped in West Africa. Pastoral farmers in Mali, Niger, and Burkina Faso sell animals in local markets, which during the late 1980s were disrupted by European beef subsidized enough to be sold at one-third of the normal price. Also in West Africa, cheap wheat imports have displaced traditional food staples in indigenous diets. Wheat imports into the coastal region increased by over 8 percent per year for the past decade, while per capita production of sorghum and millet fell. By driving down local prices, subsidized wheat exports from developed countries have done much to damage rural livelihoods.[59]

Scope for Policy Interventions

However difficult subsidy removal is reputed to be, there are some success stories. One of the best is the severe curtailment of pesticides in Indonesia and the introduction of integrated pest management (IPM). This strategy allows for limited use of pesticides as part of an overall plan deploying mixed crops, staged plantings, and natural enemies of pests. In 1985, the government of Indonesia and those of Senegal, Egypt, and several other countries were covering 85 percent of farmers' pesticide costs. In Indonesia, however, massive use of pesticides from the mid-1970s through the mid-1980s inadvertently eliminated the natural insect predators of the brown planthopper. This pest had originally been no more than a secondary and minor problem, but pesticides caused it to become a prime pest that cost Indonesia $1.5 billion in rice losses by the mid-1980s.[60]

During the brief period 1986–1989, the Indonesian government slashed subsidies from 75 percent to zero, using part of the savings of $180 million per year to fund its new IPM program. The government also banned fifty-seven of sixty-six kinds of pesticides.[61] While rice farmers' use of pesticides plunged by 60 percent, their rice yields rose by 15 percent—a phenomenon that reflected the recovery of the natural predators of the rice pests. During just the years 1986–1990, there were savings of $1 billion for rice growers and the national economy. The IPM strategy has subsequently been adopted in the Philippines, Vietnam, India, Pakistan, Egypt, Ghana, and most Latin American countries.[62]

There have also been fine results from IPM in India, China, and Brazil. In Jiangsu Province in China, pesticide use on cotton has decreased by 90 percent and pest control costs have declined by nearly 85 percent, accompanied by increases in crop yields. In Brazil, IPM use in soybean production has reduced pesticide applications by more than 80 percent.[63]

Let us note too that certain agricultural subsidies can generate positive spillovers into other sectors. In India, input supports during the 1980s totaled 17 percent of agricultural value added (25 percent for wheat and 35 percent for rice).[64] They not only achieved much for the country's Green Revolution but also generated many spin-off benefits. From the early 1970s through the early 1990s, agricultural subsidies fed into infrastructure of many sorts, with the result that the length of surfaced roads more than doubled and the number of villages with electricity quadrupled.[65]

Moreover, there are promising signs in a few countries of a shift away from extravagant subsidies. As mentioned earlier, New Zealand has phased out just about all its subsidies (Box 3.2), and Australia has gone far to follow suit in the form of reductions in irrigation subsidies. The next most promising démarche, though of far smaller scale, will probably be in the United States, where the 1996 Farm Bill, providing policy legislation for the period 1996–2002, has made the most sweeping changes in agricultural policy since the New Deal. It aims to signal a new era when farmers' decisions will be dictated by the competitive market rather than by government subsidies. Hitherto, farmers' incomes, including subsidies, have been 28 percent higher than they would have been if farmers had to operate at world market prices. The Farm Bill will also increase spending on conservation of soil, water, and on-farm wetlands via the Conservation Reserve Program.[66]

Subsidies should be not only unlinked from production but also relinked to a broad range of crops and environmental services. This should prompt farmers to adopt practices that enhance rather than degrade their farm capital.[67] It would contrast markedly with the present position, whereby price supports unwittingly foster soil erosion and other environmental ills. Indeed, subsidies send farmers far more powerful signals about how to use (or misuse) the land than do all the small grants provided for soil conservation.[68] Subsidies also encourage overuse of agricultural chemicals such as synthetic fertilizers; reducing subsidies on these fertilizers would promote alternatives such as use of organic manures in integrated crop and livestock systems.[69]

Particularly helpful would be policy measures that foster environmental safeguards, notably in the form of set-aside programs that divert erodible farmland from crop production in order to protect topsoil. These programs are strongly supported by governments, thus supplying an instance of constructive subsidies. (The measure can also serve to control the supply of food or other commodities and thus to prop up or even raise prices.) There have been some sizeable set-aside programs in recent years: in 1995 alone, 202,000 square kilometers in the United States and 81,000 square kilometers in the European Union (both equating to around 11 percent of arable land) and 7,000 square kilometers in Japan, or 16 percent of arable land. In return for setting aside land, farmers receive compensation payments, usually in the range of $35 to $125 per hectare, though occasionally as high as $1,000 for rice paddies in Japan and $6,300 for forestry in the European Union. Participation is usually voluntary, so the compensation has to be as much as a farmer would have received through crops.[70] The 1996 Farm Bill authorized expenditures of $2.2 billion during 1996–2002 on agri-environmental measures, including payments to farmers to keep highly erodible soils, wetlands, and other key habitats out of production.[71]

More helpful still would be measures that prevent the most erodible and otherwise vulnerable lands from being put under crops in the first place. But that would require a level of anticipatory land-use planning that does not yet seem feasible on a broad scale.

This leads to the question of incentives for farmers to safeguard the environmental services they derive from their lands. These services comprise nontraded public goods such as aquifer recharge, landscape amenity, flood control, riparian buffer zones, and wetland habitats. They could be developed as "crops," providing farm income as well as enriching the landscape. In fact, some American and Canadian farmers are already doing as much through programs such as the North American Waterfowl Management Plan, by which ducks as well as taxpayers foot the bills (at the ostensible behest of duck hunters). In Canada, the revenues have secured nearly 1,600 square kilometers of waterfowl habitat in the agricultural region of western Canada, a further 920 square kilometers of habitat have been restored, and 2,800 square kilometers are being managed for as many as 168 wildlife species. Much of the land continues to produce conventional farm commodities compatible with wildlife production.[72]

This approach is paralleled in certain sectors of Europe, notably the Alps, where Swiss cattle and montane meadows add to landscape attractions as part of a tourist package of expectations. There are many other such examples: the Norfolk Broads in England, the sheep moors of the Lake District and highland Scotland, and the lakes of Sweden and Norway.

All this points the way toward sustainable agriculture, a large component of which is environmentally sensitive agriculture.[73] "Eco-agriculture," as it is sometimes known, can use 60–70 percent less chemical fertilizers, pesticides, and fossil-fuel energy while maintaining crop yields; soils contain 30–70 percent more organic matter, which, apart from the fertility benefit, sequesters carbon from the atmosphere. Sustainable agriculture can also generate more jobs and result in more money being spent on local goods and services.[74]

Pushing this general approach still further, some analysts even envisage the eventual abolition of ministries of agriculture and their replacement with ministries of land resources, which will look out for conventional agriculture together with forests for timber and recreation combined; upland watersheds, hedgerows, and coppices for wildlife; sport fisheries; and soils and biotas overall as carbon sinks. After all, rural areas are crucial in terms of not only food production but also many other forms of enterprise, including leisure activities and even the "spiritual life" of countries concerned.[75]

To end on a pragmatic note, consider the policy scope to foster agricultural research. If ever there was a niche for government support, this is it. We need agricultural research more than ever if we are to feed twice as many people within another three or four decades. Hence the calls from the 1996 World Food Summit for another science-based Green Revolution. Yet the budget of the Consultative Group on International Agricultural Research (CGIAR) dropped from $319 million in 1992 to $245 million by 1994, even though its network of fourteen international agricultural research centers needed $270 million merely to maintain activities at erstwhile levels.[76] In light of the returns on research investment, which can be as high as 20 percent or even 40 percent per year, the CGIAR budget is absurdly small.[77] There is all the greater urgency in bolstering research funding at a time when agricultural planners are aiming for an annual 2 percent increase in food production, and given that there is often a time lag of ten to twenty years before breakthrough research leads to major harvest increases in farmers' fields.[78] Note that the current CGIAR budget is less than 0.1 percent of what the OECD countries spend each year on agricultural subsidies.

Chapter 4

FOSSIL FUELS
AND NUCLEAR ENERGY

We like energy, and our appetite for it keeps on growing. Since we left our caves, we have increased our numbers roughly 1,000 times, and each of us consumes roughly 1,000 times more energy, meaning that our consumption has soared one millionfold. An American uses six times as much energy, mostly fossil fuels, as the worldwide average, and seventy times more than a Bangladeshi.[1] That same American consumes twice as much energy as do Western Europeans and three times as much as do Japanese. But by increasing the efficiency with which the United States uses energy to Western European and Japanese levels, the country could save $100–$200 billion per year.[2] As Amory Lovins points out, energy saving is not only a free lunch but one we are paid to eat.

Energy production and use has become the single largest enterprise of humankind, and it is central to most economies worldwide. It can bestow abundant benefits on us. During the seventy-year start-up of the Industrial Revolution, when we began to use commercial energy in a big way, the average worker was enabled to become 100 times more productive. Energy also has great capacity to harm the environment through the polluting effects of fossil fuels, manifested through urban smog, acid rain, and global warming, as well as through nuclear fuels with their radioactive wastes. Urban smog leads to asthma, emphysema, and a host of other respiratory ills, while acid rain imposes extensive damage on biotas. As for global warming, this is widely regarded as the most important single problem in the environmental arena; half of global-warming processes are due to carbon dioxide (CO_2) emissions, two-thirds of which come from fossil fuels. Similarly, subsidies for fossil fuels and nuclear energy can harm the economy through their markedly distortional effects. So the sector as a whole has large potential for perverse subsidies.

A closely associated sector, road transportation, utilizes a fossil fuel, oil, that accounts for 97 percent of all fuel used in road transportation. At the same time, road transportation features a host of other subsidies, many of which are unusually perverse and unusually large. This entire topic is dealt with separately in the next chapter. Subsidies for oil are considered here only from the standpoint of producing the stuff, as opposed to subsidies for its use in road transportation.

However large our appetite for energy today, it is set to expand rapidly. Under a business-as-usual scenario, world demand is expected to increase by 60 percent during the period 1997–2020—and carbon emissions by 62 percent (Table 4.1). Of energy demand in 2020, fossil fuels are likely to account for more than 90 percent[3] (Figure 4.1).

Today, we derive 85 percent of our commercial energy from fossil fuels and 7 percent from nuclear power, amounts that may well persist until 2020.[4] Only in electricity have alternatives—notably hydropower, geothermal energy, and wind and solar power—made much contribution, and except for hydropower they attract little government support. It is fossil fuels and nuclear energy (including electricity) that receive the great bulk of energy subsidies. The energy sector also features many indirect and concealed subsidies in the form of environmental externalities. It generates such marked pollution that some analysts consider the environmental costs of fossil fuels to be at least equal to and possibly much greater than the more conventional and recognized costs.[5] All this, moreover, is without counting what will surely prove to be the biggest environmental externality of all, global warming (see Chapter 2), half of which is due to emissions of carbon dioxide, which stem primarily from fossil fuels.

Table 4.1. Energy Consumption and Carbon Emissions by Region, 1990–2020

Region	Energy Consumption (Quadrillion Btu)				Carbon Emissions (Million Tonnes)			
	1990	1997	2010	2020	1990	1997	2010	2020
Industrialized countries	182.8	203.7	238.7	259.9	2,850	3,039	3,563	3,928
Eastern Europe/ former Soviet Union	76.4	53.3	63.0	75.7	1,337	878	992	1,151
Developing countries								
Asia	51.4	75.3	126.4	172.6	1,067	1,522	2,479	3,380
Middle East	13.1	17.9	26.2	34.3	229	297	422	552
Africa	9.3	11.4	15.8	20.6	180	214	292	380
Central and South America	13.7	18.3	30.1	44.7	174	225	399	617
TOTAL	87.6	122.9	198.5	272.1	1,649	2,258	3,591	4,930
TOTAL WORLD (rounded)	347	380	500	608	5,836	6,175	8,146	10,009

Sources: U.S. Department of Energy, Energy Information Administration (EIA), Office of Energy Markets and End Use, *International Energy Annual, 1997,* Report no. DOE/EIA-0219(97) (Washington, D.C.: EIA, 1999); U.S. Department of Energy, Energy Information Administration (EIA), *World Energy Projection System, 2000* (Washington, D.C.: EIA, 2000).

Energy—or, rather, the production and distribution of energy—is often controlled in major measure by the state. This means that many governments play a central role in setting energy prices. The failure of governments to price energy properly means that consumption is higher, grows faster, and is more polluting than it should be. As we shall see, fossil fuels and nuclear energy cost society many billions of dollars more than their users pay directly. There is a plethora of hidden costs: tax policies supply credits, exemptions, deferrals, preferential rates, loans, loan guarantees, exclusions, deductions, research and development programs, depletion allowances, accelerated depreciation, risk insurance, and regulatory costs (see Box 4.1). While these tax policies may have served a productive purpose when they were first introduced, many have now exceeded their usefulness, yet they remain on the books. In the United States, depletion allowances were introduced to promote oil production during World War I. This was an entirely valid reason at the time, but it has long run out of rationale even though the tax subsidy persists.

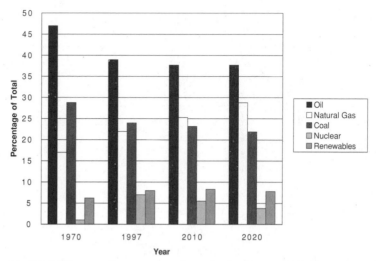

Figure 4.1. World Energy Consumption. Sources: For history: U.S. Department of Energy, Energy Information Administration (EIA), Office of Energy Markets and End Use, International Statistics Database and *International Energy Annual, 1997,* Report no. DOE/EIA-0219(97) (Washington, D.C.: EIA, 1999). For projections: U.S. Department of Energy, Energy Information Administration (EIA), *World Energy Projection System, 2000* (Washington, D.C.: EIA, 2000).

While the fossil-fuel industry is worth well over $1.4 trillion per year,[6] it is the third most heavily subsidized of all economic sectors, after road transportation and agriculture. Yet we have only a hazy idea of how large these subsidies are. Nuclear energy, being a much smaller and less diverse industry, should be accurately and precisely documented, but governments, especially those of the former Soviet Union, France, and several Asian countries, are even more loath to divulge information about nuclear energy than they are about fossil fuels. In Western Europe, nuclear-energy subsidies total around $5 billion per year, and in the United States, $7 billion.[7] Not only are fossil-fuel subsidies large; they are unusually damaging environmentally, entraining heavy economic costs both present and prospective. But as with agriculture and other sectors with huge subsidies, many governments simply do not know (or are not saying) how much of the taxpayers' money they are directing into fossil-fuel energy. Virtually

> *While the fossil fuel industry is worth well over $1.4 trillion per year, it is the third most heavily subsidized of all economic sectors, after road transportation and agriculture.*

Box 4.1. ENERGY SUBSIDIES: ALL SORTS AND CONDITIONS THEREOF

There are many direct and well-known types of subsidy that have the specific aim of altering market prices. There are also indirect subsidies—probably more numerous yet less recognized than direct subsidies—that operate via fiscal and other measures to affect investment decisions, such as favorable tax rates for oil and gas exploration. These hidden subsidies can sometimes be more influential than direct subsidies. So the term *energy subsidies* refers at some times to transfers to energy consumers via underpricing and at other times to transfers to producers via overpricing. It can even be a combination of the two.

Similarly, in the world of energy subsidies, producer subsidy equivalents (PSEs) are "direct financial aid from governments to support current production, plus price supports that result indirectly from limits to the use of other fuels to substitute for domestic coal, or from agreements between coal producers and coal users. In effect, the PSE is the direct budgetary subsidy that would make domestic production, at current costs, competitive with imports (at current levels of production and import prices)."*

* L. Michaelis, "The Environmental Implications of Energy and Transport Subsidies," in *Organisation for Economic Co-operation and Development (OECD), Subsidies and Environment: Exploring the Linkages* (Paris: OECD 1996), 175–192.

---

across the board, the database is uneven in quantity and poor in quality. Worse, such figures as are available often conflict severely. A curious circumstance, and one that makes it unusually difficult to draw policy conclusions.

Hence, the following appraisal is partial at best. At least, it presents a solid picture of how far the fossil-fuel industry is being propped up by government handouts, even though its prodigious environmental externalities and other societal spillovers suggest it should be heavily taxed. Or, as a minimum, the industry should be subjected to the full rigors of the marketplace: coal and solar energy should demonstrate their prowess on a level playing field, whereas coal is effectively awarded a start of between ten and thirty goals. Ironically, it is the communist countries of the former Soviet bloc and China that have been doing most to shed this socialistic mode of running an energy economy. One of the most energy profligate and environmentally polluting countries, the

Table 4.2. Fossil-Fuel Producers, 1998: The Top Tens

Country	Percentage of World Totals		
	Oil	Coal	Gas
Saudi Arabia	12.6		
United States	10.5	26.4	23.9
Russia	8.7	4.7	24.3
Iran	5.3		2.2
Mexico	5.0		
Venezuela	4.9		
China	4.6	28.0	
Norway	4.3		2.1
United Kingdom	3.8		4.0
Canada	3.5	1.8	7.1
Germany		2.7	
Poland		3.4	
South Africa		5.3	
Australia		6.6	
India		6.6	
Netherlands			2.8
Uzbekistan			2.3
Algeria			3.2
Indonesia			3.0
Ukraine		1.8	
TOTALS (rounded)	63	87	75

Source: BP Amoco, *Statistical Review of World Energy, 1999*
(London: BP Amoco, 1999).

United States, has not gone nearly so far to cut its subsidies, though they are smaller in relation to the size of the U.S. economy and cutbacks would be highly beneficial in both economic and environmental terms.

The problem of the poor database is helped somewhat by the fact that the fossil-fuels sector is concentrated in relatively few producer and consumer countries. The top ten producers account for 63 percent of oil, 75 percent of natural gas, and 87 percent of coal, while the top ten consumers account for 59 percent of oil, 68 percent of natural gas, and 82 percent of coal. For further details, see Tables 4.2 and 4.3. China alone accounts for almost one-third of the world's coal production, and the OECD countries account for half of all consumption. To this extent, it is a little easier to track down the major subsidizers.

In 1991 and before the former Soviet Union and a few other

Table 4.3. Fossil-Fuel Consumers, 1998: The Top Tens

Country	Percentage of World Totals		
	Oil	Coal	Gas
United States	25.2	24.0	27.3
Japan	7.5	4.0	3.1
China	5.6	27.7	
Germany	4.0	3.8	3.6
Russia	3.6	4.6	16.3
Italy	2.8		2.6
France	2.8		
South Korea	2.8		
India	2.5	6.9	
Canada	2.5		3.1
South Africa		4.0	
Poland		2.7	
Australia		2.1	
United Kingdom		1.8	4.0
Ukraine			3.1
Uzbekistan			2.1
Iran			2.3
TOTALS (rounded)	59	82	68

Source: BP Amoco, *Statistical Review of World Energy, 1999* (London: BP Amoco, 1999).

countries started to slash their fossil-fuel subsidies, the non-OECD total (including electricity subsidies of $80–85 billion) was $270–$330 billion.[8] Two-thirds of this total was in the former Soviet Union (FSU), making it far and away the single largest player in the fossil-fuels arena. While it has engaged in stringent slashing of subsidies since 1991, it still features prominently. In 1991, subsidies in the FSU amounted to an astonishing 10–13 percent of GDP; in Poland, Egypt, and Venezuela, they were over 10 percent, though in India they were "only" 2.3 percent and in China 1.8 percent.[9] Fortunately, almost all of these countries undertook deep cuts during the 1990s.

United States

The United States possesses less than 5 percent of the world's population but consumes 26 percent of the world's commercial energy.[10] It consumes roughly twice as much energy per person and per unit of GNP as do Western Europe and Japan.[11] By increasing the efficiency with which Americans utilize energy to Western European levels, the United States could save over $100 billion per year; by matching the efficiency of Japan, $200 billion per year. Overall, energy waste costs the U.S. economy over $300 billion per year—more than the military budget. Conversely, energy conservation measures since the 1970s have saved $1 trillion.[12]

The United States also emits one-quarter of all the carbon dioxide accumulating annually in the global atmosphere. In per capita terms, it emits roughly twice as much carbon dioxide as Germany, Russia, or Japan, almost three times as much as Italy, eight times as much as China, and twenty times as much as India. Fossil fuels contribute 90 percent of the United States's greenhouse gas emissions (plus 90 percent of local air pollution and acid rain and the great majority of gases leading to smog).[13] Yet by slashing fossil-fuel subsidies, the United States would cut its CO_2 emissions to 16 percent below 1990 levels by 2010, thereby surpassing its Kyoto target by a sizeable margin (and reducing pollutants such as sulfur dioxide, nitrous oxide, and particulates). It would also generate energy savings of 13 percent.[14]

U.S. energy subsidies in the mid-1990s totaled $25 billion (range $18–$32 billion), equivalent to $350 per American household.[15] (Note, however, that certain estimates vary by an order of magnitude, depending upon definitions and criteria.) Of total energy subsidies, fossil-fuels and nuclear energy subsidies amounted to $21 billion, or 84 percent of the total. Within the fossil-fuel category, the smallest subsidy went to natural gas, even though it is environmentally cleaner than oil or coal. Some minor subsidies also went to a miscellany of items, such as government-sponsored research and development and general investment tax credits.[16]

U.S. subsidies, like those in Europe, are strongly weighted against nonpolluting renewable sources of energy. Among the leading biases are specialized tax benefits for mining coal, oil, and gas (including depletion allowances of them as nonrenewable resources); exemption from minimum taxation requirements for fossil fuels; public financing for nuclear reactors, among other supports for nuclear energy; and disproportionate amounts of public research and development for conventional energy sources, primarily fossil fuels. In addition, a miscellany of minor supports, such as agricultural policies, discourage crop diversification to energy crops. The subsidy ratio for renewables versus nonrenewables is 1:10, though some experts consider it can be as high as 1:35 or even more in a few countries, such as Germany.[17] There is good cause to wonder why the major category of nonrenewables, fossil fuels, deserves any subsidies at all.

Table 4.4. Energy Subsidies in Western Europe

Country/ Region	Fossil Fuels ($ Million)	Nuclear Energy ($ Million)	Renewables ($ Million)
European Union	520.7	428.3	131.3
Austria	4.7	1.4	35.7
Belgium	61.6	146.8	5.5
Denmark	368.2	2.8	108.8
Finland	68.7	8.9	129.0
France	280.5	563.3	459.3
Germany	6,890.4	314.6	149.3
Greece	1.3	0.0	5.2
Ireland	32.4	0.0	5.6
Italy	11.0	147.3	37.1
Luxembourg	0.0	0.0	6.9
Netherlands	31.0	48.0	88.4
Norway	20.7	7.6	5.8
Portugal	4.5	3.0	1.6
Spain	705.5	40.0	68.3
Sweden	3.4	15.9	56.5
Switzerland	13.7	61.1	104.0
United Kingdom	1,217.9	2,885.9	94.9
TOTAL (rounded)	10,236	4,675	1,493

Source: Greenpeace International, *The Subsidy Scandal: The European Clash between Environmental Rhetoric and Public Spending* (Amsterdam: Greenpeace International, 1997).

All OECD Countries

OECD countries as a whole subsidize energy (not just fossil fuels and nuclear energy) to the extent of at least $70–$80 billion a year (so the United States accounts for around one-third).[18] In Western Europe, the total is $16 billion;[19] the most extreme instance is German coal, supported to the extravagant tune of some $7 billion per year (Table 4.4 and Box 4.2). Subsidies to fossil fuels and nuclear energy in OECD countries, leaving aside minor forms of energy, total $71 billion (range $66–$76 billion).

The Former Soviet Union and Eastern Europe

Of all non-OECD subsidies to fossil fuels (including electricity) in 1991, totaling $270–$330 billion,[20] roughly two-thirds were in the former Soviet Union (FSU) and Eastern Europe.[21] Just coal subsidies amounted to 50 percent of the world price—and of course these high subsidies led producers to extract poor-quality coal with low caloric

Box 4.2. COAL SUBSIDIES IN GERMANY

Coal is the most polluting of the fossil fuels, whether through production or consumption, so it should rationally be taxed rather than subsidized. Yet production is heavily supported in industrialized countries such as Germany and Japan in order to help high-cost producers compete with imported coal.

There could hardly be a more remarkable instance of perverse subsidies than coal mining in Germany.[*] Germany has practically no oil and very little gas, so there is a strong security case in favor of coal. In 1982, the German government supplied subsidies of $30 for each tonne of coal, a figure that by 1995 had soared to $119 per tonne (68 percent of production costs), while the subsidies total had climbed from $2.9 billion to $6.9 billion (in terms of producer price supports but omitting tax credits for antipollution equipment and other hidden subsidies). This meant that the subsidy cost of protecting each of the country's 90,000 mining jobs for one year had risen from $15,400 to $72,800 (1995 dollars). The price subsidy for coal as a percentage of the international price is around 230 percent, by contrast with that in countries of the European Union, 150 percent.[†]

It would now be cheaper for the German government to retire all its miners and pay them their regular salaries to stay at home, leaving taxpayers and electricity users much better off. Making electricity from coal in Germany levies further costs on consumers for disease and death caused by air pollution. (If German utilities had to pay those costs too, wind power would suddenly become much more competitive and profitable.)[‡] Furthermore, the limited contribution of the outsize subsidies is demonstrated by the fact that during the period 1985–1995, the German mining workforce still fell by half, albeit while constituting nearly 2 percent of the national workforce.[§]

Moreover, France and Belgium have virtually eliminated their coal subsidies, while Spain, the United Kingdom, and Japan have radically reduced theirs. As a result, coal miners in the United Kingdom now constitute less than 0.2 percent of the national workforce, down from an average of 1.4 percent in the early 1980s, and in France they account for less than 0.1 percent.[||] Since most of these countries are still burning as much coal as ever, however, phasing out subsidies has mostly exported the environmental problems of coal mining to producers abroad.

[*] K. Anderson, "The Political Economy of Coal Subsidies in Europe," *Energy Policy* 23 (1995): 485–496; Data Resources Inc., *The Energy, Environment, and Economic Effect of Phasing Out Coal Subsidies in OECD Countries*

(Paris: Organisation for Economic Co-operation and Development, 1994); S. Dunn, "King Coal's Weakening Grip on Power," *World Watch* 12, no. 5 (1999): 10–19; R. P. Steenblik and P. Coroyannakis, "Reform of Coal Policies in Western and Central Europe: Implication for the Environment," *Energy Policy* 1995: 537–553.

† Organisation for Economic Co-operation and Development (OECD), *Reforming Energy and Transport Subsidies: Environmental and Economic Implications* (Paris: OECD, 1997); D. M. Roodman, *Paying the Piper: Subsidies, Politics, and the Environment* (Washington, D.C.: Worldwatch Institute, 1996).

‡ D. M. Roodman, *Getting the Signals Right: Tax Reform to Protect the Environment and the Economy* (Washington, D.C.: Worldwatch Institute, 1997); see also Anderson, "Political Economy of Coal Subsidies"; D. M. Newbury, "Removing Coal Subsidies: Implications for European Electricity Markets," *Energy Policy* 23 (1995): 523–533; Steenblik and Coroyannakis, "Reform of Coal Policies."

§ International Energy Agency (IEA), *Energy Policies of IEA Countries* (Paris: IEA, 1996).

‖ Anderson, "Political Economy of Coal Subsidies"; IEA, *Energy Policies of IEA Countries.*

content and high polluting impacts while also discouraging consumers from saving energy. As a result, the FSU has been hopelessly inefficient in its use of fossil fuels. In 1993, it emitted 502 tonnes of carbon for each $1 million of GDP, way above China's 238 tonnes, the United States's 238 tonnes, India's 183 tonnes, and Japan's 144 tonnes.[22]

Subsequently, Russia and several other FSU countries have steadily removed many of their subsidies together with their energy controls and regulations.[23] The FSU is still a "biggie" in the fossil-fuels picture, being the world's second largest energy producer after the United States.[24] During the brief period 1990–1991 to 1995–1996, price supports for fossil fuels in Russia were greatly reduced[25] (Table 4.5). The slashing of subsidies, together with the country's persistent economic troubles, mean that energy consumption fell during 1990–1997 by 45 percent.[26] Today, Russia's energy prices for industry (though not for households, which received two-thirds of energy subsidies in 1994) are moving closer to world market levels.[27]

Complete elimination of Russia's fossil-fuel subsidies would reduce energy consumption by 18 percent, carbon dioxide emissions by 17 percent, and particulate emissions by 40 percent while increas-

Table 4.5. Fossil–Fuel Subsidy Reforms in Non–OECD Countries, 1990–1996

	Subsidy Rate (Percentage of Market Price)		Total Subsidies ($ Billion)	Total Subsidies (Percentage of GDP)
	1990–1991	1995–1996	1995–1996	1995–1996
Russia	45	31	9.4	1.5
Eastern Europe	42	23	5.8	3.2
Asia	33	16	13.4	1.2
China	42	20	10.3	2.4
India	25	19	2.7	1.1
Thailand	10	9	0.5	0.4
Oil Producers	56	42	19.3	2.3
Iran	86	77	9.6	8.7
Saudi Arabia	66	34	1.7	1.4
Venezuela	76	66	2.4	4.0
Mexico	32	16	2.3	0.7
Indonesia	29	21	1.3	0.9
Others	17	2	0.5	0.06

Source: World Bank, *Expanding the Measure of Wealth: Indicators of Environmentally Sustainable Development* (Washington, D.C.: World Bank, 1997).

ing economic efficiency by an exceptional 1.5 percent of GDP.[28] But Russia will find it difficult to reduce its subsidies much further in certain sectors. Complete removal would mean that household costs for heating and gas would have to be raised tens of times over the 1994 level.[29] Meantime, the economic travails of the 1990s, plus the breakdown of many government systems, have resulted in widespread failure to pay energy bills, amounting to as much as $85 billion in 1997—a huge implicit subsidy in that it means a consumer price of zero.[30]

Total fossil-fuel subsidies in Russia now amount to $7 billion per year. That the figure is probably a severe underestimate is indicated by the nonpayment of energy bills just discussed. With the recovery of government authority, this indirect subsidy is presumably being reduced and will eventually be phased out entirely, so it is here viewed as an "eccentric one-off" and excluded from the overall reckoning of $7 billion.

Next, Eastern Europe, where there was an even greater cut in price supports for fossil-fuel use between 1990–1991 and 1995–1996 (Table 4.5). In Poland (albeit an OECD member since 1996), industrial coal prices quintupled in January 1990; before then, sulfur dioxide output per head was two and one-half times as high as the European Community average, and pollution of air, water, and soils was among the worst in the world. Something similar applied in several other countries of Eastern Europe. Largely as a result of the sudden upheaval in the region's economies from 1990 onward, however, energy use has declined by about 20 percent across the board and annual fossil-fuel subsidies have declined from $13 billion to less than $6 billion, though several countries have left their coal prices at an average of 23 percent below world prices and use four or five times as much energy per head as countries with the same income levels in Asia and Latin America.[31]

Other Non-OECD Countries

China is a fossil-fuel giant to match Russia, mainly because of its coal, which provides 74 percent of its commercial energy.[32] With nearly 30 percent of the world's coal output and employing coal for over 60 percent of its commercial energy, China is the number one coal burner, having pulled ahead of the United States (Table 4.3). Every month, it installs a new coal-fired power plant with a capacity of 1,000 megawatts.[33]

During the period 1971–1995, energy use in China grew a whopping fivefold.[34] Unfortunately, end users were not encouraged to conserve energy because prices were artificially low, which in turn was due to the government's wish to supply energy at prices way below production costs. Since the mid-1980s, however, and due to deep subsidy cuts, many fossil-fuel prices have been rising more rapidly than prices for food, clothing, and other daily-use articles. Between 1990 and 1996, subsidy rates were slashed by 50 percent[35] (Table 4.5). In some sectors and regions, China's energy prices are now comparable to those in several OECD countries.[36] All this should help to reduce the widespread pollution that has been costing the country $54 billion a year through damage to productive resources, plus sickness and premature deaths (178,000 such deaths in major cities each year).[37]

But so extensive are China's fossil-fuel deposits and so ambitious are the country's plans to exploit them that China projects a three-fold expansion in its energy use between 1990 and 2025.[38] Subsidies in 1998 still pushed prices to 11 percent below world market levels; in that year, the cost of reduced efficiency amounted to $4 billion.[39] If the government were to eliminate fossil-fuel subsidies entirely, this would reduce energy consumption by 9 percent and cut carbon dioxide emissions by 13 percent[40] (Table 4.6). Nonetheless, and even if energy efficiency efforts were to be greatly expanded, China's carbon dioxide emissions would still be projected to increase from about 10 percent of global emissions in 1989 to 20 percent in 2010.[41]

Next, consider another leading player in Asia, India, where coal contributes over half of commercial energy.[42] India too reduced its price supports for fossil fuels, from $4.2 billion in 1990–1991 to $2.7 billion in 1995–1996 (Table 4.5). The government was no longer willing or able to sustain large budget deficits, and it likewise wanted to attract capital to meet growing energy demands.[43] But today its subsidies still set prices at 14 percent below the world market, at a cost of $1.5 billion.[44] In the petroleum products sector, however, prices have risen to the world level or above, with the notable exception of kerosene, a fuel widely consumed by households, especially poorer households, and subsidized at 53 percent.[45] Were all fossil-fuel subsidies to be removed, this would reduce energy consumption by 7 percent and cut carbon dioxide emissions by 14 percent[46] (Table 4.6).

In summary, fossil-fuel subsidies in non-OECD countries, including the FSU and Eastern Europe, totaled $190–$245 billion in 1991.[47] When electricity subsidies of $80–$85 billion are included, the total rises to $270–$330 billion. An alternative analysis estimated fossil-fuel subsidies of $106 billion in 1990–1991, which, in the wake of stringent energy price reforms, plunged by one-half by 1995–1996.[48] Of this precipitous decline, Russia accounted for $19 billion, Eastern Europe $7 billion, and China $14 billion, with other sizeable amounts on the part of oil producers such as Saudi Arabia and Iran[49] (Table 4.5). According to the International Energy Agency, the benefits of full-cost pricing in eight non-OECD countries (including China, India, and Russia) reveal a subsidy of $17.2 billion in 1998. If we include the other countries of Eastern Europe, Asia, the oil-producing countries, Argentina, and Brazil, the total for non-OECD countries is $30 billion.[50]

On top of this are covert subsidies in developing countries in the form of potential budgetary savings from inefficient energy production, with avoidable power losses amounting to roughly $30 billion.[51] These various hidden subsidies not only prove a burden on the public purse. They also help to create a host of inefficient and

Table 4.6. The Benefits of Full-Cost Pricing of Energy

| | Population (Million) | Average Subsidy (Percentage of Reference Price) | Cost of Subsidy ($ Billion) | Economic Efficiency Gain (Percentage of GDP) | Effects of Subsidy Removal | |
					Reduction in Energy Consumption[a]	Reduction in CO_2 Emissions
China	1,254	10.9	3.6	0.4	9%	13%
Russia	147	32.5	6.7	1.5	18%	17%
India	987	14.2	1.5	0.3	7%	14%
Indonesia	212	27.5	0.5	0.2	7%	11%
Iran	66	80.4	3.6	2.2	48%	49%
South Africa	43	6.4	0.08	0.1	6%	8%
Venezuela	24	57.6	1.1	1.2	25%	26%
Kazakhstan	15	18.2	0.3	1.0	19%	23%
TOTAL	2,748	21.1	17.2	0.7	13%	16%
WORLDWIDE					3.5%	4.6%

Source: International Energy Agency (IEA), *World Energy Outlook: Looking at Energy Subsidies: Getting the Prices Right* (Paris: IEA, 1999).

[a]Lower-bound estimate.

fragile industries, and they tend to freeze technology, although these sizeable costs remain unquantified. Conversely, reduction of subsidies has contributed to more rational pricing and reductions in energy intensity. Brazil, which retains hardly any energy subsidies, has one of the lowest energy intensities in the developing world.[52]

All in all, today's non-OECD total can be put at $60 billion per year. This total relates only to fossil fuels. It does not include anything for nuclear subsidies, since non-OECD countries do not have (as yet) many of the world's nuclear facilities.

Nuclear Energy

While nuclear energy is an energy source that is eminently renewable, it can cause major environmental problems in the form of highly toxic and long-lasting waste products. There is also the risk of accidents like the one at Chernobyl, which, in Ukraine alone, is projected to levy a cost by 2015 of $26–$34 billion, more than the value of all nuclear-generated electricity in the FSU.[53] On top of all this, there is the threat of nuclear materials getting into the hands of terrorists and rogue states. These are formidable externality costs. There is also the question of whether nuclear power can compete in a marketplace with a level playing field. In the United States, no new nuclear power stations have been ordered since 1978: they are not up to commercial snuff. Japan has only one new reactor under construction. Worldwide, ninety-four nuclear plants have already been retired and decommissioned after an active service life of under eighteen years. Even in France, the world leader in this industry, nuclear expansion has been outpaced two to one by a more cost-effective solution, energy efficiency.[54]

These problems notwithstanding, nuclear energy has attracted much government support in countries such as France and Belgium, both of which are poor in fossil fuels. All together, there are 430 nuclear plants in thirty-two countries, including sixteen OECD countries with 85 percent of the world's reactor capacity. Nuclear energy now provides 17 percent of the world's electricity (and 7 percent of all energy), compared with hydroelectric power, at 25 percent, and renewables such as solar and wind power, at 3 percent.[55]

Because nuclear energy was viewed in the late 1950s and early 1960s as likely to become "too cheap to meter," many governments subsidized it through research and development outlays, public indemnification of nuclear facilities from accidents, and public management of both the production of nuclear materials and the disposal of nuclear waste. The United States government has spent at least $7 billion a year on subsidies.[56] In industrialized countries as a whole, governments still spend over half their energy research budgets on nuclear power, by contrast with less than 10 percent on renewables. All nuclear subsidies in OECD countries documented here amount to at least $12 billion per year,[57] or 17 percent of the $71 billion in subsidies to fossil fuels and nuclear energy. Regrettably, there are no data for subsidies in non-OECD countries, but that does not matter much here since there is little nuclear power there as yet, except in the FSU.

Despite its early promise, nuclear energy has not lived up to expectations. By 2000, it will comprise only one-tenth of the lowest official forecasts made a quarter century ago. Throughout the 1990s, it was the slowest-growing energy source, with no advance at all in recent years and with no prospect of improvement. In the United States, nuclear technology has absorbed $1 trillion in research funding and sundry other subsidies, yet it delivers less energy than wood: "It died of an incurable attack of market forces."[58]

Nuclear energy, and also much coal, is used to generate electricity—which is itself highly subsidized. Certain of its subsidies are decidedly perverse; for instance, support for centralized transmission systems imposes a formidable obstacle to those many renewable energy sources that are decentralized. For a brief review of electricity, see Box 4.3.

Box 4.3. ELECTRICITY

Fully one-third of commercial energy is used to generate electricity, and more than two-thirds of that energy comes from fossil fuels, primarily coal. In the United States, almost 90 percent of coal goes to generate electricity. Electricity is one of the world's largest businesses, with annual revenues of $800 billion, twice as much as the world's automobile industry.[*]

Subsidies are still prevalent in those many developing countries that price electricity at only three-fifths of the full cost. When prices are low, saving energy becomes less attractive. Developing countries use 10–20 percent more electricity than they would if consumers paid the full cost. In addition, too much capital is spent on energy-demanding projects, while investment in new, cleaner technologies and more energy-efficient processes is discouraged.[†]

At least 2 billion people, two-fifths of the world's population, lack access to electricity. We can expect that demand will keep on growing,

(continues)

Box 4.3. CONTINUED

all the more as developing-country populations keep on increasing. There is much scope for governments to pursue a course that allows them to expand electricity supplies with less overall cost to their economies and environments.

Electricity is also subsidized in a few developed countries, notably Britain, Italy, and Australia. Direct subsidies amount to at least $10 billion per year, and indirect subsidies account for another $6 billion.[‡]

Electricity production is the largest source of greenhouse gas emissions in the United States, producing almost 30 percent; it is ahead of the transportation sector, which is responsible for 26 percent.[§] One-fifth of all electricity is used in lighting. If every commercial building in the United States installed state-of-the-art lighting systems, this would cut lighting bills by nearly half and virtually halt the rise in American carbon dioxide emissions.

[*] C. Flavin and N. Lenssen, *Powering the Future: Blueprint for a Sustainable Electricity Industry* (Washington, D.C.: Worldwatch Institute, 1995).

[†] H. R. Heede and A. B. Lovins, "Hiding the True Costs of Energy Sources," *Wall Street Journal* (17 July 1985): 28; see also A. J. Krupnick and D. Burtraw, "The Social Costs of Electricity: Do the Numbers Add Up?" *Resource and Energy Economics* 18 (1997): 423–466.

[‡] A. P. G. de Moor, *Perverse Incentives: Hundreds of Billions of Dollars in Subsidies Now Harm the Economy, the Environment, Equity, and Trade* (San José, Costa Rica: Earth Council, 1997).

[§] President's Council on Sustainable Development, *Towards a Sustainable America: Advancing Prosperity, Opportunity, and a Healthy Environment for the Twenty-First Century* (Washington, D.C.: White House, President's Council on Sustainable Development, 1999); see also S. Dunn, *Micropower: The Next Electrical Era* (Washington, D.C.: Worldwatch Institute, 2000).

Environmental Externalities

Fossil fuels cause many environmental problems apart from the better-known forms of pollution, including landscape scars, mining tailings, and oil spills. While these are generally local in scope and often ephemeral in nature, they can cause considerable loss of amenity to immediate communities. Their collective cost, in billions of dollars worldwide, is not to be dismissed just because it does not match the more widespread injuries deriving from fossil fuels, such as urban smog, acid rain, and global warming.

It is the grosser-scale types of pollution, however, that we shall consider here, notably from sulfur dioxide, nitrogen oxide, particulates, and carbon dioxide, all of which stem primarily from use of fossil fuels. (Certain of these costs are covered in the next chapter, on road transportation, so they are not touched upon here in order to avoid double counting.) In Indonesia, elimination of energy subsidies of $2.5 billion per year would entrain $490 million worth of health benefits, or $0.20 per $1.00 of subsidy removed. In India, removal of $2.6 billion in energy subsidies (earlier estimate) would translate into $1.7 billion in additional health benefits, or about $0.65 per $1.00 of subsidy removed (the pollution intensity of coal in India is much higher than that of subsidized fuels in Indonesia).[59] In many other countries too, there would be abundant health benefits from reduction of fossil-fuel subsidies that help generate pollutants such as nitrogen oxides, sulfur dioxide, and particulates.[60]

Acid rain has long been attributed to fossil-fuel pollutants, among other factors. The environmental harm imposed by acid rain is well known, though there are only a few estimates of economic costs. For example, the health benefits of controlling acid rain in the United States are in the order of $12–$40 billion per year[61]—to be compared with U.S. subsidies for fossil fuels, estimated at $14 billion per year. (In Britain, a program to reduce sulfur dioxide emissions, the main source of acid rain, confers benefits worth $29 billion per year, mostly in terms of human health.)[62] Then there is acid rain damage to forests. In Europe, there is an annual loss of commercial timber worth $30 billion.[63] There is also some emergent injury to tropical forests, as manifested already in southern China, where "acid haze" causes $14 billion worth of damage per year.[64] It should shortly affect several other sectors of tropical forests, notably those that have acidic soils and hence are very vulnerable to acid rain, with a total expanse of more than 1 million square kilometers, or over one-eighth of remaining tropical forests.[65] Extensive as this tropical forest damage could be, there is no indication of how costly it could eventually become.

There are still other costs from air pollution. Each year, Germany loses $4.7 billion in agricultural production, especially crops; Poland loses $2.7 billion; Italy, $1.8 billion; and Sweden, $1.5 billion.[66]

More important is pollution from fine airborne particles, that is, those that have an aerodynamic diameter of ten microns or less and are able to move thousands of kilometers (carbon particulates from smokestacks in Beijing have been tracked to Hawaii), whereupon they cause severe and even lethal respiratory infections. These pollutants (together with other contaminants from fossil fuels) are taking one year off the lives of American people living in cities,[67] and as many as 60,000 people die prematurely each year from particulate air pollution.[68] The putative "life value" of these deaths is $240 billion.[69] Worldwide, at least 460,000 avoidable deaths occur every year as a result of particulates, and by 2020 there will have been over 8 million such deaths if current patterns of fossil-fuel use continue. In California alone, particulates cause 3,000 deaths per year and an additional 60,000–200,000 cases of respiratory infections in children.[70]

Relatively small reductions in fossil-fuel emissions worldwide, together with their fine particulates, could save some 700,000 lives annually by 2020. While four out of five of these saved lives would be in developing countries, the number in developed countries such as the United States would equal the number of projected deaths from traffic injuries or infection by HIV.[71] This analysis does not take account of health benefits through avoidance of illness and lost workdays, nor does it consider deaths associated with pollutants other than particulates.[72]

Because of these fine particulates, urban residents in China will, under a business-as-usual scenario, face health costs rising from $32 billion (or $129 per resident exposed) in 1995 to almost $98 billion (or $197 per resident) in 2020; these costs include 600,000 premature deaths, 5.5 million cases of chronic bronchitis, more than 5 billion restricted-activity days, and 20 million cases of respiratory illness each year. When adjusted to the projected increases in income, the costs in 2020 will total more than $390 billion, or 13 percent of China's GDP.[73]

By far the biggest environmental externality is, or rather will be, global warming. There seems little doubt that it is indeed on its way, if not already arriving, and that it is due in major measure to fossil-fuel emissions, not just carbon dioxide but also methane and nitrous oxide. Uncertainties lie in the speed of its onset and its regional manifestations.[74] Nor is there much doubt about the scale (though not the size) of its economic costs, at least as minimally reckoned in trillions of dollars in the long run (see Chapter 2). Regrettably, no estimate can be advanced here, not even in the form of a range, as to the size of ultimate costs of global warming beyond preliminary assertions that it could eventually cost the United States at least 1–2 percentage points of GDP. Extrapolated to the rest of the world, this means that the total cost could readily reach $1 trillion per year and probably much more (supposing, of course, that there is no rapid phase-out of fossil fuels forthwith). Suffice it to say here that global warming is far and away the greatest environmental problem we can expect within the foreseeable future. From this standpoint, let alone other pollution effects, all use of fossil fuels is here regarded as environmentally adverse to a significant extent. But because of lack of solid estimates of costs and insofar as this will be a cost in the mid- to long-term future, the hidden subsidy levied on our descendants is left out of further consideration.

Leaving aside global warming, we still find that in the case of the United States, less than 20 percent of subsidies can be classified as improving environmental quality, even when "gray" areas are included (and surely far less than 20 percent in non-OECD countries). Those few subsidies that benefit the environment include those for financing the remediation and closure of contaminated sites, researching energy-related externalities, addressing energy-related health and safety issues, and accelerating market transition to cleaner energy sources and improved efficiency.[75] At most, they would have only a marginal countervailing effect on the adverse consequences of global warming.

Despite these many instances of environmental externalities stemming from fossil fuels (let alone nuclear energy), there is no way to come up with a quantified estimate of all environmental externalities in the fossil-fuel sphere. But several items are certainly indicative: annual health costs from air pollution in Indonesia, $0.5 billion, and in India, $1.7 billion; health costs from acid rain in the United States, $12–$40 billion (say $20 billion), and in Britain, $29 billion; timber losses from acid rain in Europe, $30 billion; agricultural costs from air pollution in four European countries, $10.7 billion; health costs in China, $32 billion; acid haze damages in China, $14 billion; and cost of lives lost to particulate pollution in the United States, $240 billion. Let us exclude the last item, valid though it is in itself; if we considered all such premature deaths in the developed countries, that item alone would approach, if not exceed, $1 trillion, making it an extreme "outlier." The other items total $138 billion.

The calculation of these other items is limited to a degree. For instance, they cover only three developing countries and almost entirely with respect to health costs. They cover only four European countries with respect only to agricultural costs, and they cover Europe as a whole with respect to acid rain damage only to timber supplies. So a reasonable estimate, albeit very rough and ready, for all environmental externalities worldwide surely runs to several hundred billion dollars. Conversely, not all the pollutants stem from fossil fuels, just the majority. The reader will readily think of various other qualifications. In order to come up with an estimate of some order, the authors postulate a total of $200 billion per year. Preliminary and exploratory (even speculative) as this is, it is more realistic than to say we cannot quantify these externalities in worthwhile fashion at all and hence imply that their value is nil.

Subsidies Worldwide

While the OECD countries use most of the world's commercial energy, they appear to employ the fewest types of energy subsidies and only about half of all such subsidies—though there could be many subsidies that remain undocumented or unidentified. In any event, their fossil-fuel and nuclear subsidies are estimated to amount to at least $71 billion per year.[76] The non-OECD countries have engaged in such drastic cutting of subsidies that their total is now less than that for OECD countries, $60 billion per year.[77]

The present annual total for fossil-fuel and nuclear subsidies worldwide—being subsidies of the formal sort—can be put at $131 billion (range $126–$136 billion). True, this estimate is not nearly so precise as it seems. It reflects many different modes of analytic assessment by governments with their abundant covert subsidies, leaving the estimate distinctly conservative. Then there are the informal, that is, indirect and covert, subsidies implicit in environmental externalities, at $200 billion per year. Overall total: $331 billion per year (Table 4.7).

How many of these worldwide subsidies shall we say are perverse by exerting adverse effects on both the economy and the environment? As we have seen, subsidies have many adverse consequences in the economic sense. In the energy arena generally, they slow economic development by distorting production and consumption decisions, and in the economy overall, they draw capital and labor away from more profitable opportunities.[78] In non-OECD countries in particular, removal of subsidies would foster economic growth by improving the efficiency with which these countries use their energy resources.[79] To this extent, all subsidies can surely be viewed as somewhat perverse from an economic standpoint.

This is not to contend that energy subsidies cannot have any positive effect on the economy. Energy plays a vital part in economic development, and it may sometimes deserve a measure of government support. All depends on the types of energy and support. Subsidies for fossil fuels tilt the energy playing field in favor of energy sources that are heavily polluting, artificially cheap, and nonrenewable. Fossil fuels are plainly worse than geothermal energy,

Table 4.7. Fossil Fuel and Nuclear Energy Subsidies Worldwide

	Subsidies ($ billion)	Externalities ($ billion)	Totals ($ billion)	Perverse Subsidies ($ billion)
United States				
Fossil fuels	14.0			
Nuclear energy	7.0			
TOTAL	21.0		21.0	
Canada				
Fossil fuels	5.9			
Nuclear energy	0.1			
TOTAL	6.0		6.0	
Western Europe (17 countries)				
Fossil fuels	10.0			
Nuclear energy	5.0			
TOTAL	15.0		15.0	
Other OECD				
Fossil fuels	29.0 (range 24–34)		29.0	
OECD				
Fossil fuels	59.0			
Nuclear energy	12.0			
TOTAL OECD	71.0 (range 66–76)		71.0	
Non-OECD				
Fossil fuels	60.0		60.0	
WORLDWIDE		200.0	200.0	
TOTAL SUBSIDIES WORLDWIDE	131.0 (range 126–136)	200.0	331.0	300.0

hydropower, solar energy, and wind power; among fossil fuels, the most polluting is coal, yet it was the most heavily subsidized until recent reforms. Subsidies inflict further economic injury by inhibiting energy efficiency and conservation and by deferring a shift to renewable forms of energy. While coal and natural gas may remain available in acceptable quantities for a long time to come, oil stocks are likely to become scarce within a matter of decades. The time to start the shift to alternatives is today—and the longer subsidies work to blind us to the crunch point, the more disruptive will be the inevitable shift when it arrives.[80]

Subsidies for energy production have further drawbacks. They stimulate energy consumption at a time when there are many benefits to energy conservation and energy efficiency. They encourage the construction of unnecessary power projects. They waste scarce capital on capital-intensive supplies of energy when it is far cheaper to simply save energy through efficiency and conservation. They deepen intergenerational inequities by hastening the depletion of nonrenewable resources. On top of all this, they set back the recycling cause, which often saves remarkable amounts of energy, as much as 95 percent in the case of secondary versus primary aluminum.[81] They also diminish the value of the energy embedded in the recycled commodity, hindering the substitution of recyclables for primary materials as well.[82] In sum, and to cite a stringent critic,[83] they inflate the government deficit, they cheat the taxpayer, they steer investment dollars into bad options, and they undermine business competition. They also promote oil imports, which erode national security, as demonstrated in the next chapter.

There is an employment aspect too. For every $1 million spent on oil and gas exploration, only 1.5 jobs are created, and for coal mining, 4.4 jobs. But for every $1 million spent on making and installing solar water heaters, 14 jobs are created; on manufacturing solar electricity panels, 17 jobs; and on generating electricity from biomass and waste, 23 jobs.[84]

It might appear too sweeping in some eyes, however, to count all subsidies as perverse in the sense of this report. The evidence is extensive and substantive but less comprehensive and conclusive than one might wish. Certainly, the subsidies reviewed here feature abundant documentation that they are harmful to the economy. In the case of U.S. subsidies, only 20 percent were shown not to be harmful to the environment, even though the United States has built up an impressive record for environmental protection in many areas—a stronger record than most other industrial countries, let alone developing countries. For the sake of being conservative and "safe," let us suppose that 75 percent of all formal subsidies are perverse in the economic sense. We consider that a strong case could be made for at least 90 percent worldwide. Other observers might assert that in order to

> For every $1 million spent on oil and gas exploration, only 1.5 jobs are created, and for every $1 million spent on coal mining, only 4.4 jobs are created. But for every $1 million spent on making and installing solar water heaters, 14 jobs are created; for every $1 million spent on manufacturing solar electricity panels, 17 jobs are created; and for every $1 million spent on generating electricity from biomass and waste, 23 jobs are created.

be correctly cautious, one should offer a lower estimate of, say, 60 percent. Clearly, the point cannot be established in definitive terms one way or the other. The authors believe that on the basis of the substantial but limited evidence presented here, 75 percent is a defensible estimate, within a range of 60–90 percent. This works out to a worldwide annual total of $100 billion per year.

From the environmental standpoint, all $200 billion of externality subsidies are to be judged, by definition, as decidedly perverse.

To summarize: subsidies that are perverse economically total $100 billion per year, and those that are perverse environmentally total $200 billion. Grand total: $300 billion per year of the $331 billion in fossil-fuel and nuclear subsidies.

Policy Options

The predominant purpose must be to reduce and eventually eliminate those subsidies that are harmful to both economies and environments, that is to say, the perverse subsidies. There are various modes to that end, focusing on (1) removing producer grants and price supports in question, (2) removing consumer subsidies and sales tax exemptions, and (3) removing tax and trade barriers, among other restrictions that discourage energy forms with fewer or no environmental injuries.[85]

Certain of these measures will have the effect of internalizing some of the egregious environmental externalities, notably emissions of carbon dioxide (unevaluated though they remain in agreed economic terms). This can be further helped by direct intervention through reformed pricing policies so that consumer prices reflect all costs, both private and social. There would be plenty of economic advantages, as documented earlier through analyses of perverse subsidies. Nor need there be a loss of business competitiveness.[86] The principal environmental payoff would lie with the front-rank measure of cutting carbon dioxide emissions, together with a decline in urban smog, acid rain, particulate emissions, and other pollution impacts.

Yet governments seem singularly reluctant to seize the manifold benefits available. In just Western Europe, well over $10 billion has been spent on subsidies for fossil fuels every year since 1990, meaning that since 1992, when the governments signed an international treaty at the Rio Earth Summit to protect global climate, they have spent over $80 billion on fossil-fuel subsidies. By contrast, environment-favoring solutions such as solar electricity, wind power, and the like have received only $1.5 billion per year and energy conservation only $3.2 billion per year.[87] Thus, subsidies for fossil fuels have been slowing if not suppressing the competitiveness of renewable and non-polluting energy sources and rejecting the climate safeguards implicit in tackling carbon dioxide emissions.[88]

Within the overall context of slashing fossil-fuel subsidies, there are two main sets of issues that policy measures must address: reducing emissions of carbon dioxide and promoting energy efficiency and conservation.

Cutting Carbon Dioxide Emissions

Were governments to slash fossil-fuel subsidies after the manner of the former Soviet Union, certain countries of Western and Eastern Europe, China, and India, they would generate major benefits, notably as concerns reduction of carbon dioxide emissions. That much is clear. What is far less clear is the scale of benefits. The problem of statistical divergencies is illustrated by the situation in the United States, a country for which one might expect there would be little disagreement. On the contrary, however, the economic models display wide divergencies of analysis and findings.[89] For instance, one assessment[90] proposes that if the United States were to remove its fossil-fuel subsidies, this would reduce carbon dioxide emissions by 11–14 percent over twenty years without affecting economic growth. Another assessment[91] concludes that the same measure would reduce carbon dioxide emissions by only 4 percent while causing GDP to increase by 0.1–0.2 percent. Other estimates are rather less or a good deal less. A carbon tax that induces a 35 percent reduction in carbon dioxide emissions could be expected to raise GDP over its projected baseline level by more than 1.5 percent or to reduce it by about 3 percent.[92]

As for all countries, elimination of subsidies as they were in 1991 (and assuming no change in fossil-fuel prices as a result) would reduce carbon dioxide emissions by 2010 by more than 20 percent in many of the main fossil-fuel-consuming countries and by 7.0 percent worldwide—though the emissions would still be more than 40 percent higher than in 1990.[93] In eight non-OECD countries that include 46 percent of the world's population, phasing out subsidies would reduce emissions by an average of 16 percent and global emissions by nearly 5 percent[94] (Table 4.6).

Whatever the precise costs and benefits of cutting back carbon dioxide emissions, Americans, as the number one source of the emissions, might recall that half of the carbon dioxide they release today will still be in the atmosphere—in everyone's atmosphere—at the end of the century.

Energy Efficiency and Conservation

A related step is to mobilize policy measures to foster energy efficiency and conservation.[95] With present energy technologies, a savings of 20–25 percent could be achieved, and with more efficient equipment, as much as 30–60 percent would become possible.[96]

Consider the scope for new and renewable sources of energy, all of them "clean," that is, nonpolluting. First off, solar energy. The cost of solar cells has fallen from more than $70 per watt of production capacity in the 1970s to less than $4 per watt today, and it will very likely fall to only $1 per watt as manufacturing capacity expands and economies of scale increase, $1 being often considered the threshold for competitiveness with coal and natural gas.[97] Japan, a leader in manufacture of solar cells, plans to install rooftop solar power systems with a generating capacity of 4,600 megawatts by 2010, an amount equal to the generating capacity of Chile. The United States, second to only Japan in the field, has announced a Million Solar Roofs Initiative, with the goal of installing solar panels on 1 million rooftops by 2010, allowing the roof in effect to become the power plant for the building. In Germany and Switzerland, new office buildings are incorporating photovoltaic (solar energy) cells in the windows of their south-facing facades. The European Union proposes that $650 million could kick-start a self-sustaining solar energy market by 2010, installing the equivalent of 1 million solar roofs worth 2,000 megawatts. In addition, it would eventually create 58,000 jobs and prevent 2 million tonnes of carbon dioxide emissions per year.[98] Even in the notoriously cloudy climate of Britain, putting solar cells on all the country's roofs could generate 68,000 megawatts of power on a bright day, roughly half of Britain's peak power demand.

In all these initiatives, two-way metering systems with local utilities will enable building owners to sell electricity to utilities when generation is excessive and to buy it back when generation is not sufficient.[99]

The United States spends about $100 million a year on photovoltaic research, the same cost as that of three kilometers of interstate highway. Despite this almost complete neglect through piffling subsidies, photovoltaics have made enough headway that the price of solar energy has come down precipitously. Despite this fine news, total power produced by solar cells today is only about one-tenth of that produced by wind.

Wind power is growing by 22 percent per year, making it the fastest-growing energy source anywhere (by contrast, fossil fuels are growing at only 2 percent or less per year) (Figure 4.2). The cost of wind energy in the mid-1970s was around $1.00 per kilowatt-hour, but by 1996 it had plunged to $0.05, and it is expected to fall to just $0.02 by 2010—when the world market is expected to be worth $25 billion.[100] In Britain, the potential for wind energy up to thirty kilometers from the coast is equivalent to three times the country's current annual electricity consumption. Denmark plans to meet half of its electricity needs by 2030 through offshore wind.[101]

Consider also the energy-saving capacity of long-lasting light-bulbs. These compact fluorescent bulbs feature in only 9 percent of American homes. An average American home has about thirty lightbulbs, three of them burning for five hours or more per day. If all American homes replaced just three of those bulbs with long-lasting bulbs, Americans would save electricity equivalent to the output of eleven fossil-fuel-fired power plants. In turn, that would eliminate about 23 million tonnes of CO_2 emissions per year—and save American consumers an annual $1.8 billion.[102]

> If all U.S. homes replaced just three lightbulbs with long-lasting bulbs, Americans would save electricity equivalent to the output of eleven fossil-fuel power plants.

In light of the immense potential of these new and renewable sources of energy, and given the many problems of fossil fuels, BP and Shell are investing heavily in solar power. These companies believe that the oil era is entering its twilight, and they are busily converting themselves from oil companies into energy companies. BP foresees a twenty-fold increase in the global solar market by 2010.

But again, we have the problem of the playing field tilted by subsidies in favor of fossil fuels. The foregoing analysis shows that in the United States, the ratio of subsidies between conventional sources, being largely fossil fuels, and renewable sources of energy is at least 10:1 (though an energy expert[103] proposes that the ratio is more like 28:1). Within the European Union, the ratio is often 10:1,[104] though in certain other countries it can be as high as 35:1.[105] Most governments and development agencies emphasize energy production over energy efficiency. Of energy loans by the World Bank, fewer than 1 percent have been for increased efficiency,[106] though the Bank is now

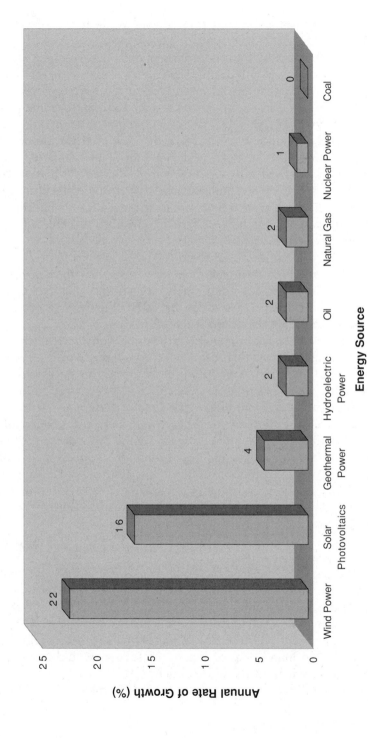

Figure 4.2. Growth in Global Energy Use, 1990–1998. *Source:* L. R. Brown et al., *State of the World, 2000* (New York: Norton, 2000).

shifting its emphasis somewhat toward renewable forms of energy and energy efficiency.[107]

Consider what could be accomplished on a level playing field. Were the U.S. Congress to fund renewable energy with the same amount in tax credits, financial incentives, and other subsidies that it provides for coal and oil, renewables would readily become competitive with fossil fuels.[108] In fact, a near-complete transition to a renewable-energy economy could be readily achieved for about $25 billion a year over the next ten years—a sum to be compared with the $21 billion worth of subsidies now supplied annually by the government for fossil fuels and nuclear energy. An earlier reckoning[109] asserted that the same transition could be achieved for $7 billion less than the government annually assigns in subsidies to coal, oil, and nuclear energy.

Meantime, renewables are enabled to supply a mere 7 percent of energy worldwide. If current energy policies persist, with their heavy emphasis on subsidies for fossil fuels, we should not expect the renewables' share to increase much by 2020 (Figure 4.1)—though with suitable incentives, it could reach 12 percent.[110]

To illustrate the scope for energy efficiency, consider the role of buildings, which all together use one-third of the world's energy, with an annual price tag of $400 billion. Cutting this energy use by half through climate-oriented designs could reduce energy pollution by one-sixth and save $200 billion per year.[111] American businesses spend almost $100 billion on energy each year to operate their buildings with lighting, heating, and cooling systems.[112] By doing more to use energy-efficient products and operational procedures, they could reduce that energy cost by $35 billion while improving the comfort and reliability of their buildings. In the early 1990s, a number of super-insulated houses in Saskatchewan were warmed during the bitterly cold winters with only the body heat of their occupants. Today, there are more than 100,000 such homes in Canada, the northern United States, and Scandinavia.

Over the past seventeen years, Americans have gained over four times as much new energy from efficiency savings as from all net increases from supply—and of the increases from supply, one-third has come from renewables. Americans' energy bills have fallen by $160 billion per year.[113] If the United States had adopted energy efficiency in 1974 to match that of Japan, the savings would have been large enough to wipe out its national debt.[114]

There are similarly large savings to be made in the electricity field.

In Brazil, the Balbina Dam, which flooded 2,360 square kilometers of Amazonian forest to generate a mere 112 megawatts of electricity, would not have needed to be built if electricity were sold at a rate that reflected its true cost.[115] In Thailand, the $10 million investment needed to build a small advanced window factory would, from the first year's production alone, save enough electricity to eliminate the need to commission a $1.5 billion power plant.[116] Similarly, if Thailand had pursued energy efficiency rather than build its Moe Moh lignite power plant, it would have saved $400 million from not having to install antipollution equipment.[117]

Developing countries as a whole could do much to avoid reliance on fossil fuels, by pursuing energy efficiency and conservation. By investing $10 billion a year over the next thirty-five years, they could eventually eliminate the need for $1.75 trillion worth of power plants, oil refineries, and other energy infrastructure, with gross savings of $53 billion a year for thirty-five years. At the same time, they would greatly reduce the pollution burden for themselves and for the world at large.[118]

Developing countries together with transition countries (those shifting from socialist to capitalist economies) are expected to account for two-thirds of the world's increased energy demand between 1999 and 2020. So let us conclude this chapter by looking again at the prospect for eight major non-OECD countries with 46 percent of the world's population: China, India, Indonesia, Iran, South Africa, Venezuela, Russia, and Kazakhstan. In the late 1990s, despite many subsidy cuts, energy prices in these countries averaged 21 percent below world market prices, ranging from South Africa's 6 percent to Iran's whopping 80 percent. If these eight countries were to eliminate their fossil-fuel subsidies, they would reduce their energy consumption by 13 percent per year, increase their GDPs by almost 1 percent, reduce their CO_2 emissions by 16 percent, and sharply reduce their local air pollution (Table 4.6). At a global level, their efforts would reduce energy consumption by 3.5 percent and reduce carbon dioxide emissions by 4.6 percent.[119]

A strategy of getting the energy prices right would revitalize energy industries in all these countries, discourage waste, stimulate development and adoption of new technologies, and promote more entrepreneurial capacity across the board. In addition, the countries could potentially earn vast sums by selling their CO_2 reductions. If carbon were to be valued at $27 per tonne (a frequently cited figure), they could earn as much as $7.8 billion (China more than $3 billion,

Russia $1.8 billion, and Iran $1 billion).[120] Of course, and as noted earlier, we should give credit where it is due: fossil-fuel subsidies in non-OECD countries overall were slashed by fully one-half during the brief period 1990–1996.[121]

Chapter 5

ROAD TRANSPORTATION

We have developed an ardent love affair with cars, especially in the United States. In 1900, there were only 8,000 cars in the United States; today, there are over 160 million. To accommodate them, there were 15 kilometers of paved roads in 1900; today, there are over 6 million kilometers. Yet increased numbers of motor vehicles do not always give greater mobility. In the United States, traffic congestion causes more than 6 billion hours lost per year, costing the economy at least $48 billion.[1] In the Los Angeles region, daily commute times are projected to double by 2020, and "unbearable" present conditions on the freeways will become even worse. By 2020, drivers are expected to spend 70 percent of their time in stop-and-go traffic, compared with 56 percent today.[2] Airborne carcinogens in Los Angelenos' air, invisible compounds in vehicle exhaust that target humans' internal organs and may be behind the region's stubbornly high cancer levels, are 426 times higher than is considered safe, even though the city already has the country's toughest car emissions standards. Perhaps cars should now carry public health warnings.

Road transportation is the main mode by which a fossil fuel, oil, is used by large numbers of people every day. (For a comment on air travel, see Box 5.1.) Of the top fifty manufacturers worldwide, no

In the United States, traffic congestion causes more than 6 billion hours to be lost per year, costing the economy at least $48 billion.

fewer than thirteen are car companies. The auto industry produces 40 million new cars a year, and there are 530 million already motoring around.[3] The global car fleet is expected to double during the next twenty to thirty years, mostly in developing countries; in 1996, over three-quarters as many cars were manufactured and sold in Asia as in the United States. China alone plans to increase its car fleet from 2.7 million in 1993 to 22 million by 2010.[4]

Road transportation has long conferred sizeable benefits. Without

---

Box 5.1. AVIATION FUEL

By contrast with all other fuels used in travel, aviation fuel carries a tax of zero. Generally speaking, airlines pay only one-sixth as much for a liter of fuel as do motorists. The alleged reason for this massive concealed subsidy is that we would need an international treaty to set up a tax, and that would be too difficult. As if there weren't all kinds of international treaties governing air travel, from safety regulations on up (so to speak).

Aircraft emissions are responsible for 4–10 percent of global-warming processes. Half of these come from carbon dioxide (CO_2); the rest are from vapor trails, nitrogen oxides, and other gases. This contribution to global warming is more than that of all greenhouse gas emissions from Britain. In the United States, domestic flights alone are largely to blame for the country's accounting for 40 percent of all aircraft pollution worldwide.[*]

Jet aircraft are the ultimate fuel guzzlers. Fuel makes up no less than half the weight of a Boeing 747 taking off on a long-haul flight. The amount of CO_2 emitted for each passenger kilometer is four times as much as would have been produced if the passenger had traveled by car and twelve times as much as if by rail. This means that a passenger's round trip from London to Florida may well exceed his or her average car use for a year.

Super-jumbo jets are a mixed blessing: the same innovations that have reduced fuel consumption, and thus cut CO_2 emissions, have caused an increase in emissions of nitrogen oxides, which can be at least as damaging to the atmosphere. Fortunately, the turbofan engines that power most of today's aircraft have improved dramatically in recent years. Fuel consumption per passenger kilometer is half what it was twenty years ago. However, this has not been enough to prevent a continuing rise in greenhouse gas emissions, as many more people are traveling by air. In recent times, there has been a doubling or more of air travel per decade. Such travel is projected to grow by 5 percent annually until at least 2015, with fuel consumption expected to rise from 130 million tonnes in 1992 to 300 million tonnes in 2015 and 450 million tonnes in 2050.[†]

[*] Intergovernmental Panel on Climate Change (IPCC), *Aviation and the Global Atmosphere* (Geneva: IPCC, 1999).

[†] IPCC, *Aviation and the Global Atmosphere.*

an efficient transport system to "lubricate" modern economies, there would have been far less geographic specialization in production and economies would not have grown nearly as much.[5] But the "car culture" is now levying appreciable costs, both environmental and economic. In just the United States, road transportation generates one-quarter of all carbon dioxide emissions (and one-twentieth of all such emissions worldwide).[6] Economic costs include those of road building and maintenance, traffic management, congestion, road accidents, and pollution, among many other items. To reiterate a point central

By contrast with all other fuels used in travel, aviation fuel carries a tax of zero.

to this book: it can be artificial, if not arbitrary, to differentiate between environmental and economic costs, and in the road transportation sector there is no clear-cut division all along the road. Environmental costs often carry monetary price tags, and economic costs often reflect environmental problems.[7]

At the same time, the sector has become such a lifestyle icon that it has spawned huge subsidies for large cars, cheap gasoline, highway construction plus infrastructure, and a host of other supports (including the implicit subsidies of environmental externalities). Ironically, transportation subsidies can be put to better environmental and economic use than can subsidies in most other sectors if used correctly, that is, for public road transport and railways. Because of their huge popularity with motorists and hence large numbers of voters, these subsidies rank among the most difficult for politicians to control. Subsidies tend to go where the votes are, and the votes are in the driver's seat.

United States

The situation is best illustrated in the United States, which has over 230 million motor vehicles for 278 million people, by far the highest proportion in the world.[8] All Americans could be accommodated in cars at the same time (as often seems the case during rush hour) and nobody would need to be in the back seat. Roads total over 6 million kilometers, or 1,250 times the distance from New York to Los Angeles. They occupy 2 percent of the country's land, more than that given over to housing and with an aggregate expanse greater than Florida.[9] Roads and other motor vehicle supports, such as parking, garages, and fuel stations, cover between one-third and one-half of space in American cities, and in "car-saturated" areas such as Los Angeles, the proportion rises to two-thirds. Americans drive 4.5 trillion kilometers per year, or an average of 23,000 kilometers per vehicle.[10] Americans are so enamored of their cars that the average household spends more on cars and gasoline than on groceries or income tax, and only a little less than on the mortgage.

Americans make 80 percent of their trips by car, whereas Europeans make 60 percent of theirs by public transit or by biking or walking.[11] Americans claim that they need their cars because they live in a big country, where car travel is essential. But Canadians and Australians, who also live in big countries, drive much less. Americans travel 60–100 percent farther by car than do Europeans, yet an average car trip in either region is no more than 15 kilometers, so it is the frequency of car travel rather than distances per se that boosts Americans' travel.[12] All in all, Americans now average 4.3 one-way trips and 62 kilometers per day, up from 2.9 trips and 42 kilometers per day in 1977. Long-distance trips (160 kilometers or more from home) have increased from 2.5 round trips in 1977 to 3.9 in 1995.[13]

> Americans make 80 percent of their trips by car, whereas Europeans make 60 percent of theirs by public transit, biking, or walking.

Because of their size and especially since the arrival of sport utility vehicles (SUVs), American cars use 25–33 percent more gasoline per kilometer than do those in Europe.

Whatever their (limited) benefits, cars are widely perceived as a vital part of the American dream, and not only for Americans. In China, which is intent on Americanizing itself, motor vehicle numbers have been growing since 1993 at an average of 18 percent per year (compared with 2 percent in the United States), while in 1994 public transport use decreased by 6.5 percent.[14]

In the United States, the automobile industry and related industries account for one in six jobs nationwide. Road transportation accounts for 80 percent of energy use in the transportation sector as a whole, which in turn uses 66 percent of all oil consumed in the United States. Road transportation also accounts for 25 percent of the country's carbon dioxide emissions, having become the fastest-growing source of these emissions. So too it causes half of nitrogen oxide emissions and three-quarters of carbon monoxide emissions (as applies in OECD countries as a whole).[15]

Despite the car culture's many problems, many Americans are driving in a decidedly wrong direction. SUVs have caught the fancy of so many Americans that in some parts of the country they make up half of all vehicles sold. During the 1990s and the SUVs fashion, gasoline consumption surged by one-quarter. In 1999, Americans purchased a record 17 million such vehicles, which had the lowest fuel efficiency in nearly twenty years. The SUV exemption from the gas guzzler tax, which would run as high as $7,700 for one of the larger cars, encourages the purchase of such vehicles, even though they are one-third less fuel efficient and up to five times more polluting than conventional cars.[16]

Subsidies to the Oil and Car Industries

The U.S. car culture is supported by myriad direct subsidies, meaning that the subsidies comprise financial payments and other monetary transfers of the sorts listed in Chapter 1. They are designated as direct subsidies in order to differentiate them from the five categories of implicit subsidy listed in Table 5.1, but like the other categories they conceal the true costs of gasoline and driving. They include government funding of infrastructure and services, research and development supports, domestic tax breaks, foreign tax credits, depreciation of machinery and equipment, low sales taxes on gasoline, and a multitude of corporate income tax credits and deductions. All in all, these supports amount to $9–$18 billion, say $15 billion, per year,[17] and they result in an effective income tax rate of 11 percent for the industry, compared with the non–oil industry average of 18 percent.[18]

Then there are subsidies for the car industry, for example, tax credits for research and development support and a government initiative known as the Partnership for a New Generation of Vehicles. In addition, there is government support for iron, steel, aluminum, glass, plastic, and other products vital to auto manufacture and deductible advertising and marketing costs for the auto industry. Regrettably, there is no good documentation of what these amount to, though they might well total as much as subsidies for the oil industry.

First, let us examine a readily recognizable subsidy.

Road Building and Infrastructure

Two-fifths of the costs of road building and related services come from revenues unrelated to transportation. Internalizing this subsidy to motorists through a gasoline tax would cost $0.22 per gallon.[19] The overall cost of roads, highway patrols, emergency teams, and related services, when calculated as costs over and above what drivers pay in gasoline taxes and other fees, amounts to more than $91 billion a year, worth another $0.64 per gallon of gasoline.[20] An alternative estimate includes capital outlay at $143 billion (including land-use effects), highway maintenance at $20 billion, and administration (half of which includes traffic police) at $14 billion, for a total of $177 billion per year.[21] In light of this final figure, which is more comprehensive and hence much higher than other estimates, the authors posit a minimum estimate of $135 billion per year, within a range of $91–$177 billion. One could argue in any case that the total should be increased in order to reflect the pressing need for expanded police efforts to reduce the steadily increasing cost of vehicle thefts.

Free Parking

Next, let us consider the cost of free parking supplied by businesses for some 80 million American workers.[22] The government allows businesses to assign up to $1,860 worth of free parking per year to each employee tax free, by contrast with only $780 for mass transit coupons.[23] This exemption, being a covert subsidy, has been variously calculated to be worth $45 billion per year,[24] $67 billion per year,[25] $85 billion per year,[26] $50–$100 billion per year,[27] or $75–$223 billion per year.[28] The divergencies reflect mainly the categories of parking space involved, the last estimate being the most comprehensive. A midpoint of this last total is $149 billion, say $150 billion, which is accepted for this chapter.

Road Congestion

In thirty-nine metropolitan areas with populations of 1 million or more, one-third of all vehicle travel takes place under congested conditions in which speed averages half of the free-flow rate. The delay amounts to 6 billion vehicle-hours each year. Within these areas, 75 million drivers average 16,000 kilometers per year, making up 1.2 trillion kilometers. Through their choices, these drivers demonstrate a willingness to pay an average of at least $1.33 (1994 dollars) to save ten minutes of travel time, or $8.00 per hour. The annual cost of these driving delays comes to $640 per driver, for a total of $48 billion.[29] Were congestion delays to be considered in the many other urban localities apart from the thirty-nine metropolitan areas, the total would a good deal larger, possibly twice as large.

An alternative reckoning, allowing also for extra consumption of gasoline by idling engines and for wear and tear on vehicles, proposes that Americans lose more than 8 billion hours per year to traffic delays, at a cost exceeding $80 billion.[30] Still another estimate[31] calculates $44–$98 billion per year; another one[32] proposes $74 billion per year; and yet another one[33] speaks of $34–$146 billion per year. When we include all costs of congestion on roads (though excluding pollution externalities, as discussed later in the chapter), the total in 1990 came to at least $100 billion.[34] For present purposes, a figure of $100 billion per year is accepted even though it is surely much higher today. That this estimate is realistic is borne out by the situation in Los Angeles, where traffic delays levy costs of $12 billion per year. Similar pro rata sums obtain in the San Francisco Bay Area and in greater Washington, D.C.; costs in the three areas combined may well total $20 billion per year.[35]

Parallel findings arise elsewhere. In central London in 1990, each driver in peak traffic cost all other road users about $0.50 in wasted time, or four times as much as the actual expense of driving.[36] The average speed of a London car today is akin to that of a horse-drawn carriage a century ago.[37]

Accidents, Injuries, and Deaths

A further economic cost and hence an indirect subsidy lies with vehicle accidents and associated injuries and deaths. There are 3.5 million injuries with 42,000 fatalities per year.[38] A detailed estimate[39] proposes a minimum cost of $139 billion per year in the late 1980s, reflecting the loss of human capital as manifested through market costs, including medical expenses and reduced worker productivity. It also values a statistical death at $500,000, which many analysts consider on the low side, and it invokes similarly low costs for injuries.

A second estimate[40] proposes an annual range of $120–$360 billion for the early 1990s. A third calculation,[41] excluding pain and lost quality of life, presents a total of $150 billion per year. A fourth estimate[42] postulates $358 billion in 1990, this being a comprehensive reckoning that covers reduced quality of life, plus pain and grief, and values a statistical death at $2–$5 million, together with comparably high estimates for injuries. But the proportion of these costs not directly borne by drivers involved in accidents, and hence borne by society, was considered to be only $55 billion.[43] A fifth estimate[44] indicates that all external costs of accidents, that is, costs borne by society rather than by motorists, add up to $33–$183 billion per year. This is far and away the most broad ranging and up to date of all the estimates, so it is the one accepted here, with a midpoint figure of $108 billion, say $110 billion, per year.

> The average speed of a central London car today is akin to that of a horse-drawn carriage a century ago.

Worldwide, some 885,000 people are killed on the roads each year, equivalent to ten fatal jumbo jet crashes every day.

Military Safeguards

Then there are the military costs of safeguarding oil tanker shipping lanes from the Persian Gulf. In 1960, U.S. oil consumption exceeded domestic production by only 5 percent, but in the year 2000 it was expected that the United States would import more than 55 percent of its oil supply, with twice as much coming from the Persian Gulf as in 1973. Never before in U.S. history, even at the height of the energy crises in the 1970s, have imports of oil exceeded domestic production. Moreover, some 45 percent of imports come from members of the Organization of Petroleum Exporting Countries (OPEC).[45]

In 1995, the United States paid almost $50 billion for its imported oil (half of which came from the Persian Gulf), with these imports accounting for 30 percent of the trade deficit.[46] The country pays about $17 for a barrel of Gulf oil, and effectively it pays several times more per barrel through military protection.[47] In 1991, the Department of Defense spent around $50 billion on military safeguards for oil, mostly with respect to the Persian Gulf.[48] (Another estimate[49] postulates $73–$227 billion for all military outlays of whatever sort associated with protection of oil in 1994, and yet another estimate[50] speaks of $11–$23 billion for just Persian Gulf safeguards in 1995.) Well over half of the Gulf oil imported into the

United States is used for road transportation, so half of the $50 billion of annual military expenditures, $25 billion, should be allocated to motorists.[51]

Ironically, in 1989 the United States imported 220 million barrels of oil from Iraq and Kuwait—an amount that would have been saved if the U.S. auto fleet had been achieving improved efficiency of just five kilometers per gallon (as could well have been stimulated through a rollback in gasoline subsidies).[52] Today, Americans would have to cut their oil use by only one-eighth in order to end their dependence on Persian Gulf imports, and this could be readily achieved by a marginal improvement in fuel efficiency, from 32 to 40 kilometers per gallon.[53] Yet the oil import bill is expected to increase by 86 percent during 1996–2005.[54]

Environmental Externalities

Finally, let us examine environmental damage, notably the externality costs of air, water, and noise pollution as they affect landscape visibility, agricultural crops and buildings, and climate in the form of global warming. These costs have been calculated for 1991 at $12–$50 billion.[55] A similar estimate[56] posits $46 billion for 1989, while still another estimate[57] proposes $12–$35 billion per year for the early 1990s. A final analysis[58] calculates $66 billion per year. Due to differences in what is measured and what is omitted, a realistic estimate is $50 billion per year.

Added to this are human morbidity and mortality costs from air pollution, estimated at $42–$182 billion for 1991.[59] Adding in the other air pollution costs of $50 billion makes a total of $92–$232 billion per year. This aggregate estimate seems realistic in light of data for air pollution in a single area, the Los Angeles basin. Not all pollution there stems from road traffic, but the bulk of it does. A report on the health benefits from meeting the federal public health standards for ozone and particulates shows that over 30 million "restricted activity" days and 1,600 deaths could have been averted annually in the late 1980s. The value of these health gains in a population of 12 million is estimated to be $14.3 billion.[60]

As many as 100 million Americans live in cities where vehicle emissions regularly push ozone levels above federal standards. There are several other health hazards from traffic pollution.[61] As a measure of the scale of values involved in air pollution from automobiles, among other sources, the Clean Air Act Amendments of 1990 are expected to prevent 23,000 Americans from dying prematurely and avert over 1.7 million cases of respiratory disease each year by 2010. The benefits will total $110 billion, whereas the costs are likely to be only about $27 billion.[62] Of course, the assessment covers all forms of air pollution, though those from road transportation (and other uses of fossil fuels) are predominant. In the United Kingdom, between 12,000 and 24,000 people die early every year as a result of air pollution, whereas only about 3,600 die in road accidents.[63]

> The Clean Air Act Amendments of 1990 are expected to prevent 23,000 Americans from dying prematurely and avert over 1.7 million cases of respiratory disease each year by 2010. The benefits will total $110 billion, whereas the costs are likely to be only $27 billion.

It is unfortunate that estimates for human health costs should span such a broad range, $42–$182 billion, while being large relative to other hidden costs. That is to say, this single component of a single sector is unusually significant for the book's entire calculations. The broad range reflects the uncertain methodology employed to calculate health values, and until it can be better substantiated and refined, we must live with it as best we can.

The overall estimate is very conservative. For instance, it considers that the factor that could eventually turn out to be the biggest environmental externality of all, possibly worth all the rest put together, namely, climate change and global warming,[64] is worth no more than $22 billion per year. This does not do justice to recent calculations by the Intergovernmental Panel on Climate Change and other preliminary estimates of the putative costs of global warming.[65] In any case, all global-warming assessments feature an uncertainty range such that the "true" value may diverge from a given estimate by anywhere from 5 percent to 2,000 percent.[66]

For purposes of the present analysis, the authors propose a median figure of $160 billion, within a range of $92–$232 billion per year. Rough and ready, but reasonable in the absence of anything better.

Total U.S. Subsidies

The estimates just presented are set out in Table 5.1, with an overall total of $695 billion per year, within a range of $425–$958 billion. Many of the supporting calculations date from the early 1990s; today's total is likely to be a good deal higher. The figure is not unduly high, however, in light of the growing documentation of externalities, even though it constitutes nearly 60 percent of global subsidies in this sector. It is to be compared with three much lower

Table 5.1. U.S. Subsidies for Road Transportation

Subsidy Type	Amount ($ billions)
Direct	
Oil and car industry	15
Road building and infrastructure	135
TOTAL	150
	(range 100–195)
Indirect	
Free parking	150
	(range 75–223)
Congestion	100 minimum
Accidents, injuries, deaths	110
	(range 33–183)
Military safeguards	25 minimum
TOTAL	385
	(range 233–531)
Externalities	160
	(range 92–232)
TOTAL SUBSIDIES	695
	(range 425–958)

Sources: As noted in the text.

Note: The total of $695 billion is 59 percent of the global total of $1,180 billion.

estimates, $174 billion,[67] $184 billion,[68] and $330 billion.[69] Other estimates are higher: $750 billion[70] and $1.5 trillion.[71] Two estimates present ranges: $120 billion–$1.1 trillion (1991 estimate)[72] and $559 billion–$1.7 trillion.[73]

Few estimates include additional costs such as land-use effects, which, in terms simply of the land used for the U.S. highway system, carry an annualized value of $75 billion (see the earlier discussion).[74] Nor do the estimates include general aesthetic degradation or social costs such as mobility loss for nondrivers in automobile-dependent communities.

The estimate presented here for the unpaid costs of road transportation, $695 billion per year, is equivalent to $2,500 per American, more than 8 percent of U.S. GDP. This is roughly consistent with a midrange figure in one of the most detailed and up-to-date assessments,[75] $480–$4,000 per American. Indeed, if Americans were to cover the entire costs of their car culture, including environmental externalities and especially global warming, they could find themselves paying much more than they now pay for their largely "free ride" provided courtesy of the hefty subsidies to road transportation. Passing the concealed costs back to drivers would require a tax of around $2–$7 per gallon of gasoline (even as high as $6–$16).[76] Such are the ultimate costs of a car culture that, through its abundant and munificent subsidies, amounts to a form of super-socialism.

Whatever the true figure, it says much about the "high" present price that Americans pay for their gasoline. Around $1.50 per gallon today (April 2000), gasoline is actually cheaper in real dollars than it has been in sixty years; it is still cheaper than milk or Perrier water. Americans might compare their gasoline expenses with those of other countries. The 1995 price was 79 percent of Canada's, and the tax component was 33 percent of the price (27 percent in April 2000), whereas Canada's 1995 price was 47 percent. Similarly, the 1995 price in the United States was 60 percent of that in Australia, where tax made up 67 percent of the price. Both Canada and Australia are geographically large countries like the United States, a factor that supposedly requires extended car driving (though 80 percent of Americans' trips are less than fifteen kilometers). Moreover, the 1995 price in the United States was only 28 percent of that in Italy, where tax made up 75 percent (Figure 5.1).[77] Not surprisingly, 1993 per capita gasoline consumption amounted to 1,600 liters in the United States, 1,124 liters in Canada, 936 liters in Australia, and less than 400 liters in Italy.[78] The 1995 U.S. motor vehicle fleet used 143 billion gallons of motor fuel, leading to 1.3 billion tonnes of CO_2 emissions.

In Western European countries generally, subsidies tend to be quite a lot lower thanks to higher fuel prices and taxes, which in Germany are as much as 80 percent, in the Netherlands 110 percent, and in France 120 percent (in France, 1991 revenues exceeded expenditures by $11 billion, in 1997 dollars).[79] Certain European countries such as Italy pay over $3 per gallon in taxes, and the amount is being ratcheted up year by year at a rate considerably faster than that of inflation. In Britain, motorists now pay $6 for a gallon of gasoline.

Other OECD Countries

Now for other OECD countries and their subsidies, both direct and indirect. In the United Kingdom, the external costs of cars, trucks,

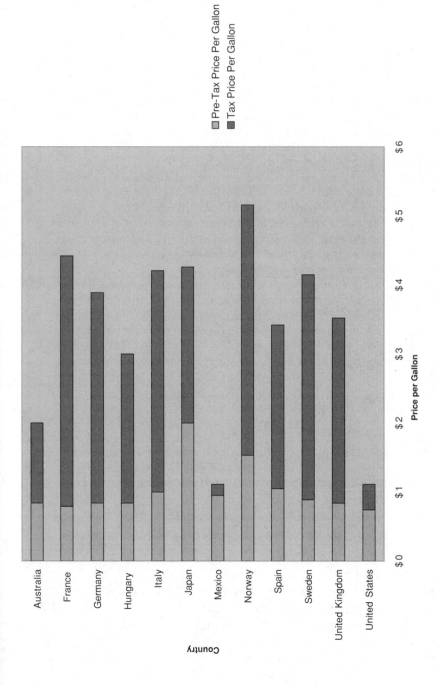

Figure 5.1. Gasoline Tax and Retail Prices in Industrialized Countries, 1995. Source: National Research Council (Transportation Research Board), *Toward a Sustainable Future: Addressing the Long-Term Effects of Motor Vehicle Transportation on Climate and Ecology* (Washington, D.C.: National Academy Press, 1997).

Box 5.2. ROAD TRANSPORTATION COSTS IN THE UNITED KINGDOM

In the United Kingdom, with 59 million people and 22 million cars, roads and their verges (shoulders) occupy 3.3 percent of land area, whereas railways occupy only 0.2 percent. Well over half the population is exposed to substantial noise pollution from motor traffic. Road vehicles account for 90 percent of carbon monoxide emissions and 24 percent of carbon dioxide emissions, with the latter proportion increasing fast.[*] At least one in five and possibly one in three persons in England is at risk from poor air quality, though not all the pollution comes from road transportation. Premature deaths due to air pollution caused by motor vehicle use total 6,000 a year, double the number of deaths from traffic accidents. Asthma affects every seventh child, and among adults it is responsible for one in every six workdays lost through work-related illness. Asthma is thought to be predominantly caused by the recent rise in vehicle emissions; in 1990, the costs to the economy were in the region of $6.2 billion, and similar costs are reported for other European countries.[†]

All together, the health effects of traffic pollution are estimated to be at least $24 billion per year, while road congestion imposes further costs of $30 billion per year. Road accidents impose costs on society of over $16 billion per year. The grand total according to this reckoning is $70 billion per year, a total to be compared with another recent estimate, over $80 billion per year.[‡] Because the first is a partial reckoning and the second is for 1993, we shall go with $80 billion.

[*] Royal Commission on Environmental Pollution, *Transport and the Environment* (London: Her Majesty's Stationery Office, 1994).

[†] W. O. C. M. Cookson and M. F. Moffatt, "Asthma: An Epidemic in the Absence of Infection?" *Science* 275 (1997): 41–42; W. Lenney et al., "The Burden of Paediatric Asthma," *European Respiratory Review* 4 (1994): 49–62; L. Strachan et al., "National Survey of Asthma Prevalence, Severity, and Treatment in Great Britain," *Archives of Disease in Childhood* 70 (1994): 174–178.

[‡] D. Maddison et al., *Blueprint 5: The True Costs of Road Transport* (London: Earthscan, 1996).

---

vans, and the like are estimated to have totaled $80 billion in 1993.[80] For details, see Box 5.2. In Germany, the estimate for 1991 was $81 billion.[81] The aggregate total of all subsidies in seventeen European countries is estimated to have been $355 billion in the early 1990s (Table 5.2).[82] In the U.K. case, one-third of the external costs are

Table 5.2. External Costs of Road Transportation in Western Europe

Germany	$81 billion
United Kingdom	$80 billion
France	$53 billion
Italy	$45 billion
Spain	$27 billion
Europe (17 countries, including the above)	$355 billion

Sources: Based on W. Rothengatter and S. Mauch, *External Effects of Transport* (Paris: Union Internationale des Chemins de Fer, 1994); D. Maddison et al., *Blueprint 5: The True Costs of Road Transport* (London: Earthscan, 1996).

taken to be covered via taxes, and if we extend this proportion to the other sixteen European countries, the subsidies are $240 billion, of which $110 billion are environmental externalities. In Japan, there was a direct subsidy for road construction and maintenance in 1991 of $19 billion.[83] Including externalities, the total could have been as high as $50 billion,[84] and that figure is accepted here.

Total Subsidies in OECD Countries

The total for the United States ($695 billion), seventeen European countries ($240 billion), and Japan ($50 billion)—cautious or even minimalist reckonings as they mostly are—comes to $985 billion per year. These nineteen countries comprise 790 million people, so the collective total of $985 billion works out to $1,250 per person per year. If we assume that the same average applies for four other OECD countries (Canada, South Korea, Australia, and New Zealand, omitting Mexico and a few other recent members) with their 100 million people, these four countries account for $125 billion in subsidies. Thus, we get an OECD total of $1,110 billion per year in subsidies for road transportation. This is to be compared with a recent estimate for just three countries, the United States, Germany, and Japan, of $85–$200 billion per year. (This estimate does not include any component for externalities, which detailed analyses suggest could be anywhere from $350 billion to $1.5 trillion per year.)[85]

Subsidies in Non-OECD Countries

If it is difficult to come up with accurate estimates for subsidies in OECD countries, it is even more difficult to find much data at all on subsidies in the transition economies of Eastern Europe and the former Soviet Union, and still more difficult to establish much evidence in developing countries. A fact frustrating in the extreme, but a fact.

All one can say is that in Russia, direct gasoline subsidies in 1998 were $0.6 billion and the cost of rehabilitating the road network would be at least $5 billion per year.[86] Plainly, this must constitute only a part and probably a small part of direct subsidies. Regrettably, there is no information on indirect subsidies or on implicit subsidies in the form of environmental externalities. It would be surprising if the true total were not in the region of $50–$100 billion, but in the absence of any substantive evidence, we must stick with a gross underestimate of $6 billion per year. As for other countries of the former Soviet Union and Eastern Europe, let us postulate a further $6 billion per year. Again, this must surely err on the low side several times over, as any observer would agree after experiencing the lamentable state of transport infrastructure overall.

As long as we lack any indication of the true situation in the countries in transition, we must settle for a joint total for road transportation subsidies of $12 billion per year. The authors would not be surprised if a comprehensive reckoning proved to be ten times greater.

As for developing countries, both the economic spillovers and the environmental externalities tend to be even worse than in developed countries, due to larger populations in many cities, inadequate infrastructure, lower safety standards, and higher accident rates and pollution levels.[87] Developing-country cities are legendary for their congestion and pollution, and rural areas are equally legendary for the disrepair of their roads. In Bangkok, there are long periods every day when traffic moves at an average speed of three kilometers per hour (little over half of walking pace), and cars spend an aggregate average of forty-four days per year stuck in traffic, costing $2.3–$9.6 billion in lost worker productivity plus $1.6 billion in energy wasted by idling car engines. Only 37 percent of trips are made by public transportation. Private auto fuel use is projected to nearly triple during the period 1990–2005, and traffic congestion is projected to reduce fuel-use efficiency by at least half. Bangkok has 1 million respiratory infections each year linked to air pollution, and cancer rates are three times higher than in other parts of Thailand.[88] Costs of damage to health and buildings from air pollution run as high as $1 billion a year.[89] These costs will eventually have to be met from the public purse and should be counted as unwitting subsidies.

In New Delhi, 7,500 people die prematurely from traffic pollution each year, and 1.2 million people receive medical treatment for pol-lution-derived ailments.[90] In India as a whole, urban air pollution levies costs of $1.3 billion per year.[91] In Cairo, particulate pollutants, largely from motor vehicles, cause morbidity and mortality costs between $343 million and $1.5 billion per year, or $38–$161 per res-ident; in Jakarta, the costs are $220 million and $27.[92] Much the same applies in Manila, Santiago, São Paulo, and Lagos, among other large developing-world cities. Total health costs of particulates in developing-world cities are almost $100 billion per year.[93] Yet pri-vate vehicle numbers are increasing at unprecedented rates in many developing countries.[94] In China, the growth rate has averaged 18 percent per year since 1993 (compare with the United States, at 2 percent), and in 1994 public transport use declined by 6.5 percent.[95]

In addition, the World Bank believes that half of developing coun-tries' roads are in such a poor state that governments need to spend $15 billion per year simply to rehabilitate their road networks, let alone to expand them for farmers wanting to get their produce to market: this means more of those effective though hidden subsidies. A coffee farmer on the eastern slopes of Kilimanjaro in Tanzania finds that the value of his crop has dropped by half by the time it has made its way along dismal roads to the export ship in Mombasa. In Africa as a whole, one-third of $150 billion invested in roads has been lost due to poor maintenance and management, and the poten-tial annual cost savings (an effective subsidy) amounts to $1.5 bil-lion.[96]

This means, of course, that governments effectively subsidize their road users by charging them only a small part of the costs of con-structing the roads and keeping them in tolerable condition. Indeed, Bangladesh and Tanzania require road users to cover only 19 percent of direct costs, and Bolivia, 20 percent (improbably precise though these figures seem). Conversely, China charges its road users 120 per-cent of the costs and Turkey 217 percent, while in countries as dis-parate as Bangladesh, Bolivia, and Tanzania, road user fees cover only 20–50 percent of direct costs.[97] But in none of these countries is there any estimate of indirect costs, let alone externalities.

Both of these latter two items can be costly. Traffic-accident deaths in India are believed to total at least 500,000 per year; the rate per 1,000 people is two to five times higher than in Europe.[98] If all such deaths in all developing countries total several million each year, regardless of how the value of life is computed, the cost and hence the covert subsidy must be exceptionally large. Regrettably, it remains unquantified for present purposes.

What are the total subsidies in developing countries? The parlous lack of information is so severe that it is difficult to come up with much that is meaningful. But to offer no assessment on the grounds that we have no "realistic" basis for saying anything is to deny the real world. We could reasonably offer a few judgments with respect to environmental externalities. For instance, we could say that traffic congestion Bangkok-style levies costs of $20 billion per year in all developing countries (the actual total could readily be several times greater). The same goes for air pollution and health costs. Then there is the $27 billion for unrepaired roads and so forth, as cited earlier. This all amounts to a total of $67 billion, and that is the figure accepted here, even though its small size seems to fly in the face of common sense. Could the environmental externalities truly be only a small fraction of those in OECD countries, instead of a lot larger?

Subsidies Worldwide

Overall reckoning for subsidies in this chapter: $1,110 billion per year in OECD countries (range $840–$1,373 billion), at least $12 billion in countries of the former Soviet Union (FSU) and Eastern Europe, and at least $55 billion in developing countries. Grand total: $1,177 billion per year, say $1,180 billion. Of this, conventional subsidies (both direct and indirect) in the United States are $535 billion, in 17 European countries $130 billion, in Japan $19 billion, and other OECD countries $68 billion. In the FSU and Eastern Europe, they are $12 billion. In developing countries, they are $35 billion. (A more realistic and less minimalist estimate for the FSU and Eastern Europe and for developing countries could well increase the total by $100 billion each, perhaps much more, but no data are available.) The total for conventional subsidies is $799 billion, say $800 billion. The rest, $380 billion, is made up of externalities (Table 5.3).

How much of the $1,180 billion should count as perverse subsidies? Recall that not all conventional subsidies are to be viewed as perverse; there are beneficial and neutral subsidies as well as adverse ones. So for the final summation later in the chapter, we shall count only a proportion of the conventional subsidies. By contrast, all the implicit subsidies of environmental externalities are regarded as 100 percent perverse (for the rationale, see Chapter 1).

What proportion of conventional subsidies should be considered perverse? The economic case is readily recognized, namely, that road transportation imposes sizeable direct costs. Let us first note, however, the positive aspect. There is the prima facie argument that road

Table 5.3. Road Transportation Subsidies Worldwide

	Total Subsidies ($ billion)	Conventional[a] ($ billion)	Externalities[b] ($ billion)	Perverse Subsidies ($ billion)
United States	695	535	160	430
Europe (17 countries)	240	130	110	175
Japan	50	19	31	40
Other OECD	125	68	57	90
TOTAL OECD	1,110	752	358	735
TOTAL NON-OECD	67	47	20	45
GRAND TOTALS (rounded)	1,180	800	380	780

[a]Perverse subsidies are 50 percent of conventional subsidies.

[b]Perverse subsidies are 100 percent of environmental externalities.

transportation serves as a basic "lubricant" for economies at many levels of development (see the opening of this chapter); hence, there will often—though certainly not always—be a need to build more roads and otherwise support the car culture. In addition, we shall continue to need regulation of traffic through highway patrols and the multiple like. So not all subsidies are economically adverse. At the same time, the severe overloading of road systems through the rapid increase in vehicles, leading to congestion, traffic accidents, and so forth, demonstrates that while increasing numbers of vehicles can liberate the individual, they can eventually enslave society.[99] As the reader will recognize from his or her own experience, driving in many cities and on rural roads is no longer a benefit but a burden. Like the Red Queen, we seem to have to run faster to stay in the same place.

Now for the environmental side of conventional subsidies. Road building has its adverse environmental factors, such as despoiling of landscapes; as mentioned earlier, in the United States, an expanse the size of Florida has been taken over for roads. Traffic congestion can likewise be said to have an adverse environmental dimension. The same applies, though sometimes in a more marginal sense, to the other categories of subsidies. (This much is apparent; perhaps not so obvious is that if the problem were entirely environmental, it would rank as an environmental externality and thus become an implicit subsidy.) There are many adverse environmental aspects to conventional subsidies, even if some of their costs, notably their nonmonetized costs, can be characterized in only qualitative fashion.

One would be somewhat justified in concluding that virtually all conventional subsidies exert adverse effects both environmentally and economically and thus are perverse subsidies. Let us allow, however, for the net benefits that still accrue from subsidies in certain circumstances, even though they may often be in accelerating decline in relation to the "disbenefits." Let us note too that while the replacement of subsidies in the United States, for example, through targeted user fees and gasoline taxes, would reduce carbon dioxide emissions by 11–14 percent over a twenty-year period (a major environmental benefit, boosted by reduction of urban smog, acid rain, and other forms of pollution), it would often induce the parallel benefit of relieving traffic congestion and other economic ills.[100] The picture is decidedly mixed, with all kinds of factors operating in some positive as well as many negative senses. On the whole, however, the evidence is decidedly downside.

As a best-judgment assessment, let us conclude that a sizeable proportion of conventional subsidies are perverse. After reviewing all the evidence, the authors have decided that the proportion is somewhere between an absolute minimum of one-third and a more likely two-thirds (if not more—the transportation experts who critiqued this chapter considered that 100 percent would not be unrealistic). It is difficult indeed to narrow the one-third/two-thirds range in strictly objective fashion. As a thoroughly informed but less than finally accurate estimate, the authors propose that roughly half of the $800 billion of conventional subsidies are perverse, that is to say, $400 billion per year.

True, this assessment is arbitrary in the extreme. Is it any more arbitrary, though, than the "assessment" now being imposed by the individual calculations and choices of the world's road users? It is idle to say that in the absence of conclusive evidence one cannot or should not offer any estimate at all of what the proportion should be. What one can truly say is that one cannot offer a definitive estimate. For want of a better assessment, one-half seems appropriate.

To this must be added the many covert subsidies, notably the environmental externalities, which are 100 percent perverse by definition (nobody benefits from pollution-related illness, etc.). In the United States, these externality subsidies are estimated to be $160 billion per year. In Western Europe, they are estimated to be $110 billion; in Japan, $31 billion; and in other OECD countries, $57 billion. In non-OECD countries, as we have seen, the total is $20 billion per year. These make up a total of $378 billion per year, say $380 billion, and

100 percent of this figure is taken to be an implicit and perverse subsidy.

In summary, conventional perverse subsidies are $400 billion per year, and covert perverse subsidies in the form of environmental externalities are $380 billion per year. Grand total: $780 billion per year (Table 5.3). This is two-fifths of the global total of all perverse subsidies in six sectors, almost $2 trillion. The authors have repeatedly asked their expert colleagues if the calculations are inflated, and the response has been a resounding no. Indeed, several of them assert that the share of conventional subsidies represented by perverse subsidies should be not 50 percent but 100 percent. Moreover, where a particular subsector, for example, road accidents in the United States, features a range of estimates, the authors have usually chosen a median or lower estimate. Many of the statistics derive from the early 1990s, and the figures for today would surely be higher. For all these reasons and for others that reflect the generally cautious and conservative approach to this chapter's assessment, the estimate of $780 billion for perverse subsidies seems realistic, even though it is far and away the largest for the six sectors considered in this book.

Policy Responses

It is commonplace to limit a listing of policy proposals to fuel taxes and other policy instruments and management measures, plus specific actions such as promotion of unleaded gasoline. Instead, we start here with what is surely the most productive and urgent option of all. In fact, it could well be worth all the other proposals together.

Establish the "True" Price of Gasoline

We need to get a secure quantified handle on all subsidies both direct and indirect, with emphasis on their numerous externalities. It is absurd that we are ostensibly expending $1,180 billion per year through subsidies worldwide, let alone $780 billion through perverse subsidies, yet we do not have a precise idea of how accurate these figures are (the limited evidence suggests on several counts that both figures could be on the low side by quite a way). The first is a sum equivalent to 3.4 percent of the global economy. It is like saying that an individual with an annual income of $30,000 is paying out a special tax of over $1,000 per year with only the haziest notion of its existence or of whether the actual amount is more, possibly a good deal more. Or suppose you were buying a car for $15,000 and then found that it would be subject to all manner of additional payments that increase the purchase price by hundreds of dollars. You would protest that it would be both fairer and more efficient for you to be told the true overall price in the first place.

We need to firm up the calculus from all angles, and with due dispatch.[101] Until we know just what is the nature and extent of the problem we are grappling with, there is limited mileage (so to speak) in formulating solutions.

When we have gained a firm understanding of the scale of subsidies, we can take measures of parallel scale to require road users to pay the full costs of what they do. In particular, we can do more to internalize the super-scale externalities inherent in road transportation. A good start could be made with rigorous implementation of the Polluter Pays Principle, a concept that is recognized throughout OECD countries. Cutting back on the underpricing of car travel can reduce vehicle use by 33 percent or more—and it would thereby reduce environmental consequences such as air and noise pollution.[102]

Adjust the Playing Field

The transportation playing field should be leveled or even tilted in favor of bus and rail transport, which are usually competitive commercially and far less harmful environmentally. The same applies, only more so, to bicycles. In Copenhagen, city managers supply 2,300 bicycles for individual citizens. Users collect them from bicycle racks against a $3 coin-box deposit, ride them to wherever they are going, and then leave them in another rack and collect a refund. As a result, one-third of Copenhagen's commuters cycle to work. Much the same type of bike commuting applies in major cities of Germany and the Netherlands, by contrast with the United States, where only 10 percent or less of trips are by bike. Shifting just 5 percent of Americans onto bikes would save at least $100 billion per year.[103]

> In Copenhagen, city managers supply 2,300 free bicycles for citizens.

Similarly, positive and constructive subsidies can promote "green" cars. In Sweden, the government has reduced taxes on electric cars, hybrid cars, and cars that run on fuel other than gasoline and diesel fuel.

Expand Traffic Management

There are many options for relieving traffic congestion.[104] When employees are in a position to decline free parking in favor of a cash payment of equal value, car commuting declines by 20–40 percent.[105] Making car insurance a variable cost (to reflect, e.g., miles driven) can reduce driving by 5–14 percent in the short term and by 16–14 percent in the long term.[106] Then there is scope to charge for road use in prime areas and during peak hours. Singapore is one of the most prosperous communities in the world, and one would expect traffic to match that in bumper-to-bumper Bangkok. On the contrary, the city government levies a $3–$6 daily user fee for cars entering the city's central zone, especially during rush hour. These various measures have decreased traffic during peak periods by 75 percent. In addition, the government taxes cars heavily and auctions the right to buy them.[107]

There is much scope too for carpooling. On an average day, 15 million Americans carpool, compared with fewer than 6 million who take all forms of public transit, though contrasted with the 84 million who drive alone.[108] Carpooling typically reduces participants' vehicle use by 50 percent.[109] Plus, carpooling just one day a week keeps the average commuter from releasing more than half a tonne of CO_2 into the atmosphere per year.[110]

Consider Al Gore's Commuter Choice program, which allows employees up to $2,880 a year in reimbursements if they carpool or take mass transit to work. Workers enjoy pretax deductions for their commuting and parking costs. If an employee spends, say, $50 a month on gasoline and car maintenance to drive to work and $50 a month to park, he or she can be reimbursed $100 a month for leaving the car at home. Employers can also offer incentives such as free passes on mass transit systems, which are exempt from income and payroll taxes. More than 8,800 companies have already given workers tax incentives and transit passes, notably in New York, Washington, D.C., and San Francisco.[111]

Increase Car Efficiency

A typical twenty-two-kilometers-per-gallon vehicle produces twice as much CO_2 per kilometer as does a standard car with its forty-five kilometers per gallon. The standard car in turn produces more than twice as much CO_2 per kilometer as do the new hybrid electric vehicles being introduced by Toyota and Honda. Were all U.S. cars to get

160–200 kilometers per gallon (as should soon be feasible in principle), that would eliminate the need for U.S. oil imports, cut the automobile sector's contribution to global warming by three-quarters, and reduce local air pollution by two-thirds or more. Similarly, persuading drivers to travel at 90 kilometers instead of 120 kilometers an hour would increase fuel economy by 25 percent (and raise survival chances in an accident). Germany aims for a 25 percent cut in average fuel consumption by cars between 1990 and 2005, while Switzerland aims for a 15 percent reduction during the brief period 1996–2001. In addition, European car manufacturers have agreed to a 10 percent reduction in average new vehicle CO_2 emissions per kilometer between 1993 and 2005,[112] and the European Parliament proposes an even higher target for the same period, a reduction rate of 2–3 percent per year. The U.S. Environmental Protection Agency has proposed new pollution standards for SUVs.

To cite an energy and automobile expert, Hal Harvey:

> Better than raising gasoline taxes would be to set fuel-efficiency standards. But both slam up against political reality. It would take a very steep gasoline tax to cut carbon emissions from American automobiles by even a half. Gasoline buying accounts for only 11 percent of the cost of running a car, considerably less than insurance. Doubling the price of gasoline would increase fuel efficiency by one third at most, far less than what is technically feasible. And doubling the price of gasoline is only slightly less tractable politically than outlawing the flag.[113]

Harvey goes on to assert:

> A more sophisticated approach lies with modest taxes, say $4–5 per tonne of carbon, whereupon the proceeds of the taxes could be used to transform energy technology, leading to a vastly cleaner system. The trick is to focus on promoting good technologies rather than punishing bad behavior. Promoting the commercialization of energy efficiency and renewable energy technologies is a far cheaper way to achieve the same effect as raising taxes, and requires a much more modest political effort.[114]

Finally, consider the success of a city of 2.6 million people in the industrial sector of southern Brazil. In the early 1970s, Curitiba designated several main roadways radiating from its center and strategic axes for busways, as well as extra-large buses for popular routes and bus-stop shelters where passengers pay their fares in advance. Although the city now has one car for every five people, two-thirds of all trips are made by bus, while car traffic has declined by 30 percent since 1974 even though the population has doubled.[115]

This success story contrasts sharply with the approach in most other cities and countries. One American commentator has remarked: "We meter and charge for water and electricity. We do not fund an airline monopoly with taxes and offer everyone free plane rides. Yet that is precisely the craziness by which we manage urban highways."[116]

Chapter 6

WATER

The water sector features abundant subsidies, making it crucial for this book. The subsidies are diverse, scattered, and often concealed; hence, they are difficult to track down. Because they are so large, however, a review is essential, even if its findings are approximate and exploratory in some respects.

In this sector probably more than in other sectors, there is a premium on equity for all beneficiaries. After all, water is a basic component of life processes and should be readily available to all users, especially the poor. This generally means that water should be subsidized for the poorest. Conversely, we cannot expect to see sound water management when subsidies are munificently dispensed to rich and poor alike, often in inconsistent fashion. The hardscrabble rice farmer on one side of the road should not have to pay for water if the car manufacturer, the swimming pool owner, and the golf player on the other side of the road do not pay the full cost of their water—or do not pay the full cost of wastewater treatment, flood protection, storm drainage, and a host of other ancillary services that support water supplies for the entire community.[1]

Water Demand and Supply

Humans withdraw water from rivers, lakes, and other freshwater bodies for three main uses: household and municipal, industrial, and agricultural (mainly irrigation) use. Worldwide, household and municipal use takes 10 percent, industry 25 percent, and agriculture 65 percent. In developed countries, agriculture accounts for less than 40 percent on average of total use, whereas in many developing countries it is over 90 percent. Most of the funds spent on the water sector each year go to financing of irrigation schemes, as is appropriate given that irrigated croplands make up only one-sixth of all croplands but supply two-fifths of the world's food, more than half of the world's grain, and nearly two-thirds of the world's rice and wheat (the only other major staple being corn).[2]

Of all agricultural water used, the developing world's share is around 70 percent. In developed countries, by contrast, industrial use of water tends to be as high as agricultural use.[3] In the United States, the single biggest user is the thermoelectric power industry (fossil-fuel and nuclear plants), which requires huge quantities of water for cooling purposes, albeit much is returned to the source in a semi-satisfactory state. Other big industrial users are the pulp and paper, iron and steel, chemical, and petroleum industries. Yet industry is not always obliged to treat its wastewater—a factor that serves as a salient example of the many major uncounted subsidies in the water sector. The same applies to wastewater from households. Both of these sets of covert subsidies arise in developed and developing countries alike.[4]

How much water does a person use each day? Counting all three main purposes, the average worldwide is 1,800 liters, though over half a billion people receive as little as 20 liters. An American uses 400 liters for personal and direct purposes and 5,100 liters including all forms of use.[5] The latter figure primarily reflects an American's consumption of grain in both direct and indirect fashion, an average tonne of grain requiring 1,000 tonnes of water and 1 tonne of beef requiring 100 times as much.[6] One tonne of water is equivalent to 1 cubic meter or 1,000 liters. Were the worldwide average daily water use to amount to 2,740 liters per day, that would work out to 1,000 cubic meters per year. So a global average of 1,800 liters per day equates to just over 650 cubic meters per year.[7]

We can reckon this in another way. A nutritious low-meat diet requires about 1,600 cubic meters of water per person per year, or 4,400 liters per day. Worldwide water use for household and industrial purposes averages about 240 cubic meters per person per year, or 660 liters per day. By reducing this level through more careful consumption and more efficient technologies, we can assume an average of 200 cubic meters per person per year, or 550 liters per day. When we add in water for food production, the total rises to 730 cubic meters per person per year, or 2,000 liters per day. A portion of water runoff must remain in rivers, however, in order to dilute pollution and meet other in-stream needs. Thus, the total amount of runoff must be two to three times higher than the amount required to meet the three main purposes. So let us postulate an average total requirement of 1,700 cubic meters per person per year, or 4,660 liters per day.[8]

When water use falls below 1,700 cubic meters per person per year, a country encounters water stress through lack of adequate supplies. When water use falls below 1,000 cubic meters, there is water scarcity, meaning a significant and often severe restriction on material welfare at the individual level and on development prospects at the national level.[9]

True, some countries manage with a good deal less than the cutoff level of 1,000 cubic meters. Israel, for example, gets by with a renewable per capita water supply of only around 400 cubic meters.[10] In part, the country manages to do this by importing much of its grain, which has been referred to as "virtual water"[11] because, as mentioned earlier, 1 tonne of grain requires 1,000 tonnes of water. The Middle East as a whole, which is the most concentrated region of water scarcity in the world, is fortunate in that its oil exports allow it to import 30 percent of its grain.[12]

Producing food takes a lot of water. One kilogram of lettuce takes over 800 kilograms of water; 1 of rice takes almost 2,000; and 1 of grain-fed chicken, 3,500 kilograms.[13] One cup of orange juice takes 220 liters of water; 1 kilogram of pasta, 2,850; and 1 hamburger, 2,775 kilograms.[14] One of the thirstiest crops of all, albeit not a food crop, is cotton: 1 kilogram of cotton needs 17,000 kilograms of water.[15]

Whatever the limitations on water supplies today and still greater shortages in the future through population growth alone, they could become even more stringent because of global warming. If mean annual temperatures rise, possibly by as much as 3–4 degrees Celsius, rainfall in the U.S. corn belt could well decline by 10 percent.[16] This would be accompanied by in-

> Producing food takes a lot of water. One kilogram of lettuce takes over 800 kilograms of water.

creased evaporation, meaning still greater loss of moisture. Worldwide, global warming could step up irrigation needs by one-quarter
simply to maintain the production level of the early 1990s, without
allowing for increased human numbers and improved diets.[17] In
addition, there could be many more droughts: those that have only a
5 percent frequency today could increase to 50 percent by 2050.[18]

Yet we need to produce 50–60 percent more food during the next
thirty years simply to keep up with the projected rise in human numbers and in human appetites. Since at least half of this increase is
scheduled to come from irrigated croplands, this places a premium
on more efficient and careful use of water. It is, after all, a renewable
resource, available for repeated recycling and thus contrasting
strongly with other natural resources such as topsoil and fossil fuels.
Almost everywhere, however, water is misused and overused, in
major measure because of subsidies that discourage people from
making efficient and careful use of water. Fortunately, through vigorous policy reform of subsidies, among other measures, developing
countries—these being where water shortages are likely to become
most pronounced—could eliminate almost two-thirds of their present water losses due to inefficient and profligate use of water. This
would be equivalent to increasing their actual water supplies by a full
one-quarter.[19]

Water Waste and Subsidies

There can hardly be a country in the world that is more dependent
on a natural resource than Egypt is on water. At the United Nations
International Conference on Population and Development, held in
Cairo in September 1994, the conference grounds were regularly
watered at midday, when the temperature was over 30 degrees Celsius. So too in California's Central Valley, where it is often the practice for highly inefficient water sprinklers to irrigate croplands at
midday, when the temperature is not much lower than in Cairo. The
reason in both cases is that government subsidies encourage wasteful
use of water and eliminate any incentive to use it sparingly, let alone
repeatedly. California is overdrafting its groundwater at a rate equal
to 15 percent of the state's annual water consumption.[20]

Water subsidies typically range from 75 percent to 99 percent of
full costs; in the irrigation sphere, governments collect an average of
under 10 percent of irrigation services via user fees (Tables 6.1 and
6.2).[21] Almost as bad, wasteful use of water means that money is
spent on lobbying and other forms of persuasion to secure further

Table 6.1. Water Prices as Share of Marginal Cost of Supply

Country	Percentage
Israel	60%±
China	25%
Egypt	20%
United States	17%
Pakistan, Indonesia, South Korea	13%
Philippines	10%
Nepal	4%
Thailand	3%
Bangladesh	1%

Sources: P. H. Gleick, "Basic Water Requirements for Human Activities: Meeting Basic Needs," *Water International* 21 (1996): 83–92; S. Postel, *Dividing the Waters: Food Security, Ecosystem Health, and the New Politics of Scarcity* (Washington, D.C.: Worldwatch Institute, 1996); I. Serageldin, *Water Supply, Sanitation, and Environmental Sustainability: The Financing Challenge* (Washington, D.C.: World Bank, 1994).

Table 6.2. Irrigation Subsidies in Developing Regions, 1983–1993

Region	Annual Costs ($ million)	Irrigation Subsidies ($ million)
Africa	6,281	5,909 (94%)
Latin America	3,598	3,386 (94%)
Asia	13,263	12,480 (94%)
TOTAL	23,142	21,775 (94%)

Sources: P. H. Gleick, "Basic Water Requirements for Human Activities: Meeting Basic Needs," *Water International* 21 (1996): 83–92; S. Postel, "Dividing the Waters," *Technology Review* (April 1997): 54–62; S. Postel, *Last Oasis,* rev. ed. (New York: Norton, 1997); World Bank, *Expanding the Measure of Wealth: Indicators of Environmentally Sustainable Development* (Washington, D.C.: World Bank, 1997).

Note: The amount of irrigation water available to plants is generally 40 percent; through efficient irrigation systems, 60–90 percent. Over the past thirty years, Israel has achieved a fivefold increase in the value of crops grown with a given amount of water.

supplies of cheap water, causing subsidies to create a second-order source of waste.[22]

A potent political reason for subsidizing irrigation water in developing countries is that agriculture often employs over half the workforce.[23] This can help to justify government measures to build yet another irrigation project or hydro works. To oblige its farmers, China plans to divert 5 percent of the Yangtze River's flow to its dry northern provinces, while Mexico pumps water as much as 1,000 meters up into its Central Valley.

Despite many water shortages, wasteful use is the order of the day. Whereas water consumption in developing countries has been increasing at 4–8 percent per year for much of the past several decades, demonstrating exceptional demand, 40–60 percent of water delivered by utilities is lost to leakage, theft, and poor accounting. In the case of irrigation, which consumes 65 percent of the world's water, half of the water supplied is lost to seepage and evaporation—in many developed countries as well as virtually all developing countries.[24] This wasteful use amounts to an effective subsidy, which in turn sends a further potent message to the consumer that water is not a scarce resource to be used frugally and efficiently but a resource in endless supply that can be used as prodigally as anyone wishes.

In short, subsidies give rise to a host of problems: chronic excess demand for water, especially through grand-scale water projects; poor operation and maintenance of water systems; inattention to scope for water conservation; and many other problems. The upshot (to cite Robert Repetto) is "inefficient, inequitable, fiscally disastrous, wasteful use of increasingly scarce water, and environmentally harmful." Because of subsidies, he notes, "neither farmers, local governments, irrigation agencies, nor international banks are financially at risk for the success of irrigation investments, so pressures for new capacity lead to a proliferation of projects, many of them being of dubious worth."[25]

This is all the more unfortunate in that water is becoming scarce in many parts of the world. Humans already use 54 percent of available water runoff, and new dams will increase this runoff by only about 10 percent over the next thirty years—a period during which population is projected to increase by 40 percent.[26] Global water use tripled during the four decades 1950–1990, and demand is expected to rise by nearly 50 percent during the period 1990–2025. In eighty-eight developing countries with 40 percent of the world's population, the problem has become a serious constraint on development, and the number of people experiencing water shortage is projected to climb sixfold to reach 3 billion by 2025 (range 2.8 billion to 3.3 billion).[27] It is unlikely that this demand will be met, if only because of practical upper limits of usable and renewable freshwater stocks. Indeed, a business-as-usual scenario for 2010 could see all countries except for Canada and the Scandinavian countries suffering water shortages in at least part of their territories and many countries encountering a high level of water stress. By 2025, the water sector is likely to be in a crisis situation in many regions of the world.[28]

The principal areas at risk include, though are not confined to, parts of China, India, Pakistan, the Middle East, Mexico, and much of Africa. (This analysis takes no account of further shortages brought on by global warming.) By 2020, China is projected to more than triple its domestic water withdrawals and to increase industrial withdrawals fourfold over the 1995 level, supposing that the water is available. In Southeast Asia, there is expected to be a doubling of domestic water withdrawals and a 290 percent increase in industrial demand by 2020. The largest increase in water demand, 309 percent, is likely to be in India, where the volume could well equal the demand increment in developed countries.

Adverse Consequences

Water shortages cause major problems for irrigation agriculture, industry, and public health. A full 80 percent of developing country disease, or 4 billion cases, are due to lack of clean water for household use, and 6 million deaths per year stem from water-related diseases such as malaria, cholera, schistosomiasis, yellow fever, river blindness, and, especially, diarrhea.[29] There are 1 billion episodes of diarrhea annually in developing countries. Moreover, when a person experiences diarrhea, malaria, or other disease, some 5–20 percent of food intake is needed simply to offset the disease's adverse effect on nutrition.[30] In India alone, poor water supplies impose health costs of $5–$7 billion per year.[31] All in all, water-related diseases are estimated to levy a total cost, just through workdays lost to sickness, of $125 billion a year (late 1970s value),[32] in contrast with the minimum of $11 billion a year cost of supplying both water and sanitation facilities by 2025 (additional funds would be required to serve growing urban communities as well as to maintain and upgrade existing systems).[33] Thus, the subsidized abuse of water exacts high costs from national economies in the health sector alone.

There are many other instances of broad-scope externalities from water pollution. Industrially contaminated wastewater used for irrigation in northern China causes a loss of 5 million tonnes of grain a year.[34] Pollution of groundwater in Yingkou, China, has almost doubled the cost of new water supplies, while in Shenyang, also in China, similar pollution was expected to cause the cost of new supplies to almost triple during the period 1988–2000.[35] Worldwide, pollution-related externalities of various sorts must collectively amount to tens of billions of dollars of covert subsidies per year, but they remain

> *Industrially contaminated wastewater used for irrigation in northern China causes a loss of 5 million tonnes of grain a year.*

unquantified by economists and hence unconsidered by policy makers. To this sizeable extent, of course, the subsidy estimates in this chapter are to be viewed as all the more cautious and conservative.

Water subsidies also exert adverse effects on the environmental cause writ large. Foremost, as noted earlier, is the wasteful use of a natural resource that is coming into ever greater demand and ever tighter supply. Other effects include, in terms of irrigation water alone, widespread agricultural pests (as well as a lengthy list of diseases); disruptions of river hydrology; water-caused soil erosion; siltation of water bodies; draining of wetlands; depletion of fish stocks; and building of unnecessary dams. All these adverse effects arise because governments find it politically easier to provide new water sources than to make users pay a price that reflects the true costs of supply, thus encouraging consumers to treat water negligently if not prodigally.[36] In India alone, 95,000 square kilometers out of 420,000 square kilometers of irrigated croplands have been lost to cultivation through waterlogging, and another 100,000 square kilometers are affected by salinization. In Pakistan, more than half the Indus Basin canal system, some 120,000 square kilometers of irrigated cropland, is waterlogged, and 65,000 square kilometers are salinized. In the former Soviet Union, 25,000 square kilometers are damaged; in China, 70,000 square kilometers; and in the United States, 52,000 square kilometers.[37] Worldwide, 454,000 square kilometers out of 2.8 million square kilometers are salinized enough to reduce crop yields, with crop losses worth almost $11 billion per year.[38] Waterlogging and salinization may now be taking as much old land out of irrigation as is being added through new irrigation networks.[39]

There are other environmental problems from excessive irrigation. In some regions, so much water is withdrawn from rivers that they start to run dry. In Asia, which will see the most population growth and greatest rise in food demand within the foreseeable future, many rivers are largely or completely tapped out during the drier part of the year, precisely when irrigation is most needed. They include most rivers in India, including the Ganges, and China's Yellow River, where the lower reaches ran dry for 226 days in 1997, resulting in crop losses of 8 million tonnes, worth $1.7 billion.[40]

At the same time, heavy irrigation leads to a decline in water tables. As far back as ten years ago, more than one-fifth of the United States's 100,000 square kilometers of irrigated land was being watered only by lowering water tables, especially that of the Ogallala Aquifer.[41] In parts of the northern China plain around Beijing and Tianjin, the water table is currently dropping by one to two meters a year. This area, roughly China north of the Yangtze River, contains nearly half a billion people, almost 40 percent of the country's populace. It also encompasses half of China's croplands, yet it features only one-fifth of the country's surface water.[42] This situation explains, even if it does not justify, the Chinese government's action in subsidizing water for agriculture.[43]

In India too, pumping of water from underground far exceeds aquifer recharge. The result has been a precipitous fall in water tables—as much as two meters per year in parts of Tamil Nadu—and drying up of the more shallow tube wells in tens of thousands of villages nationwide, while in certain coastal areas, overuse of freshwater has sucked in seawater, destroying freshwater aquifers permanently.[44] All this will surely lead to a steep decline in irrigation water supplies, thus threatening food production. As India's population has tripled since 1950, water demand has climbed to where it may now be double the sustainable yield of the country's groundwater stocks. Aquifer depletion and cutbacks in irrigation water could reduce India's grain harvest by as much as one-quarter.[45] In a country where more than half of all children are malnourished and underweight and an additional 18 million people are taken on board each year, a shrinking harvest could increase hunger-related mortality.[46]

In certain pivotal regions of the world, overpumping of aquifers now exceeds recharge by at least 100 percent, or 160 billion tonnes of water per year.[47] The countries that are the biggest users of groundwater, namely, India, China, the United States, North Africa, and the countries of the Arabian Peninsula, produce 180 million tonnes of grain (almost 10 percent of the global harvest) by depleting water supplies. If we reckon that 1,000 tonnes of water are needed to produce 1 tonne of grain, this implies that were the overpumping to be stopped, world grain production would decline by at least 160 million tonnes, equivalent to the grain needs of 600 million people.[48]

Falling water tables affect urban communities too. Water for Mexico City, for example, has been supplied at a price that implied an annual subsidy of $1 billion. This encouraged excessive pumping, with the result that the water table has fallen by 80 meters, aquifers are being compacted, and many parts of the city have been sinking (in some localities by as much as 8 meters, damaging the city's underground infrastructure of pipes, cables, and sewers and increasing the potential for earthquake damage).[49] Fortunately, there have been major reforms of irrigation water subsidies in Mexico, yet the price of irrigation water to farmers is only 3–8 percent of their production costs, a typical range for irrigated agriculture.[50]

Perhaps the best-known example of subsidy-driven degradation of a water resource occurred in the former Soviet Union, in the decline of the Aral Sea. In the late 1950s, much of the water basin that was centered on the Aral Sea—once the world's fourth largest lake—was given over to cotton growing with heavily subsidized irrigation water, requiring the diversion of two of the sea's main feeder rivers. As a result, the sea's expanse declined by 50 percent and its water volume declined by three-quarters between 1960 and the early 1990s. The sea's fishery, which once produced 44,000 tonnes of fish a year, has all but disappeared, taking with it 60,000 jobs. Within another decade or two, the Aral Sea is likely to dwindle to a few residual brine lakes, worsening water shortages in an extensive sector of central Asia and contributing to political tensions.[51] To rehabilitate the area's salinized lands could cost at least $1 billion.[52]

There are further environmental problems from water subsidies, albeit of less precise and graphic impact. For instance, subsidies foster agriculture on marginal lands, where cultivation requires excessive use of chemicals, hence contributing to degradation of rivers, contamination of aquifers, destruction of wetlands, and toxic pollution of fish and wildlife.[53] Yet these environmental externalities, like the others listed earlier (rivers running dry, water tables plunging, etc.), remain almost entirely unquantified in economic terms and hence unnoticed in policy terms—even though they effectively constitute perverse subsidies of exceptional size.

Another way to get a handle on what is at stake is to consider the putative value of major benefits derived from water and then to reflect on what will be lost as water supplies decline in relation to fast-growing demand. According to a recent assessment,[54] water supplies from watersheds, aquifers, and reservoirs generate benefits worth $1.7 trillion per year, and water for agricultural irrigation, industrial processes, and waterway transportation is worth $1.1 trillion per year worldwide. Even if these benefits, totaling $2.8 trillion, were reduced through water waste, pollution, and the like, by only 1 percent per year, the annual economic loss would be $28 billion, as discussed later in this chapter.

That the $2.8 trillion estimate is in the right ballpark is demonstrated by a further recent assessment. This shows that dilution of pollutants, as measured by the cost of removing all contaminants and nutrients from wastewater by technological means, is worth $150 billion worldwide per year (this estimate applies only to municipal water and does not consider the dilution function that removes pesticides, nitrates, and other contaminants from agricultural drainage water). Then there is the value of transportation by freshwater, generating revenues in the United States of $360 billion per year and in Western Europe of $169 billion per year, this being a lower-bound estimate that also does not consider the rest of the world. In addition, there is the value of freshwater systems for sport fishing, worth $46 billion per year in the United States alone; the global value of fish, waterfowl, and other goods taken from freshwater systems amounts to at least $100 billion per year, possibly several times as much. The marginal value of these benefits is increasing in many countries as more people spend time and money on outdoor pursuits and as freshwater systems become more scarce. The economic value of the services listed amounts to $825 billion per year, while "the entire benefits and services provided by freshwater systems almost certainly amount to several trillion dollars annually."[55]

Finally, consider what could prove to be the biggest potential externality of all: water wars. This is not so improbable within the foreseeable future,[56] mainly because of water stocks that straddle international frontiers. Of 214 major river basins around the world, three-quarters are shared by two countries and one-quarter by three to ten countries. (See Table 6.3, which presents further information about international interdependence on water supplies.) Almost half of the Earth's land surface is located within international river basins, supporting 40 percent of the world's population; two-thirds of these basins are in developing countries, which generally have less water per citizen than do developed countries. Nearly fifty countries have more than three-quarters of their territory within such areas. Within countries too there is scope for conflict. In India's Punjab, there have been constant violent clashes as Sikh nationalists claim that too much of their water has been diverted to the Hindu states of

Table 6.3. Dependence on International Water Supply

Country	Share of Total Water Flow Originating in an Upstream Country or Countries
Egypt	97%
Botswana	94%
Uzbekistan	91%
Cambodia	82%
Syria	79%
Sudan	77%
Iraq	66%
Bangladesh	42%
Thailand	39%
Jordan	36%

Sources: P. H. Gleick, ed., *Water in Crisis: A Guide to the World's Freshwater Resources* (New York: Oxford University Press, 1993); S. Postel, "Dividing the Waters," *Technology Review* (April 1997): 54–62.

Haryana and Rajasthan.

Tensions and violence have erupted too in the river basin of the Mekong, shared by Thailand, Laos, Cambodia, and Vietnam; in that of the Amur, shared by China and the former Soviet Union; in that of the Paraná, shared by Brazil and Argentina; in that of the Lauca, shared by Bolivia and Chile; and in that of the Medjerda, shared by Tunisia and Libya.[57] Were confrontation over water shortages to give way to conflict and outright violence, this would quite likely be the biggest and most costly single externality of all, yet it does not figure in the economic calculations of policy makers in the water sector.

Water as a Free Good

Why this dismal state of affairs from both economic and environmental standpoints? Much of the essential reason is that nations and individuals alike tend to regard water as a free good, which places an ostensible burden on governments to supply it without charge. (The free-good approach is explicitly enshrined in the Koran, which may account for grossly wasteful use of water in Muslim lands of the Middle East—though in the largest Muslim country, Indonesia, the government gets around the problem by charging for the container in which the water is delivered.) The overall result is that water is generally used inefficiently because it appears to cost next to nothing if not nothing at all. What is priceless is taken to be valueless. As a further result, governments squander large amounts of taxpayers' money in building new water-supply systems.[58]

A subsidiary reason is that all governments recognize a basic responsibility to make sure their citizens are fed, preferably with home-grown food. Fully two-fifths of the world's food is produced on irrigated lands, even though they constitute only one-sixth of all croplands. But if agriculture were to compete openly with industrial and domestic needs for water, it would often be outpriced. So governments support agricultural water use with one subsidy after another, certain of them of indirect character and difficult to discern. In particular, governments sponsor water-demanding crops. In California's Central Valley, with its desert-like climate, three of the main crops are alfalfa, cotton, and rice, crops more suitable to a much moister climate. In an increasing number of semi-arid countries, the main use of water is to grow crops that are worth less than the water itself. In Cyprus, for example, three-quarters of crops grown are uneconomic, produced only because of water subsidies.[59] In Jordan, one of the driest countries anywhere, subsidies encourage overuse of irrigation water, whereupon strict rationing is required because of the resulting scarcities.[60] A further subsidy lies with the electricity used to drive irrigation pumps, a virtually universal practice in developing countries.

In most thirsty regions, water management can account for as much as 14–18 percent of all public investment. This should supply a massive incentive to ensure that farmers make the best use of every last drop of water. But from California to Indonesia and along the banks of the Nile, the Ganges, and the Yangtze, farmers rarely pay more than one-fifth and sometimes only one-tenth of the operating costs of irrigation schemes, let alone their capital costs.[61] Much the same applies in Canada, Greece, Spain, and Italy, though most other developed countries cover their government outlays with consumer charges (whereas capital costs are often subsidized to an average of 20–40 percent).[62] In Australia, the government of the state of Victoria has engaged in reforms and now mostly recovers the delivery costs of irrigation water, but the government of New South Wales manages far less. Because of massive overuse of water, irrigated lands in New South Wales's portion of the Murray-Darling Basin—especially important because they produce 90 percent of the country's irrigated crops with just 6 percent of the country's water runoff—feature broad-scale salinization, water pollution, rising water tables, and soil erosion.[63]

Inefficiency and Waste

Let us take a closer look at the degree of subsidy-induced inefficiency and waste in many developing countries. In China, water prices are believed to be only 25 percent of the marginal cost of supply, while the cost of infrastructure (dams, piping, etc.) is left out of accounting altogether. In Egypt, supply-cost recovery is 20 percent or less; in Pakistan, Indonesia, and South Korea, it is 13 percent; in the Philippines, 10 percent; in Nepal, 4 percent; in Thailand, 3 percent; and in Bangladesh, 1 percent (compare these with the United States, at 17 percent) (Table 6.1). Irrigation charges as a percentage of economic benefits to farmers work out in Indonesia to 21 percent and in Pakistan to 6 percent.[64] This means that were governments to steadily increase the cost of water supply, it would make only marginal difference to farmers' overall costs.

Because farmers are implicitly encouraged to be prodigal in their use of irrigation water, it is generally the case that only a small fraction of water actually becomes available for plants' use—typically 40 percent at best, compared with 60–70 percent in more advanced systems. The rest of the water seeps or evaporates from unlined or obstructed canals and distributories.[65] In India, as much as 45 percent of irrigation water seeps through unlined field channels, while another 15 percent is applied beyond what is needed.[66] So wasteful is water use by outmoded irrigation systems that they often use twice as much water per hectare yet achieve crop yields only one-third as high as their more advanced counterparts.[67]

Even in more efficient irrigation systems, however, generally only half of the water is used by crop plants. Farm distribution systems lose 15 percent, irrigation systems lose another 15 percent, and field application methods lose another 25 percent.[68] Irrigation efficiency can be improved by several techniques, including the simple expedient of irrigating at night in order to reduce evaporation.[69] This is not to say that farmers do not value their irrigation water; rather, the situation discourages them from valuing it much at all in financial terms. In India, farmers in areas where irrigation water is supplied by private instead of public bodies have been willing to pay six to nine times the water charges levied for official supplies.[70] This means, of course, that subsidies are strictly unnecessary insofar as farmers are willing to pay high prices for their irrigation water.

The same applies to inefficiency and waste in municipal communities. The water supply in Manila, for example, loses 58 percent of its volume through leakage from pipes between the treatment plant and the consumer, whereas Singapore, with its hefty water charges, loses only 8 percent. In most Latin American cities, water losses through pipe leaks and other sources of unaccounted-for loss amount to fully 40 percent, while the average municipal loss in many countries is as high as 50 percent. As a result, Latin America as a whole forgoes $1.5 billion in water revenues each year.[71] As noted, developing countries could readily avoid two-thirds of their water losses.

Three Case Studies

Let us now look at three illustrative instances: a large developing country, a small developed country, and one of the biggest water users in the world—the United States. All three are exceptionally dependent on irrigation water for several sectors of their economies.

India

Some 93 percent of India's water use is for agriculture, mostly irrigation. Revenues from irrigation farmers cover only 7.5 percent of the cost of operating and maintaining irrigation systems, while subsidies cost Indian taxpayers $735 million in 1991.[72] Yet there is not enough public money even to repair and desilt irrigation canals, so the whole canal network is deteriorating. The system encourages farmers to misuse and overuse irrigation water, and years of excessive soaking of irrigated farmlands have led to much waterlogging and salinization, as detailed earlier.

There are further subsidies at work in India, this time indirect ones. State electricity boards supply electricity for irrigation pumps at a 1992 cost to the states of around $1.5 billion a year, yet farmers pay only one-eighth of the cost (in three southern states, the power is given for free).[73] Ironically, farmers in the Punjab, the country's number one breadbasket, could cut back on irrigation water use by 15 percent without reducing crop yields simply by eliminating overwatering.[74] Since water charges are typically 2–5 percent of the harvest's value, they have very little impact on the farmers' financial planning.

The two figures, $735 million and $1.5 billion, add up to $2.2 billion. They date from 1992 and 1991, and at the time of the lead author's latest visits to India, in early 1996 and early 1998, there was no sign of the subsidies being reduced—rather the opposite. Allowing for expansion of the subsidies (and not counting other subsidies, notably the many indirect and otherwise concealed items), we can suppose that a realistic minimum estimate for India's irrigation subsidies in 1996 was $2.5 billion. This is the same as was alternatively estimated for 1992.[75]

Israel

Israel is an instance of a country that tries to do things properly, or at least better. It has come a long way, but it has quite a way to go. Over the past thirty years, it has achieved a fivefold increase in the value of crops grown per unit of water, yet in a flooded or spray-irrigated field, at least half the water never reaches plants' roots but seeps underground or evaporates. This is to be contrasted with an Israel-innovated technique, drip irrigation, which utilizes long lengths of hose with pinholes that drip water close to plant roots; the technique cuts water losses by half.[76] As far back as the early 1980s, at least 5,000 square kilometers of Israel's irrigated lands were being watered by drip irrigation and other water-efficient techniques. True, this area was small compared with the total expanse under irrigation, but half of the remaining irrigated lands were being subjected to a moderately efficient technique known as micro-irrigation.[77] Today, over half of Israel's irrigated lands are served by drip irrigation. It is a measure of Israel's pioneering efforts that only 1 percent of irrigated lands worldwide feature any form of trickle or drip irrigation.[78]

In addition, Israel recycles 70 percent of its wastewater for use on farms, where wastewater accounts for 30 percent of all water supply (a figure planned to rise to 80 percent by the year 2025). As a measure of the significance of Israel's efforts, note that if all countries were to recycle 65 percent of their domestic and municipal wastewater, they could theoretically boost their agricultural output by 350 million tonnes of wheat, or almost 20 percent of all grain grown today.[79]

As a result of excessive pumping from water reserves over many years, however, Israel now faces an acute hydrologic deficit.[80] The source of the problem lies with water subsidies of numerous sorts, plus special interests' control over water-use decisions, faulty pricing assumptions, and rigid use patterns that penalize users of low-cost stocks of water. Water subsidies amount to $120 million annually, which means that they are the most expensive subsidy in the country apart from that for public transportation, but they reduce the price of agricultural water by only 17 percent after tax exemptions. On top of this, there is an indirect subsidy with respect to underpricing of the pumping and distribution services of the main water agency, Mekorot Water Company Ltd.[81]

In marked contrast, Saudi Arabia spent $40 billion during the 1980s on developing its farming, thanks largely to extravagant subsidies, mostly for water. The country also spent $10 billion on desalinization plants that provide just 15 percent of drinkable water for its citizens, the rest coming from groundwater. Because of poor irrigation techniques, more than two-thirds of water pumped to the surface to irrigate fields of wheat, alfalfa, and date palms never reached plants' roots but was lost to evaporation.[82] Yet the country contrived to increase its wheat output from virtually nil in 1980 to more than 4 million tonnes in 1992, even producing an exportable surplus thanks to huge subsidies that reduced the price from a level ten times that of American wheat.[83] Following the recent decline in oil prices, however, the Saudi government slashed its agricultural subsidies, and grain output dropped by 60 percent.[84]

United States

Irrigated lands in the United States account for one-ninth of the country's croplands, one-third of the value of its agricultural output, and two-fifths of the country's water withdrawals.[85] They also feature some of the largest irrigation subsidies in the world. Since the cost recovery from Bureau of Reclamation irrigation projects in the early 1980s averaged only about 17 percent of total costs, the implied subsidy to farmers using Bureau water was about $1 billion per year.[86] The total is estimated to have risen to $2.5 billion per year.[87]

Remarkably enough, it is impossible to estimate the total value of all U.S. water subsidies because government agencies (others are involved besides the Bureau of Reclamation) do not maintain records that would permit such calculations. There is general agreement, however, that irrigation subsidies in the western United States alone amount to $4.4 billion per year.[88] Well over half of all federally irrigated lands are in the West (with three-fifths of that total in California). In this dry region, irrigation accounts for 86 percent of water use.[89] Ironically, irrigation is used primarily to grow crops that are officially in surplus and subject to other expensive federal programs to reduce production.[90]

To gain a clearer picture of subsidies at work, consider California and its Central Valley Project. So extravagant are subsidies here that one hectare of agricultural land can sometimes use roughly as much water as one hectare of houses and offices (albeit most farmers get their water from groundwater wells rather from subsidized sources). Although agriculture accounts for only 3 percent of the state's economic production, it consumes 85 percent of the water. Were urban users to cut their water consumption by one-third (swimming pools and all), that would do no more than farmers' cutting their consumption by a mere 10 percent. Grand-scale irrigation enables California to grow 8 percent of U.S. agricultural output (and half of the country's fruits and vegetables) on less than 1 percent of U.S. farmland. Each California farmer feeds 130 people, of whom nearly 100 are Americans and the rest are foreigners. But without virtually unlimited supplies of artificially cheap irrigation water, most farmers could not continue with their traditional cropping patterns (though there is plenty of scope for them to shift to less water-demanding crops and to use scarce water more productively).[91]

The water subsidies derive from fifty-year contracts for cheap water signed early in the twentieth century, many of them still in operation even though they have long exceeded their "shelf life." By the mid-1980s, farmers had repaid only 4 percent of the original capital cost of almost $1 billion, with U.S. taxpayers footing the rest of the bill. The subsidies ensure that many farmers now pay around $25 per hectare-foot for water that costs ten times as much to pump it to them, by contrast with $575 for the same hectare-foot in San Francisco and more than $750 in Los Angeles. On top of that, California farmers collect direct subsidies of $400 million to grow such thirsty crops as rice, cotton, and alfalfa.[92] This curious circumstance is by no means confined to California; in neighboring Arizona, farmers pay only one-twenty-fifth as much for their water as do residents of Phoenix.[93]

Fortunately, there is vast scope for water savings in California, and not just in agriculture. They are urgently needed. Demand already exceeds supply, and a business-as-usual scenario projects that the gap will steadily increase until at least the year 2020. But through water-use efficiency and conservation, fostered by water markets, as discussed later in the chapter, supply could easily exceed demand by 2020. Thanks to existing technologies, industrial water-use efficiency could increase by 20 percent over today's level within twenty-five years; residential water use could decline by 46 percent; and use of reclaimed water could expand fivefold.[94] There is potential for similar grand-scale savings throughout the United States. Were subsidies to be phased out and Americans required to pay the full social cost of their water, they would be more inclined to install efficient technologies. Use of improved showerheads alone would effectively save water equivalent to the output of ten large dams, while the resulting electricity savings would equal the output of three Chernobyl-sized power plants (they would also reduce CO_2 emissions by 20 million tonnes a year).[95] The cost of water from a plumbing-retrofit program is only half the average cost through conventional suppliers.

So attractive are water savings that in the state of Washington, the Seattle Water Department is relying on improvements in water-use efficiency as the sole source of additional water for its expanding population during the 1990s. It will actually give away water-efficient showerheads. It will also audit home water use, promote the installation of water-efficient toilets, and implement many other similar water-saving programs. By 2002, this is expected to supply over 30 million liters of water per day at an estimated cost of almost $16 million, whereas water from conventional supplies, notably that obtained by diverting a river, would cost almost three times as much per liter.[96]

Subsidies Worldwide

What is the scale of water subsidies worldwide? To reiterate a key point: governments do not usually keep systematic records of all their financial supports for any of the three main categories of water use. So the true total remains a black hole. For the purposes of this chapter, however, it is pertinent to attempt a best-judgment estimate of the scale of these government outlays.

We have just noted the annual $4.4 billion spent on irrigation in the western United States. Let us suppose that other irrigation subsidies in the United States bring the total up to $5 billion (though it could be much more). In Australia, the government has supplied a financial subsidy to irrigated agriculture in order to cover a deficit in operation and maintenance of water-supply systems, totaling Austral$3.3 billion, or approaching U.S.$2 billion, per year. Let us suppose too that several other developed countries such as Japan, Russia, and Ukraine (leaving out other former Soviet Union republics in Asia) practice irrigation subsidies of similar scale, making another $6 billion. That makes a developed-world total of $13 billion (probably much more) per year. This is rather a "heroic extrapolation," but it is cautious and conservative. Then there are subsidies not related to irrigation. In Canada, for instance, the additional annual costs of operation, maintenance, and improvement of the municipal water (and wastewater) system are estimated at $4.5 billion for the period 1993–2003, or an average of $0.45 billion per year.[97] So the total of $13 billion is certainly well below the true figure for all developed-country subsidies of all types. These could readily be twice as large, but there is no way to establish that with any accuracy.

In developing countries, the cost recovery of providing water for household use averages around 35 percent. The fiscal burden of this underpricing can be conservatively calculated at $13 billion for 1993[98] (and rather more today, if only because of the booming growth of cities and other urban communities). Then there are savings to be made from eliminating illegal connections, worth perhaps $5 billion in 1993, and savings available through increased efficiency, worth $4 billion. This makes a total of $22 billion.[99] By today, the total could well have risen to $25 billion per year, and this figure is used for present purposes.

More important than subsidies for household water use in developing countries are subsidies for irrigation, particularly in Asia. Ten years ago, the general cost recovery was no more than 20 percent at best, often only half as much.[100] There is scant reason to suppose it is better today except in a few countries and abundant evidence to suggest it is worse in most countries. Given total costs in 1985 of $25 billion, and using the conservative recovery figure of 20 percent, effective irrigation subsidies in 1985 could be put at $20 billion.[101] Fifteen years later, they are likely to have risen to at least $29 billion if only because there are an extra 1 billion people in developing countries, over 60 percent of them in the humid zones of Asia, where most rice is grown. That this figure of $29 billion is conservative, perhaps extremely so, is demonstrated by seven-year-old estimates of annual subsidies of $0.5 billion in Pakistan, $1.5 billion in India, and $5 billion in Egypt,[102] while China in 1997, with its 25 percent cost recovery rate, is estimated to have had effective subsidies of $13 billion.[103]

There are similar subsidies in non-Asian developing countries where irrigation is widespread. In Mexico, for instance, annual subsidies for operation and maintenance of irrigation systems (i.e., not including capital costs) have been estimated to be 0.5 percent of GDP, or almost $4 billion,[104] although recent reforms will have reduced this somewhat (see the discussion later in the chapter). Again, such subsidies must exist in many other large developing countries, but no data are available.

Thus, subsidies in developing countries are here estimated to be at least $54 billion ($25 billion for households and $29 billion for irrigation), and those in developed countries are estimated to be at least $13 billion, for an overall total of $67 billion per year. (The figure of $54 billion per year for developing countries is to be compared with a World Bank estimate for minimum water investments in these countries over the next decade, an average of $60 billion per year.[105]) The true subsidies total could readily be twice as big, conceivably several times bigger were we to consider all forms of water use. (No account is taken here, for example, of subsidies for industry, the sector that often uses the most water in developed countries and surely receives implicit subsidies, if only through its disposal of untreated wastewater, worth tens of billions of dollars worldwide.) Given the harm that these subsidies impose on economies and environments alike, at least three-quarters of them, or $50 billion worth, are considered to be perverse. True, this is a very preliminary and approximate estimate, even an exploratory guesstimate, though it reflects a strong consensus of opinion among water experts consulted in Europe, North America, Israel, India, China, and Australia. It is advanced solely with the aim of getting a handle, however rough and ready, on the scale of a matter of paramount importance to developed and developing countries alike.

In addition to these formal or conventional subsidies are the implicit subsidies of environmental and other externalities. Notable instances are water pollution and water deficits, both of which relate strongly to disease in developing countries. We have already noted the cost of workdays lost to water-related diseases, $125 billion per year.[106] In 1991, a cholera outbreak in Peru cost the country at least $1 billion, while a 1994 plague in India deprived airlines and hotels of $2–$5 billion.

A further way to shadow price the cost of water shortages is to estimate the numbers of people—at least 550 million[107]—who trek long distances each day to fetch clean water for their homes. Suppose the average time spent at this task is two hours (some estimates propose three hours), and suppose too that the "time opportunity cost," that is, the cost of time that could more usefully be spent on tilling crop fields, is $0.10 per hour. Result: an externality cost of $40 billion a year.

There are still other environmental externalities arising from water shortages. As we have already seen, the value of leading water benefits worldwide—from watersheds, aquifers, and reservoirs and from water for agricultural irrigation, industrial processes, and waterway transportation—can be roughly reckoned to be $2.8 trillion per year.[108] A parallel reckoning[109] postulates that these and

Table 6.4. Water Subsidies Worldwide

Region	Direct Subsidies ($ billion)	Externalities ($ billion)	Total Subsidies	Perverse Subsidies
Developed countries	13		13	10
Developing countries	54	165	219	205
WORLDWIDE		15	15	15
TOTAL	67[a]	180[b]	247	230

[a]Total is 75 percent perverse.
[b]Total is 100 percent perverse.

other water benefits—including pollution mitigation, sport fishing, and waterfowl habitat—are worth at least $779 billion per year. If the overall benefits were reduced through water waste, pollution, and so forth by only 1 percent per year, the annual economic loss would be between $28 billion and $7.8 billion. A median figure would be almost $18 billion. Some of this loss has already been accounted for in the foregoing disease calculation. Let us accept an exploratory though conservative estimate of $15 billion.

These three implicit subsidies alone total $180 billion per year, or nearly three times more than the formal and conventional subsidies. As argued in Chapter 1, these implicit subsidies are to be counted as 100 percent perverse. So the combined total for perverse subsidies in the water sector amounts to $50 billion plus $180 billion, or $230 billion, per year (Table 6.4).

Scope for Policy Reform

The main priority is to reduce and eventually phase out water subsidies. This chapter has demonstrated that there is plenty of scope to do this, especially in agriculture. Australia has implemented increases in water prices, working toward full cost recovery, and similar measures are envisaged in France, Italy, and Canada.[110] California landowners can buy water for only one-tenth as much as it costs the federal government to deliver it—and this water can be worth six times as much on the open market.[111] Nor need farmers fear the gradual elimination of subsidies. For most agricultural commodities, water is such a small component of overall costs that steadily climbing water prices would have negligible effects on crop prices. Far from undermining farming, the disappearance of subsidies would foster more sustainable agricultural practices in the long term. In fact, by growing less thirsty crops and making more careful use of water, farmers could increase their revenues by 12 percent while using 12 percent less water.[112]

There is lots of scope too in the urban and industrial sectors. An increase in the water tariff in Bogor, Indonesia, from $0.15 to $0.42 per cubic meter has resulted in a 30 percent decline in household demand for water.[113] In the industrial sector, increased water prices led to investment in water recycling and conservation technology. In Goa, India, increased water tariffs have induced a 50 percent reduction in water use by a fertilizer factory over a five-year period. In São Paulo, Brazil, three industrial concerns have reduced water consumption by 40–60 percent in response to effluent charges.[114] For a detailed account of what is being achieved in South Africa, see Box 6.1.

Water conservation in households can also be accomplished through efficiency measures. U.S. cities large and small are investing in water-efficient showerheads and faucets, reduced-flush toilets, and the latest washing machines, which together reduce water use by 20–30 percent, sometimes more. As an indication of what has already been achieved, water use in the United States dropped by 9 percent during the period 1980–1995, the first decline in decades, even though the population grew by 16 percent (one community in San Diego reduced its water use between 1987 and 1997 by a whopping 90 percent).[115] Efforts such as these could markedly slash the costs of future infrastructure projects for water, which otherwise will need as much as $200 billion during the next two decades. Reduction of water demand through efficiency and conservation costs $0.02–$0.45 per cubic meter, while treatment and reuse of wastewater for irrigation costs $0.36–$0.60. By contrast, desalinization of brackish water costs $0.43–$0.68, and desalinization of seawater, $0.98–$1.48. Development of marginal water sources comes in at $0.52–$0.83—a high cost partly because there are few good dam sites left.[116]

Much the same applies in other developed countries. In Denmark, a water tax, which currently accounts for only 20 percent of the average price of household water, will double the price over five years. This measure should reduce household water consumption by 25 percent.

In developing countries, removal of water subsidies would reduce water use overall by 20–30 percent; in parts of Asia, by as much as 50 percent. That would make it possible—without large, environmentally destructive water development projects—to supply safe drinking water to most of the people now lacking it.[117]

Box 6.1. SOUTH AFRICA: A SUCCESS STORY IN THE MAKING?

South Africa is a thirsty country. Two-thirds of the country receives less than 500 millimeters of rainfall per year, regarded as the minimum for sustainable dryland farming, and evaporation is often greater than precipitation. Only 13 percent of the country is suitable for cultivation. Due to water shortages, the industrial sector sometimes endures months of water restrictions. Two-fifths of all citizens lack access to drinkable water, and one-half do not enjoy water sanitation. At the same time, the population is growing at 1.6 percent per year; its current total of 43 million is projected to surge to 47 million as early as the year 2010. Regrettably, there is little incentive for consumers to use water sparingly, given the multitudes of subsidies pushing them in the opposite direction. South African farmers pay some of the cheapest water prices in the world.

Much depends, however, on how many people want how much water. An affluent citizen consumes at least 1,750 liters of water per day for household purposes alone, whereas a shantytown dweller makes do with only 15 liters, not much more than a single flush of the rich citizen's toilet. In metropolitan Cape Town and the rest of the Western Cape region, there are 400,000 households, plus schools and the like. If they were all to switch to low-flow showerheads and dual-flush toilets, they would save more water than is to be delivered by a huge new dam and would do it with one-quarter of the capital investment and none of the operational costs. The dam is being built primarily to satisfy the "needs" of affluent Cape Towners, who make up 5 percent of the populace.

Fortunately, South Africa's new minister of water affairs and forestry is embarking on a program to (1) phase out the many subsidies that encourage abuse of water and (2) charge consumers the "full economic costs" of water, that is, the cost of replacing each liter consumed. He is also encouraging water marketing and mandating that water suppliers adopt conservation measures such as recycling.

It is sometimes objected that to reduce water subsidies for household use in developing countries would penalize the poor. There is much evidence, however, that these people are willing to pay high costs for dependable water supplies. In many cities, street vendors sell water at prices four to twenty times higher than those of public utilities.[118]

A further policy initiative lies with water rights and water markets.[119] As we have seen with respect to areas as disparate as California, the central United States, India, China, and central Asia, when farmers have motivation to view water as "cheaper than dirt," they treat it as such. They also face the choice of "use it or lose it," meaning that if they behave with public spirit and reduce their consumption through conservation measures, the water merely becomes available to other users. If, by contrast, the farmers could sell their water to higher-value users, the opportunity cost of using the water would immediately rise and the farmers would have an incentive to conserve it. But they will not be willing to consider this positive prospect unless they are accorded some form of ownership of their water. Hence the vital issue of water rights.[120]

Fortunately, these rights are now being made available in many areas, and in turn this opens up the scope for a highly promising phenomenon: water markets. As soon as water rights become tradable, they achieve several things: they empower water users, provide investment motivation, improve water-use efficiency, increase flexibility in resource allocation, and reduce incentives to degrade the environment.[121]

Water markets state in effect that water is an economic good and should be treated as such—whereupon there are many opportunities for imaginative husbandry of the resource.[122] The gap between the value of a liter of water to a farmer and its value to a thirsty industrialist or city dweller is so large, and agriculture's use of water is so extensive, that there is abundant opportunity for trading deals.[123] After all, 1,000 tonnes of water can be used in California agriculture to produce 1 tonne of wheat worth $200—or it can be used to expand industrial output by $14,000.[124] Similarly, 1 cubic meter of water used in China's industries generates more jobs and seventy times more economic value than the same quantity used in agriculture.[125]

Since the late 1970s, a vigorous water market has sprung up in the western United States, allowing urban authorities to buy up farmers' water rights and thus provide extra water for city communities. Los Angeles, for instance, has made a deal with Imperial Valley farmers: by paying for improvements to reduce wastage from irrigation channels, the city has acquired more water at less than half the cost of the cheapest alternative, while farmers have received cash and suffered no reduction in their irrigation supply.[126] Annual savings of more than $200 million could be achieved in California through regional reallocation of water from agriculture to urban areas.[127]

This all epitomizes the saying "Water flows uphill to money." Similar water markets are emerging not only in other parts of the United States but also in Australia, New Zealand, Algeria, Morocco, Tunisia, Brazil, Peru, Mexico, Chile, China, India, and Pakistan.[128] In Chile, for instance, water companies supplying urban communities, with their fast-growing populations, can now buy water from farmers who have surpluses, thanks to their efforts to improve efficiency.[129] The Mexican government has turned over 30,000 square kilometers of irrigated land to water user associations, and water fees have soared (by 50–180 percent in several districts), thus reportedly lifting the rate of irrigation financial self-sufficiency from 37 to 80 percent.[130] As for Asia, assume that water demand falls in proportion to a rise in its price; then a 10 percent increase in the price of irrigation would double the amount of water available to industrial and residential users while still leaving Asian agriculture with the largest share of water withdrawals in the world.

As a measure of how far water markets can stimulate conservation, note that farmers in northwestern Texas, trying to cope with falling water tables caused by depletion of the Ogallala Aquifer (which waters one-fifth of irrigated land in the United States), have reduced their water use by 20–25 percent by adopting more efficient sprinkler technologies, surge valves to even out distribution, and gravity systems, among other water-saving practices. Farmers in various countries who have switched from furrow or sprinkler irrigation to drip systems, which deliver water directly to the roots of crops, have cut their water use by 30–70 percent while increasing their crop yields by 20–90 percent, often leading to a doubling of water productivity.[131] By the mid-1990s, 13 percent of California farmland was irrigated with drip systems, up from 5 percent in the mid-1980s.[132]

That irrigation subsidies can be removed with benefit to the economy and environment alike is demonstrated by the experience of several republics of the former Soviet Union, where these subsidies have largely been ended, leading to a marked shrinkage of irrigated areas. During just the period 1990–1993, Russia phased out more than 7,000 square kilometers of irrigated cropland, or 13 percent of its former expanse. This contraction is expected to continue for perhaps another decade or however long it takes for governments in the region to recover their fiscal health.[133] The governments of Vietnam and Indonesia, both heavy water users, have recently legislated to recover all costs of water supplies.[134]

Let us conclude this chapter with a remarkable success story made possible through innovative policy measures, albeit with respect to water for city use rather than irrigation agriculture. In the mid-1990s, New York City found its water demand rising so much that it faced the prospect of having to build a new filtration plant. The plant would have been the largest in the world, with a capital cost of $6–$8 billion and operating costs of another $3 billion over ten years. Fortunately, there was an alternative. The city could rehabilitate a watershed in the Catskill Mountains, where water purification has traditionally been carried out by the vegetation's root systems and soil microorganisms; these filtration functions have been sufficient to cleanse the water to the standards of the Environmental Protection Agency (EPA). In recent years, however, soil pollutants in the form of local sewage, fertilizer, and pesticides have reduced the efficacy of the process below EPA standards. So the city was faced with a choice: build an expensive new filtration plant or restore the watershed ecosystems. In other words, invest in either physical capital or natural capital.[135]

Investment in natural capital meant buying 5,200 hectares of land (fifteen times the area of Central Park) in and around the watershed so that land use could be restricted—for instance, no more farming methods that cause pollution. The investment would also entail subsidizing the construction of better sewage treatment plants for the homes of watershed residents. The total cost would be $1–$1.5 billion, between one-sixth and one-eleventh of the alternative. This would give an internal rate of return of 90–170 percent and a payback period of four to seven years—a return an order of magnitude higher than is normally available, particularly on relatively risk-free investments. Moreover, these calculations were conservative because they considered only one service of the watershed, namely, water purification, even though watersheds generally provide other important services such as flood control, biodiversity habitat, and recreational opportunities. In 1996, the city floated an environmental bond issue, using the proceeds to restore the functioning of watershed ecosystems and to undertake better sewage treatment for watershed residents. The cost of the bond issue is to be met by savings produced, that is, the avoidance of a capital investment of $6–$8 billion plus an annual $300 million in operating costs.[136]

The EPA estimates that over the next twenty years, ensuring safe and adequate drinking water throughout the United States will require infrastructure investments of $138 billion (the equivalent figure worldwide will be in the trillions of dollars). Watershed conservation could cut these investments substantially, while securitization or privatization could ensure that much of the balance remaining is provided by the private sector.[137]

Chapter 7

FISHERIES

One of the world's greatest fisheries lies off Newfoundland and New England. Known as the Grand Banks and Georges Bank, it has been fished for over 400 years. First came the Newfoundlanders and local Americans; then came the British, French, and Norwegians, together with fisherfolk from other maritime provinces of Canada. In 1954, there arrived on the scene a $3 million British "factory trawler" that could process and freeze fish onboard at the rate of 600 tonnes per day. It was followed by Russian and French factory trawlers and then by still bigger Spanish ships.

That was the beginning of the end for cod and other once bountiful species. A single netting could capture 50–60 tonnes of fish. During the period 1961–1972, Spanish ships alone hauled up more than 200,000 tonnes of fish a year. The biggest catch of all was in 1968, when all the fishing countries brought in 810,000 tonnes. But during the period 1970–1990, the catch fell by almost one-third. As the catch dropped year by year, the governments concerned, especially the Canadian and U.S. governments, supported their suffering fishing communities with ever greater subsidies—which merely served to foster still more overfishing. At the same time, many fleets compounded the irrationality by heavily exceeding their quotas. By the early 1990s, the northern cod stock had dropped from 400,000 tonnes to 2,700 tonnes.[1] In 1992, the fishing grounds had to be closed, at a cost of 42,000 jobs and $8.1 billion in unemployment payments plus widespread bankruptcies for fishing businesses.[2]

As fisheries expert Carl Safina has pointed out,[3] there is no longer as much truth as there used to be in the proverb "Give someone a fish and you feed them for a day; give them a net and you feed them for a lifetime." Marine fisheries are fading in many regions, primarily because of massive government subsidies that foster overfishing.

Marine Fisheries in Decline

These fisheries produced a worldwide catch averaging around 85 million tonnes during the 1990s. After four decades of steadily expanding catches, they appear to have exceeded their sustainable output in many instances despite—or, rather, because of—fishing fleets bigger than ever and fishing technology more sophisticated than ever. Worse, there have been marked declines in populations of cod, haddock, plaice, and other fishes that make up the bulk of the catch and are preferred for human consumption.[4]

The declines are regrettable not only from the conventional economic and environmental standpoints. Some 20 million fishermen, mostly small-scale operators, fish for a living, and ultimately as many as 200 million people depend directly on ocean fisheries for their livelihoods.[5] Of the 1993 catch of 84 million tonnes, 55 percent was taken by just eight countries: China, 12 percent; Peru, 9.7 percent; Japan, 9.6 percent; Chile, 7.2 percent; United States, 7.1 percent; Russia, 5.3 percent; Spain, 2.1 percent; and Canada, 1.8 percent.[6]

Still more to the point, marine fishing supplies 16 percent of all animal protein consumed.[7] Fish is the prime source of animal protein for 1 billion people in developing countries, where it supplies 86 percent as much animal protein as do the four terrestrial livestock groups combined, namely, cattle, sheep, pigs, and poultry.[8]

Since 1950, the world's marine fish catch has increased almost fourfold.[9] But as noted, the steady forty years' growth appears to have peaked a full decade ago (Figure 7.1). Worse, if the catch were measured by value instead of by weight, the decline would be even more marked: as the most valuable stocks are fished out, fishermen have to hunt other, less valuable species. Most fisheries are fully exploited if not heavily overexploited, and many are depleted to var-

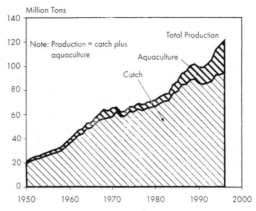

Figure 7.1. World Fish Production, 1950–1996. Source: A. P. McGinn, *Rocking the Boat: Conserving Fisheries and Protecting Jobs* (Washington, D.C.: Worldwatch Institute, 1998).

ious degrees. Indeed, nine of seventeen major fishing grounds are in precipitous decline, and four are commercially "fished out."[10]

For illustration, the stocks of cod and haddock in Europe's North Sea fell by 83 percent during 1971–1990; the stock of mackerel crashed fiftyfold during 1960–1991; and the herring fishery, closed altogether in 1977–1982, has not recovered to anywhere near its former levels. Catches in the Gulf of Thailand have been maintained only because an expanding trawler fleet has been fishing the stocks ever more intensively, a situation that cannot persist indefinitely.[11]

> *Nine of seventeen major fishing grounds are in precipitous decline, and four are commercially "fished out."*

Worse, a depleted fishery may not recover regardless of how long it is relieved of exploitation pressure. Other species may fill the ecological niche left open and keep the recovering stock from resuming its place in the ecosystem. There is much evidence to support this, as witnessed by the North Sea haddock population, which was wiped out in the 1950s and has never recovered, as well as similar ecosystem shifts in the Baltic Sea, the northeastern Arctic Ocean, the Gulf of Thailand, and the Grand Banks.[12]

Because of the unpredictable variations in and unknown status of many fishery stocks, many experts now believe that even with optimum management, the ultimate maximum sustainable yield probably could not exceed 100 million tonnes per year and the annual catch should be limited to about 80 million tonnes.[13] As a result of the failure of stagnating supply to match fast-rising demand, the worldwide per capita consumption of seafood, which rose from nine kilograms in 1950 to nineteen kilograms in 1989, had declined by 12 percent by 1998. As a further result, international prices for seafood have been rising by an average of 4 percent per year in real terms over the past decade. Whereas export prices for pork in late 1991 were 55 percent above the 1975 price and those for beef 75 percent above, those for marine fish were 235 percent higher. Demand for fish in 2010 is projected to be at least 45 percent higher than in 1990, meaning that prices can be expected to climb even higher still.[14]

There is a further problem, significant in some areas while not comparable to the decline of fisheries overall. Modern industrial fishing can lead to disruption and degradation of marine habitats through, for example, dredging, trawling, long-hauling, and use of explosives, all of which deplete structural formations on otherwise relatively featureless seafloors. There can also be widespread destruction of tropical coral reefs, temperate oyster and polychaete reefs, and seagrass beds.[15]

Reasons for Decline

The fundamental issue here is the "tragedy of the commons," as well as the related problem of obstacles to collective action. These generic problems probably have no more graphic, widespread, or intractable manifestation than in marine fisheries.[16]

For much of fishing's history, there have been enough fish in the world's oceans and there have been few enough fishing enterprises that each country could take its catch without depleting the stocks. The built-in inducement for a country to take more than its share has proven too potent, however, given that the benefit has accrued exclusively to the overfishing country while the cost has been borne by all fishing countries. Once an individual country has begun overfishing, others have followed suit. The upshot is today's deeply depleted stocks. In addition to the problem of a common property resource vulnerable to "open access," or free-for-all exploitation, there is a problem with the market rate of discount, which has generally been high enough to further encourage fishermen to view the fisheries within a foreshortened time horizon and to overexploit the resource.[17]

Subsidies Worldwide

One might suppose that the fisheries decline would send a clear message to governments that their fleets should reduce their excessive fishing. On the contrary, however, governments have preferred to put off the day of reckoning by stepping up their subsidies to the fishing industry. When fishermen's livelihoods are in danger, governments provide plentiful incentives for them to catch more rather than fewer fish—thus exacerbating the problem from top to bottom.[18] The solution lies with a severe reduction in subsidies and an eventual phasing out of them, paralleled by a collective decision to protect remaining fish stocks through collective action, suitably enforced. If only.

Instead, governments have been inclined to engage in ever heavier subsidies—which have served only to prolong the agony. Subsidies have proliferated in both type and quantity. They have included financial contributions from governments in the form of transfers of funds (grants, loans, equity infusions), potential transfers of funds (loan guarantees), forgone government revenues (tax incentives and preferences), discounted or free marine insurance, fuel-tax credits, research and development supports, payments to foreign countries for access to their fisheries, and financial transfers to a funding mechanism or to a private body to perform any of the above. On top of these financial contributions have been price- and income-support programs (other than tariffs), social benefits, export promotion programs, port facilities, and housing or other community infrastructure for fishermen.[19]

These state supports have primarily helped to pay for more and larger boats. The global fishing fleet expanded from 585,000 registered vessels in 1970 to 3.5 million in 1998, worth $320 billion. The largest factory trawlers are twenty-five meters long and weigh over 100 tonnes. Industrial ships make up only 1 in every 100 vessels, yet these giants constitute well over half of the total fishing capacity. There is a need to cut the global fishing capacity by at least 25 percent forthwith and another 22 percent later on.[20]

Other subsidies have helped supply longer and larger nets. A typical trawl net is one kilometer long and big enough to hold twelve jumbo jets. Some of these nets scoop up 400 tonnes of fish at a single go, or 80–90 percent of a fish population in a year.[21] Other advanced equipment includes radar and remote-sensing devices. Given the sophisticated technology of the 1990s fishing industry, only half of the world's fishing fleet would have been needed to catch the maximum sustainable yield of fish.

According to calculations by the Food and Agriculture Organization of the United Nations,[22] the 1989 catch was worth around $70 billion at dockside. Yet the fishing effort to land the catch—boats with their crews, equipment, and so forth—cost $124 billion. The difference, $54 billion, was almost entirely made up of government subsidies, including price controls, fuel-tax exemptions, low-interest loans, and outright grants for gear and other infrastructure.[23] This has meant that every $1 earned from fishing has carried a cost of $1.77.[24]

Such, at least, was the understanding of fishery subsidies during much of the early 1990s. But critics have been pointing out that the 1993 assessment did not define or analyze the subsidies themselves; rather, it merely inferred them from revenues and costs in 1989. A recent assessment includes a more detailed and comprehensive review.[25] It shows that while subsidies conform for the most part to the categories listed, the total is more likely to be $14–$20 billion per year, equivalent to at least one-fifth of global revenues from fisheries. Half of the subsidies are dispensed by OECD countries.

Note that this estimate is highly conservative. For instance, it takes only incomplete account of environmental externalities. It excludes subsidies for reducing overcapacity and excess fishing effort. It acknowledges that not all countries are included in the reckoning. It does not include those many subsidies underwritten by authorities at less than national government level, such as provincial and state governments. Most important of all, it accepts that certain leading countries, such as Japan, Russia, and China, are severely underreporting their subsidies;[26] in the case of several countries in 1996, less than one fishery subsidy dollar in ten was reported, conceivably as little as one in twenty.[27] As acknowledged by analyst Matteo Milazzo, the estimate "probably errs on the low side, perhaps by a considerable margin."[28] A more realistic estimate is $20–$30 billion (25–38 percent of revenues of $80 billion).[29] For the purposes of this chapter, then, let us accept a midpoint of $20–$30 billion, $25 billion per year.

Subsidies arise from the efforts of governments to preserve their fishermen's jobs. Regrettably, these incentives have long induced investors to finance more industrial fishing ships than the fish stocks could possibly sustain. During 1970–1989, the world's fishing fleet grew at twice the rate of the global catch, until it amounted to twice the capitalized capacity needed to catch what the oceans could sustainably produce, after allowing for rebuilding of fish stocks (Figure 7.2).[30]

Because this excessive capacity has rapidly depleted the amount of fish available, profitability has generally plunged, reducing the ships' value. Unable to sell their chief assets without major financial loss, shipowners have found themselves forced to keep on fishing—or, rather, overfishing—in order to repay their loans. They are caught in

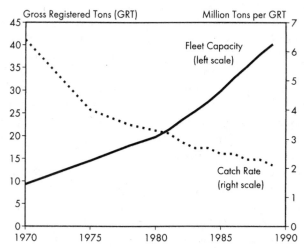

Figure 7.2. World Fleet Capacity and Catch Rate, 1970–1989. Source: A. P. McGinn, *Rocking the Boat: Conserving Fisheries and Protecting Jobs* (Washington, D.C.: Worldwatch Institute, 1998).

an economic trap. In response, they have mobilized political pressure on governments to refrain from cutting the inflated fishing quotas.[31]

The costs to fisheries are substantial. If, in the case of the United States, the principal fish species in question were allowed to rebuild to their long-term potential, sustainable harvesting would add $8 billion to GDP and provide some 300,000 jobs.[32] Within U.S. federal waters, today's catch is only 60 percent as valuable as it could be if fish stocks were allowed to recover.[33]

In addition, subsidies encourage gross wastage. Fishermen make enough profit on their subsidized operations, albeit at the cost of progressively depleted fisheries, that they throw away many fish that could be marketed but do not command best prices. (For details on this bycatch, see Box 7.1.) Because the most favored species have often been exploited to commercial extinction, many fishermen are now content to catch "trash" fish for sale, with several such species now fetching $3 or more per kilogram. But again, trash fishing means that the structure of marine food webs, that is, the proportion of organisms at each trophic level, is shifting. To cite a leading analyst, Elliott Norse, "We've eliminated the marine equivalent of lions and bears,

> Within U.S. federal waters, today's catch is only 60 percent as valuable as it could be if fish stocks were allowed to recover.

Box 7.1. FISHERIES BYCATCH

Every fourth creature taken from the sea is unwanted. Worldwide, these discards total at least 27 million tonnes per year, equivalent to one-third or even one-half of fish landings. Discards, or bycatch, could be as much as half of the entire catch by weight, but nobody really knows because they do not have to be recorded and it is in the fishermen's interests to keep quiet about them. In fact, if we were to include all sea urchins, sponges, and other marine life hauled up with commercial fish and then discarded, the amount would readily be several times greater.* Discards of king crab in the Bering Sea in 1990 amounted to 16 million individuals, more than five times the number landed and weighing 340,000 tonnes. Off the northern coast of Norway in the 1986–1987 season, as many as 80 million cod, weighing almost 100,000 tonnes, were discarded because they were too small. In Europe's North Sea, about half of the haddock and whiting caught for human consumption each year is discarded, usually because the fish are too small or of inferior quality.† In some U.S. shrimp fisheries, 10 tonnes or even 15 tonnes of fish are dumped for every 1 tonne of shrimp landed, making up 175,000 tonnes per year; in the Gulf of Mexico during the past twenty years, this bycatch has contributed to an 85 percent decline in populations of seafloor species such as snapper and grouper.‡ Most of the bycatch is thrown back either dead or in such a weakened state that it forms easy prey for predators.

* A. P. McGinn, *Rocking the Boat: Conserving Fisheries and Protecting Jobs* and *Scaling Back to Promote Sustainable Fisheries* (Washington, D.C.: Worldwatch Institute, 1998).
† E. Bonino, "Fishing for Ever," *Our Planet* 8, no. 4 (1996): 13–15.
‡ C. Safina, "Where Have All the Fishes Gone?" *Issues in Science and Technology* 10, no. 3 (1994): 37–43.

---

and we are moving towards taking rats, cockroaches and dandelions."[34] If current trends continue, fishermen could eventually find themselves obliged to catch jellyfish, krill, and even zooplankton.

As noted, total subsidies today are estimated to be $25 billion per year.[35] If one is cautious, one can view perverse subsidies primarily as those that enhance the capacity and effort of fishing fleets, making up some 80 percent of all subsidies, or almost $20 billion per year. But virtually all fishery subsidies can be considered perverse, for three reasons: (1) because subsidies are far and away the principal cause of overfishing; (2) because of the parlous and fast-deteriorating state of fisheries, a state that is worsened by subsidies; and (3) because of the adverse repercussions of fisheries decline for both the economies and the natural resources concerned. Indeed, a recent review by Milazzo concludes that "just as trade experts insist that . . . all subsidies are bad from a trade point of view, . . . practically all subsidies are bad from a conservation standpoint."[36] Thus, the figure for total subsidies, $25 billion per year, is accepted here as the figure for perverse subsidies.

Nevertheless, the subsidy figure, being 31 percent of revenues, means that ocean fish are hardly more supported than are certain other protein foods.[37]

Policy Responses

While the $25 billion figure is small compared with perverse subsidies for agriculture, fossil fuels and nuclear energy, and road transportation, the fisheries sector is nonetheless the most politically volatile of all sectors reviewed in this book. This is evident from the numerous fishing disputes during the past few years, notably the conflicts over tuna in the northeastern Atlantic Ocean, crab and salmon in the North Pacific Ocean, squid in the southwestern Atlantic, and pollock in the Sea of Okhotsk.[38]

Fortunately, there are signs of improvement in the situation, albeit far less than are required.[39] In the United States, depleted stocks on both coasts are prompting the U.S. Congress to consider allocating $421 million for programs such as boat buybacks and job training. The Canadian government is spending Can$2 billion over a five-year period on unemployment handouts for its fishery workers who were laid off as part of a government effort to restore depleted fish stocks. While a much more sustainable gesture would be to offer alternative employment to these workers, retraining them if need be, the measure does at least supply scope for the fisheries to recover and perhaps employ future fishermen.[40]

On a still larger scale, the European Union (EU) set aside $2.2 billion in 1996 to pay for job retraining and other economic aid for fishery workers. Following intense pressure from the fishing industry and politicians, however, EU ministers dragged their feet on fleet reductions and postponed the reforms.[41] Fortunately, the EU has slashed cod catches by two-thirds in the Irish Sea and by almost two-fifths in the North Sea, while haddock and whiting hauls are being reduced by 13 percent and 23 percent, respectively. Were the EU's fisheries to be allowed to rebuild, they could eventually yield a fur-

ther $2.5 billion worth of fish a year. At present, the EU spends
nearly $780 million a year on fishing subsidies, almost all of it to
support the bloated fishing fleets.[42] If governments feel politically
obliged to make payments to their fishermen, they would do far better by creating incentives, such as retraining for alternative employment, than by fostering ever greater capacity to chase ever fewer
fish.[43]

Governments could also go far to reduce fishing capacity while
increasing employment. The key is to redirect subsidies and convert
them from perverse to constructive by, for instance, phasing out the
more highly mechanized ships and using
the released funds for more productive
purposes.[44] Each $1 million of invest-
ment in industrial-style fishing provides
only 1–5 jobs, whereas the same investment in small-scale fishing could
employ anywhere from 60 to 3,000 people. The United States has been leading
the way in promoting management efficiency through catching inefficiency. In Chesapeake Bay, for instance, oyster-dredging boats are
now required by law to be powered by sail alone. Similarly, half of
the U.S. bluefin tuna fishery is now allocated to the least capable
gear, such as hand lines or rod and reel, whereupon almost 80 percent of jobs are supplied by ships with labor-intensive tackle, by contrast with 2 percent on the part of ships with large nets.[45]

> *Were the EU's fisheries to be allowed to rebuild, they could eventually yield a further $2.5 billion worth of fish a year.*

The United States's fisheries situation has been helped too by the
1996 amendments to the Magnuson-Stevens Fishery Conservation
and Management Act. The act is crucially limited, however, in that it
does not define and prohibit overfishing. Nor does it direct fishery
managers to take a series of other vital steps: to rebuild depleted
populations, to protect habitats for fishery resources, to reduce
wasteful and harmful bycatch of nontarget organisms, and to consider predator–prey and other important ecological relationships.[46]

There are still further policy initiatives and management options
available to governments. They are not directly related to subsidies,
but they would be helped if undertaken in conjunction with phase-
out of subsidies. Only 10 percent or so of the world's catch is found
in international waters, the rest being within 200 nautical miles of
some country's shoreline. Yet governments do not generally charge
fishermen for the right to catch off their shores. The few governments that impose such charges set the price far too low, typically at
no more than 5 percent of the catch's value. If governments were to

charge fishermen an appropriate price for access to their fisheries (and if they were also to manage their fisheries as communal rather than commons resources), the results would be formidable—some $3–$7 billion a year for access alone.[47] For instance, the Falkland Islands' fisheries are exploited mostly by foreign fleets. When the Islands introduced charges of up to 28 percent of the catch's value, the result was vigorous protest from foreign fishermen. But the increased fees yielded revenues enough to quadruple the Islands' GDP—and they supplied a stream of revenues that could be used to pay for still better management and policing of the fisheries.

A final policy response could lie with tradable fishing rights for individual fishermen, a system known as individual transferable quotas (ITQs). Again, this would be reinforced if accompanied by a reduction in subsidies and would be much less useful if perverse subsidies continued to pull in the opposite direction. ITQs can help both to curb overfishing and to boost fishermen's incomes. The strategy would allow individual fishermen to buy and sell rights to shares in a fishery's potential catch and thus would give them a financial stake in the fishery's health. Also, fishermen obliged to leave the industry would receive implicit compensation by being able to sell their rights to the fishermen remaining.[48]

An approach along these lines—controversial as it is in some quarters, and largely unproven as yet—could hold promise for matching fishing investment with fishery productivity and sustainable catches. A number of pilot programs have had some success, for example, a 30 percent drop in the Australian bluefin tuna catch and improvements in the halibut and sable fish fishery of British Columbia, in conjunction with stabilizing investment returns and compensation for unemployed workers.[49]

Finally, note that despite numerous assertions to the contrary, a country can manage with no subsidies at all. New Zealand derives a good part of its income from fishing, yet it has long since abolished every last subsidy.

Chapter 8

FORESTRY

Forests are the glory of the earth. They are the finest celebration of nature to grace the face of the planet since the first flickerings of life, almost 4 billion years ago. They contain at least three-quarters of all species, and their ecological processes are more diverse and complex than we have the wit to comprehend. They also afford exceptional sites for leisure pursuits: who does not enjoy a walk in the forest?

Forests used to cover two-fifths of the earth's lands. Today, they have been reduced by at least one-third, and the most exuberant forests, the tropical rain forests, have lost over half their expanse. Much of the decline has been a result of subsidies that foster deforestation on many a side. True, forestry subsidies are not remotely on the scale of those in agriculture, road transportation, and other leading sectors considered in this book. They are significant nonetheless. They reveal how exploitation of a natural resource that should be eminently renewable can quickly become nonrenewable, thanks to their distortional impact.

The subsidies come in many shapes and sizes. They include tax breaks, low-interest loans, reduced royalties, and underpricing for commercial loggers; government outlays on forestland infrastructure (surveys, roads, mapping, etc.); losses in state-owned enterprises; and inducements for agriculturalists to settle in tropical forests. For example, when forestry subsidies were first introduced in the western United States, a century ago, they helped to foster settlement of extensive territories and thus served a valid purpose. In developing countries too, when subsidies started to be set up in the mid-1960s, they played a constructive role in promoting investment. But in both regions, most original subsidies have long exceeded their shelf life. They persist in part because certain governments remain unaware of the all-around and enduring values of their forests and hence tend to view the forests as capital to be liquidated.[1] Most such subsidies are implicit rather than direct and are not intended to foster deforestation. Rather, they support activities that inadvertently lead to deforestation. Moreover, many forestry subsidies are partially concealed and thus difficult to recognize.[2]

Forestry in the sense of the wood products industry is worth well over $400 billion per year. Global trade in forest products has grown from $80 billion in 1985 to $152 billion in 1995, four-fifths of it on the part of developed countries.[3] Just three countries—Canada, Russia, and the United States—account for more than half of all commercial timber worldwide.[4] More important, forests supply many nonwood products and an array of environmental services, some of them much more valuable than commercial timber.[5] We shall come back to these diverse outputs toward the end of this chapter.

Regrettably, there is much overcutting of forests, often fostered by a plethora of subsidies. In turn again, this will be adverse for demand-and-supply patterns of timber in the foreseeable future (not to mention the abundant environmental services). In fact, there are already signs of timber shortages ahead in certain areas. Demand is projected to increase during 1993–2010 by 56 percent.[6] In particular, there is a growing shortage of specialty hardwoods from the Tropics. Tropical-forest countries used to earn as much from timber exports as from cotton and twice as much as from rubber. Because of overharvesting of timber stocks, however, this income is falling away steeply, imposing a severe economic limitation on those many tropical-forest countries where timber revenues have made a sizeable contribution to GNP.[7]

As a measure of burgeoning timber demand, consider the situation in China. A nationwide construction boom has brought on a severe timber shortage for a country with 21 percent of the world's population but only 3 percent of the world's forests. Timber imports doubled during the decade 1984–1993, reaching more than 10 million cubic meters of roundwood equivalent—a figure that is predicted to soar to

60 million cubic meters by shortly after the year 2000.[8] Per capita consumption of two main timber products, sawn wood and panels, amounts to less than two-thirds as much as Asia's average and less than two-fifths as much as Indonesia's. Were China to increase its consumption to match Indonesia's, its share would amount to almost 60 percent of Asia's total—and if it ever matched Japan's, 280 percent of Asia's total.[9] In short, China seems poised to become the world's leading importer of wood, with all that will mean for forest supplies in regions from Southeast Asia to Siberia and beyond.

This brief introduction highlights the role of subsidies that foster overexploitation of forests. The great majority of the world's forests are state owned. In theory, the state should be a better owner of forests than the private individual or company, since its time horizon can and should be longer than that of the private owner. But in practice, a forest may be managed by political appointees whose time horizon is no longer than the tenure of their jobs and who may therefore be inclined to turn a blind eye to deforestation that will not impose its full penalties until the longer-term future.[10] As a result, logging fees in countries such as Indonesia, Malaysia, and the Philippines are often set too low to reflect the full costs of replanting. Such stumpage fees, being only a share of replacement costs, have covered less than 15 percent of total costs in Ivory Coast and Kenya.[11] In the United States, the federal government has long sold logging rights in national forests for sums that not only fail to reflect the environmental cost of such activities but even underestimate their commercial value.[12]

Example of Overlogging: Indonesia

As an illustration of logging subsidies in tropical forests, consider Indonesia, a country with 10 percent of the world's remaining tropical forests. The country's commercial forestry sector contributes $8 billion to the domestic economy, and exports of forest products are second only to those of oil and gas as a foreign exchange earner.[13] Almost half of Indonesia's 215 million people depend on the forests, whether directly or indirectly, through, for example, forest products and watershed services. The value of these socioenvironmental benefits is estimated to be equal to the economic value of timber production.[14] But during the past fifteen years, one-quarter of the forests have been destroyed, an expanse equal to that of Florida. The country now experiences deforestation of 16,000 square kilometers per year, a rate of at least 1.8 percent.[15]

Timber concessions cover 600,000 square kilometers, or two-thirds of remaining forests. Logging rates are far beyond the government's calculation of the maximum sustainable yield.[16] So widespread is overlogging (in the sense of overheavy and destructive logging that eliminates the bulk of woody biomass) that it now accounts for well over half of deforestation, possibly much more.[17] Some observers[18] believe that if present trends persist, Indonesia could be obliged to import a large proportion of its timber needs within two decades—a period much shorter than the time since the logging boom began.

The recent upsurge in deforestation is mainly a result of illegal logging. This logging has now reached epidemic proportions; it is rampant even in the national parks. The Ministry of Forestry admits that the level of illegal logging in 1998 was 2.7 times higher than that of legal logging, which in turn was down by 30 percent from its 1997 level. This illegal logging accounts for 73 percent of total timber production and constitutes virtually all domestic consumption of logs. In turn, the problem derives from excessive expansion of the forest products industry, encouraged by a series of governments over past decades as a way to increase exports and provide jobs in the world's fourth most populous nation. Result: today there is a huge overcapacity in the forestry industry and a demand for ever more logs. The pulp industry expanded its mill capacity from just over 600,000 tonnes per year in 1988 to almost 4 million tonnes in 1998.

Satellite imagery shows that on the large islands of Kalimantan (Borneo), Sulawesi, and Sumatra, more than 170,000 square kilometers of forest disappeared in just the period 1986–1997. So extensively and rapidly has deforestation increased that there may soon be an end to lowland forests (the most valuable commercially), despite many official assertions to the contrary. These forests are essentially defunct as a viable resource on Sulawesi and are likely to be eliminated on Sumatra by 2005 and on Kalimantan by 2010.[19]

Overlogging has been greatly stimulated by subsidies both direct and indirect. So pervasive are subsidies that it is instructive to look in some detail at the effects of fiscal and other incentives that foster overlogging. The prime repercussion of subsidies is that they have caused the government to extract only a small part of the taxes and royalties that should have been charged in terms of natural resource rent, that is to say, the value of the trees before they were cut. In addition, underpricing (another covert subsidy) has induced loggers to take trees that would otherwise have been uneconomical to cut.[20]

During the early 1980s, the rate of rent capture, that is, the gov-

ernment's performance as a percentage of the actual rent from logging, was no more than 37 percent, often a lot less.[21] Moreover, if
unreported timber harvests for 1980–1985 had been subjected to the
relatively low 1980 tax, the actual revenues of $1.55 billion would
have been increased by an additional $1.2 billion, or an average of
$200 million per year.[22] During 1988–1990, the government recov-
ered only 8–17 percent of economic rent. The situation had hardly
improved by 1990: if the government had captured the same percentage of the market value of its timber resources as it did from its
oil resources (85 percent), it would have received an additional
$1.9–$2.5 billion.[23] In 1993, the government was capturing one-
third or less of economic rent from timber concessions.[24] As recently
as the mid-1990s, government forest concessions to logging companies were still pricing timber well below market levels, with government fees and taxes capturing only 25–35 percent of potential economic rent.[25] All this has encouraged logging companies to heavily
overexploit the forests.

In addition, there are inefficiencies in wood-processing industries,
this being a further reflection of subsidies. Many processing mills
have been established in response to fiscal incentives, among other
subsidies, to the point that Indonesia now controls 90 percent of the
world's tropical plywood market.[26] As a result of subsidies, however,
its processing mills have tended to be small and wasteful, with conversion rates of logs into sawn lumber and plywood only about two-
thirds of industry standards.[27] Largely because of processing short-
comings, during just the two-year period 1981–1982 Indonesia's
economy lost over $400 million in potential revenues, equivalent to
27 percent of the timber rent.[28] Moreover, for every $1 gained in ply-
wood exports, $4 was sacrificed in log exports.[29] During the 1980s
overall, while the government was subsidizing the sawn-wood and
plywood industries, log production fell by 20 percent and timber
exports by 14 percent, while fewer jobs were created net.[30] It was not
until 1988 that the value of plywood exports exceeded the 1979 log
export earnings of $2.1 billion.[31]

How far have forestry subsidies been maintained on this scale?
While there has been some drop-off since the heights of the early and
mid-1980s (certain tax credits were abandoned in 1988), there is still
a plethora of supports of one sort and another, many of them hard
to identify. Despite a lengthy list of fine publications on Indonesian
forestry in recent years,[32] there is next to no specific indication of
how much was being spent on subsidies in the late 1990s. Rent capture increased from a mere 5 percent in 1986 and only 17 percent in

1990 to at least 30–40 percent in 1995 and possibly as high as 65 percent in 1996—even though there is little reason in principle why the amount should not be nearer 100 percent.[33]

This recent advance notwithstanding, timber corporations still enjoy large, if not excessive, profits. To cite a British forestry expert, Alastair Fraser:

> There is in effect a huge subsidy to the wood processing industry, which is very wasteful, using only the best logs and a limited number of tree species. It also means the wood processors can sell their products on the world market at low prices, which then means that large volumes can be sold, meaning in turn again that large areas of forest are logged to supply the raw materials. [The heavy wood-processing subsidies arise] primarily as a consequence of lack of data and analytic tools to monitor what is going on. In addition, the unintended subsidy has the effect of undervaluing the forest timber resource, and this in turn reduces the apparent impact on the economy of clearing forest for other land uses, which look so much more economically attractive as a consequence. It is difficult for the Forest Department to resist pressure to release forest for agriculture. It also results in waste all along the chain from tree stump to plywood mill. At the same time, it takes the attraction out of investment to minimize logging damage and foster regeneration.[34]

What shall we make of this account of Indonesian forestry and its subsidies? While a good number of studies of the timber industry have been undertaken, notably by the World Bank, the Asian Development Bank, and the Food and Agriculture Organization of the United Nations, as well as the World Resources Institute and several other nongovernmental organizations, they diverge widely in their findings on subsidies, mainly because of differences in analytic methods and baseline assumptions. But the World Bank[35] seemed able to conclude that fully two-thirds of deforestation in Indonesia, amounting in 1994 to 10,000 square kilometers per year (cf. today's 16,000 square kilometers), has been a result of programs either sponsored or encouraged by government supports, primarily subsidies.

What level of subsidies shall we suppose for the late 1990s? They were surely as much as $1 billion per year, and certain experts[36] have postulated more, conceivably as much as $3 billion. It is most unsatisfactory to end this Indonesia review in such an imprecise manner. The authors propose a median figure of $2 billion per year. This is very much a best-judgment assessment, and it is advanced solely in order to come up with an indication of any sort, however rough and ready. If no estimate were offered at all, some observers might infer that subsidies were effectively nil. A figure of $2 billion may not sound like much in relation to subsidies such as those for road transportation in the United States, but in relation to the future of forestry in Indonesia, it is certainly significant.

Still further covert subsidies arise with respect to corporate debt to the Indonesian Bank Restructuring Agency. This debt amounts to almost $52 billion, of which nonperforming debt accounts for $34 billion. At least $2 billion and more likely $3.6 billion in bad debt is due to be written off. In principle at least, debt write-off amounts to a direct capital subsidy to the forest conglomerates (together with some estate crop conglomerates),[37] but in practice it is so far apart from the subsidies considered in this chapter that it is not included in the calculation of the more readily accepted forms of subsidies.

In addition to its logging subsidies, the Indonesian government has spent large amounts on inducements to persuade small-scale farmers in overpopulated Java, Bali, and Madura to migrate to the "outer islands" of Sumatra, Kalimantan, Sulawesi, and elsewhere. The Transmigration Programme was once so heavily subsidized that the government costs of moving just a single family were as high as $10,000 in 1986 dollars—and that in a country with a per capita GNP of little over $600 at the time.[38] All in all, the program resettled some 8 million people in 17,000 square kilometers of state forestland.[39] Even though the program added significantly to Indonesia's deforestation, it was not a result of forestry subsidies, so it is not counted here as part of the overall calculus.

Example of Cattle Ranching: Brazil

Most of the extensive deforestation of Brazilian Amazonia can be traced directly to government-financed subsidies. Starting in the early 1970s, hefty subsidies became available for entrepreneurs wanting to ranch cattle in cleared forestlands. Generous tax and credit incentives created over 120,000 square kilometers of large cattle ranches in Amazonia, with the typical ranch covering more than half its costs through the subsidies. By supplying funds on exceptionally easy terms, the Brazilian government invited investors to acquire and clear large tracts of forest. During the period 1979–1984, a typical ranch in Amazonia incurred costs of $415 per hectare and earned revenues of only $113 per hectare, or little over one-quarter of the costs. Yet it stayed in business; in fact, it made a commercial killing, thanks to the many subsidies at work.[40]

All in all, the Brazilian government spent $2.5 billion in subsidizing ranchers' investments through long-term loans, tax credits and other fiscal incentives, monetary inducements, and duty-free imports of capital equipment.[41] This support meant that many ranches, no matter how inefficient, made a vast profit, even to the extent that hardly any ranchers bothered to sell the timber felled to make way for the pasturelands. Virtually every ranch proved a financial success for the individual entrepreneur but an economic setback for the national economy. An activity that was privately profitable was socially unprofitable. The combined costs of tax credits, subsidized credit, and timber revenues forgone from destroyed forestland totaled $4.8 billion during the period 1966–1983, an average of $266 million per year.[42]

Government subsidies were also the driving force behind other forms of large private-investment ventures in Amazonia, with a focus on crop agriculture or mixed cropping and ranching enterprises.[43] In the state of Rôndonia alone, settlers received an implicit subsidy of $3,200 per person, making an aggregate of $163 million by 1990. Subsidized settlers cleared 25 percent more forests than those not benefiting directly from government programs.[44] Overall, the net value of future income available from unlogged and otherwise undisturbed forests may be 50–200 percent higher than the net present value of income from forest conversion through cattle ranching among other forms of agricultural settlement.[45]

In recent years, deforestation subsidies in Brazilian Amazonia have become "largely a thing of the past."[46] This is especially the case for cattle ranching and some other forms of agricultural settlement. Now that it has been stripped of most of its subsidies, ranching offers a net annual return of only $6 and sometimes a mere $2 per head of cattle.[47] There is one prime reason for this recent shift: deforestation has long been seen to be a massive drain on government coffers.

A reduction in deforestation was eventually recognized as being in Brazil's interests as well as in the interests of the world.[48] Way back in 1987, many rural-credit subsidies were abolished, and today the degree of subsidization is far from what it was.[49] The government has decided there will be no more subsidies for new ranches, though such supports continue for established ranches covering 120,000 square kilometers, these being ranches that have already cost the Brazilian treasury more than $2.5 billion in revenues forgone.[50]

Other Examples of Subsidized Deforestation in the Humid Tropics

Deforestation has been fostered by multiple subsidies in tropical-forest countries and regions as diverse as Colombia, Ecuador, Peru, Bolivia, Central America, Mexico, West Africa, Myanmar, Thailand, and the Philippines.[51] Few of these countries have captured more than half the economic rent of their timber resources.[52] In 1991, Malaysia captured 35–53 percent of economic rents for its logs.[53] If state governments in Malaysia had captured the rents on logging that were actually captured by loggers during the period 1966–1989 and invested the money in an account earning 10 percent interest, they would have accumulated an additional $90 billion by 1990, or an average of almost $4 billion per year.[54]

So too in other countries. In Vietnam, lost revenue from logging in 1992 was around 17 percent of all government revenues, while in Cambodia, revenues forgone from timber concessions have amounted to an extraordinary 63 percent of the government's entire revenues each year.[55]

Consider just a single calculation of further detrimental costs entailed. In Costa Rica, forests have been widely cleared for agriculture, especially cattle ranching. If we subtract the loss of forests from the gain in secondary forests in order to determine a net change in timber, we find that in 1984 the net value of forests eliminated was $167 million, or $69 for each Costa Rican citizen—in a country with a per capita GNP of only $1,280 at the time.[56] At the same time, Costa Rica emphasizes many environmental values such as carbon sequestration, water conservation, biodiversity protection, and "natural beauty," with a worth of $58 per hectare per year for primary forest and $42 per year for secondary forest (two-thirds attributable to carbon sequestration).[57]

Costa Rica also demonstrates how subsidized deforestation often reflects the unintended impacts of policies outside the forestry sector—particularly road development and land distribution, as well as subsidized credit and fiscal incentives for cattle ranching and crop cultivation. As a result, deforestation can proceed at a rate way more than is socially optimal—which, according to many observers, should surely be zero, given that most of Costa Rica's forests have already disappeared.[58] At the same time, successive governments in Costa Rica have made exemplary efforts to set aside as much as 25 percent of the country's territory, mostly forests, under some form of protected status—a uniquely successful achievement among tropical-forest countries of Latin America. The parallel deforestation in Costa

Rica demonstrates how an enlightened government can inadvertently tolerate measures that undercut its conservation efforts. When subsidies are indirect and covert, they can be especially insidious.[59]

Total Subsidies in Tropical Forestry

What, finally, is the scale of subsidies promoting deforestation in the humid Tropics? It is worthwhile to attempt some sort of estimate, even an informed guesstimate, insofar as no estimate at all might be construed in some quarters as meaning that there are no subsidies of any consequence. We have noted the $2 billion per year in Indonesia. Despite the extreme paucity of recent data, the authors hazard the best-judgment assessment that timber subsidies throughout the humid Tropics may now be on the order of $3–$5 billion a year, say $4 billion—a figure that reflects the various statistical analyses presented earlier, partial and approximate though they are. In reality, the subsidies could be somewhat less, and they could also be a lot more. Cattle-ranching subsidies are assumed to be small only as compared with logging subsidies. If both sets total only around $4 billion a year together, this is very little by contrast with the other types of subsidies addressed in this book. But they are significant for the economies of the countries concerned.[60] In light of their overall adverse impacts, they are all considered perverse.

Tropical deforestation has ranked high as an environmental and development concern since the late 1970s, yet the forests are declining faster than ever. A 1987 survey of seventeen countries with over 70 percent of all tropical forests found "sustainable" logging practiced in fewer than 10,000 square kilometers, or less than 0.2 percent of the forest area surveyed.[61] Two main reasons were adduced. First, government policies often helped establish or perpetuate unsound logging practices. Second, governments collected only a small fraction of the rents (especially windfall profits) accrued by loggers, and this both fostered corruption and deprived the governments of a large stream of revenues. Such government policies often have a political basis. Almost all tropical forests are government owned, enabling public officials to preside over the distribution of logging permits, which in turn assume a form of political patronage by public officials who thereafter undertax and underregulate the clients gaining these permits. Hence, government leaders rarely have much concern about unsustainable logging.[62]

Fortunately, a few efforts are being made to tackle the problems of tropical deforestation in a manner that should counter perverse subsidies to some extent.[63] The Asian Development Bank, for instance, plans to use its forestry loans as leverage to give logging rights to whichever logging company offers to post the highest guarantee bond. The bond will be invested for the life of a logging project and will be forfeited if the logger fails to protect the forest. Another option advanced by the Asian Development Bank is to award perpetual leases for an annual rent to be reviewed every five years and revoked if the holder fails to adhere to the agreement. Making the leases tradable will offer an incentive for timber concessionaires to maintain the value of their concessions.[64]

In the wake of these efforts to improve the situation, there have been a few advances. The Philippine government, for instance, began reforming its timber-pricing policies in the mid-1990s and now captures 25 percent of the value of its timber, as opposed to 11 percent in 1990.[65] In addition, a number of countries have embarked on reforestation—though this is not always so helpful as it sounds. Because reforestation subsidies are often overpriced, the upshot of these efforts can be further deforestation. In Indonesia, for instance, a reforestation fund turned out to be "a slush fund for highly questionable investments outside the forestry sector, with virtually no contribution to reforestation."[66]

Examples of Overlogging in Developed Countries

Let us now look at three major forestry countries: the United States, Canada, and Russia.

United States

Now let us examine the situation in a leading forestry country in the developed world, the United States. The USDA Forest Service supports logging in its national forests with an array of subsidies, many of them indirect or otherwise semi-concealed and hence hard to track down.

About one-third of the United States is forestland, though "frontier forests," or forests comprising original vegetation, are almost entirely restricted to the Pacific Northwest and Alaska and account for a mere 6.3 percent of original forest cover.[67] The National Forests cover 780,000 square kilometers, an expanse twice as large as that of California, though only half of them are actually forested. For decades, they have been "managed" by the Forest Service primarily for logging by private contractors. The principal factor has been the government's subsidization of road building to smooth the way for loggers. By the late 1990s, the Forest Service had installed 610,000 kilometers of roads, enough to stretch fifteen times around the world and a distance eight times longer than the interstate highway system, albeit at a per-kilometer cost a tiny fraction of that for a multi-lane highway. Some observers believe that the Forest Service has become the largest road-building agency in the world.

Thanks to abundant subsidies, road building has enabled a large proportion of the National Forests to be logged, even though many of the areas in question are considered commercially unsuitable for sustained timber production. In just 1994, for instance, the U.S. government spent over $100 million of taxpayers' funds on building and maintaining roads in National Forests, largely for the use of timber companies that contributed nothing to the cost. By eliminating the construction of new roads in these forests as well as other "management" activities, the government could save $475 million.[68]

In addition, the Forest Service subsidizes logging by selling timber at prices way below its own costs of timber marketing as well as by providing other subsidies, such as the $811 million in tax breaks that the forest industry enjoyed in 1991.[69] During the period 1992–1994, timber sales lost the agency $1 billion in direct costs alone (road building, surveys, mapping, etc.), let alone a lengthy list of environmental problems.[70]

Timber sales in most National Forests lose money every year. In 1992, 95 of the country's 120 National Forests operated at a heavy loss because the Forest Service spent more money on administering timber sales than it received in revenue from those sales.[71] In the following year, government subsidies for below-cost timber sales alone amounted to $323 million, including $35 million for the Tongass National Forest in Alaska.[72] In 1996, timber sales produced a net loss to U.S. taxpayers of $791 million while providing less than 4 percent of the nation's wood supply. A major share of the subsidies supported not only road building, timber sales, and the like but also administration of the Forest Service bureaucracy.[73]

These annual losses would have been even higher had they reflected transfer payments to states and long-term capital expenditures for road construction. When we combine all subsidies identifiable and quantifiable, we find that in 1999, the Forest Service spent $2.26 billion and received only $268 million, meaning a net loss to the Treasury and hence the taxpayer of $2.15 billion.[74]

The resulting deforestation has contributed to widespread soil erosion, water depletion, fisheries decline, loss of wildlife habitat, and several other environmental problems, all which have constituted further subsidization (albeit unquantified) in the form of environmental externalities. It has also been to the detriment of still other prominent benefits from the forests, notably recreation, which, despite the degradation of forest amenity, jumped from 560 million visits in 1980 to 860 million in 1996. These visits generated 2.6 million jobs and added almost $100 billion to the national economy, whereas logging added only 76,000 jobs and $3.5 billion.[75]

The key question of whether the Forest Service makes a reasonable profit, as it claims, or loses by a large margin is beset by the curious accounting procedures adopted by the agency. It employs several different methods for making its calculations, which look like a convoluted accounting system that overlooks many costs while including certain revenues that never actually accrue to the government.[76] During the shorter period 1992–1994, when the agency claimed a profit of $1.1 billion, the General Accounting Office showed a loss of nearly $1.0 billion. Yet the more the Forest Service has sold timber and the more the Treasury has lost money on logging operations, the more the agency's budget has grown. As some critics argue, it would be cheaper to pay loggers directly out of the Treasury than to continue subsidizing the depletion of an increasingly scarce asset.[77]

The subsidies problem is exemplified especially by the Tongass rain forest in Alaska, which is both the biggest forest and the biggest money loser in the National Forest System. With 68,000 square kilometers (an area the size of West Virginia), it is the most extensive temperate rain forest on Earth; it is home to the world's greatest concentration of grizzly bears and bald eagles, and its rivers support spawning grounds for all five species of Pacific salmon (a fishery that contains more wild salmon than in all the "lower forty-eight" states and that is vital to Alaska's economy). The forest contains groves of spruce trees that were already growing tall when the Pilgrims arrived in New England. They still have not stopped growing. Here are sizeable stands of old-growth trees that rank among the rarest of all natural wonders and deserve to be preserved as national monuments. Instead, many are exported to Asia to be milled into rough building materials or even chopsticks, sold by the Forest Service at a fraction of their full economic worth (sometimes as little as $2 each, even though management costs to the Forest Service have been many times more).[78]

The Tongass rainforest is being depleted through overlogging more rapidly than are most rainforests in Amazonia or on Kalimantan. Between 1982 and 1988, the U.S. government spent $389 million on roads and other services for private clear-cutting operations there yet earned only $32 million in return. In 1990, the U.S. Congress passed the Tongass Timber Reform Act, aimed at curbing the absurdly botched management. But during 1992–1994, the timber program's outlays exceeded revenues by $102 million, more than twice as much as in any other national forest, the deficit being made up by the American taxpayer. This represented $1,325 for each hectare cut, a figure that rose to $2,030 by 1995–1997.[79] Whether from the standpoint of the environment or that of the economy, the so-called management of the Tongass does not make sense. Commercial loggers regularly buy trees for a few dollars each, whereas management costs to the Forest Service have been dozens of times as much, most of them going toward road construction.[80] Timber sales cannot even accomplish their stated goal of safeguarding timber industry jobs, even though each job that is created costs taxpayers an average of $12,000.[81] To cite Wisconsin senator William Proxmire, "Japan gets the logs and the United States gets rolled."[82]

Fortunately, there now seems to be a prospect of better times ahead for the Tongass—better in principle, at least. Although the forest remains open to logging for the time being, it has been targeted for "special study."

For the purposes of this chapter, and reflecting the assessment presented earlier, we can conclude that formal subsidies in U.S. forestry are large and climbing. Reckoned simply in terms of what comes out of the Treasury and what is returned to it (a partial calculation), these subsidies topped $2 billion for the first time in 1992, reached $2.6 billion in 1997, were estimated to be $2.7 billion in 2000, and may well exceed $3.0 billion in 2001.[83] A present-day total of $3 billion is accepted for the present purposes, and all subsidies are considered perverse in view of their persistent depletion of a valuable resource and their downside repercussions for the environment.

There are many more covert subsidies in the form of environmental externalities, being uncompensated costs levied by the Forest Service and loggers on society. Examples include degraded watersheds, reduced flood control, soil erosion, reduced nutrient cycling, depleted fisheries, decline of wilderness amenity and recreation, elimination of species habitats, and loss of carbon sinks. These are so widespread and significant that their collective value exceeds that of the formal subsidies many times over. In areas adjacent to the National Forests, human communities benefit through supply of clean water worth more than $3 billion a year, while pollution filters are worth nearly $3.4 billion. As the principal habitat for thousands of insect pollinators, the forests contribute $4–$7 billion to U.S. agriculture.[84] Total: $11–$14 billion. Local communities also benefit from forest-dependent activities such as recreation, hunting, and fishing worth tens of billions of dollars.[85] Because the environmental values of forests worldwide are dealt with later in this chapter, we shall not consider these benefits further here.

The amount of income and the number of jobs generated by these ecosystem services far outweigh the income and jobs from logging. In Alaska, for instance, jobs related to the environment outnumber logging jobs sixteen times over—yet timber sale programs ignore these services while exaggerating the value of timber.[86]

Meanwhile, Americans' tax dollars are hard at work propping up a timber industry that should, at the very least, be paying handsomely for the right to cut the country's last best trees.[87]

Fortunately, it now looks as if a fresh strategy for the forests is to be attempted, meaning that many of the unwanted subsidies should eventually be reduced, if not abandoned. The new head of the Forest Service, Michael Dombeck, has proposed an eighteen-month moratorium on building of new roads in roadless areas. These areas still cover 240,000 square kilometers, or 30 percent, of the National Forests, while another 140,000 square kilometers are officially designated as wilderness areas. The Forest Service has recommended that the expanse be increased by another 24,400 square kilometers in order to retain parts of the National Forests in pristine condition. But many of these protected forests are remote, are inaccessible, or do not have many trees, so they are unlikely ever to be logged anyway. The main logging battleground is a much smaller area, and for political reasons some of it could end up exempt from the order.[88]

More important, the National Forests are henceforth to be managed for several purposes apart from logging, notably watershed health, recreation, wilderness, and forest health through prescribed burning. The greatest priority will be given to the first of these; more than 60 million people in 3,400 communities and thirty-three states obtain their drinking water from National Forest lands.[89] The new policy will help eliminate flooding, soil erosion, siltation of rivers, and destruction of fisheries, all of which are problems associated with clear-cutting. Under the new policy, the timber harvest, which reached an all-time high during the 1980s, has already been drastically reduced.[90] Moreover, the new long-term vision was supported by President Bill Clinton, who asserted in late 1999 that the forests have purposes higher than timber supply.[91] All in all, this policy démarche will mark one of the biggest ever advances for the country's natural heritage.

Canada

Canada contains over one-third of the world's boreal forests and one-tenth of the world's forests of all kinds.[92] The most valuable forests, however, are the temperate rainforests of British Columbia. The province's forestry industry is its second largest economic sector, supplying the world's largest timber exports. Two-thirds of the province is made up of forests, almost all of them owned by the provincial government. British Columbia is also Canada's most biologically diverse province, with over 7,000 native plant species in an area twice the size of Britain, with its 1,400 native plant species. The province is home to 70 percent of Canada's mammal and bird species, half of which are found there exclusively.[93]

Regrettably, logging has not been carried out in a sustainable fashion for decades, thanks largely to plentiful subsidies.[94] Most forests are leased out as "forestry tenures" to large timber companies. In British Columbia, forest concessions have long been awarded to companies that undertake to build sawmills and pulp mills. This has resulted in overcapacity, which in turn has fostered overlogging.[95]

The divergence between log prices and stumpage fees, probably the best example of an ongoing subsidy to the forestry sector, estimated to have topped Can$1 billion by 1991.[96] Companies have sold logs for 80 percent more than stumpage, which means that the logs have been highly subsidized indeed. In eighteen out of twenty-five years during the period 1970–1994, the province underpriced stumpage fees at an average of only 17 percent of economic rent captured.[97] It may have made sense to give away the trees when the aim of public policy was to attract investment capital to kick-start the provincial economy, as was the case in the 1930s. But it does not make sense today, when the appropriate policy should be to move the forest economy away from old-growth liquidation and primary processing to secondary-growth management and value added, thus relieving the pressure to log the remaining old-growth forests and creating more forest-sector jobs.[98]

According to a recent calculation,[99] the British Columbia government's subsidies to the timber industry averaged nearly Can$3 billion annually from the late 1980s to the early 1990s, with net benefits to the industry after payment of stumpage fees of around Can$1 billion per year. Another recent analysis[100] proposes that the province has been forgoing potential revenues of between Can\$1 billion and Can\$2.6 billion, for a median figure of Can\$1.8 billion. Still another estimate[101] postulates that in 1998, the forest industry lost Can\$1 billion. According to these diverse estimates, British Columbia's subsidies to the timber industry work out at rather more than Can\$1 billion per year.[102] When we add in further subsidies for transportation, energy, and water, the total could well be one-third higher, equivalent to U.S.\$1 billion per year.

The most recent and detailed analysis, averaged across four pricing methodologies,[103] calculates that the shortfall in 1997 stumpage fees was between Can\$842 million and Can\$2.6 billion, with an intermediate figure of Can\$1.8 billion. The highest estimate[104] available reveals that the full economic rent in 1997 should have been between two and four times greater than the Can\$1.8 billion of stumpage fees paid. This would have resulted in rent forgone totaling between Can\$1.8 billion and Can\$5.3 billion. All in all, subsidies to the forest industry—not only rent forgone but also tax abatement, a profits reduction program, reduced property taxes, and tax deferrals and credits—now total Can\$2.9 billion (range Can\$1.7 billion to Can\$4.2 billion) per year.

Then it is necessary to add in the costs of natural capital depletion due to overlogging. These costs include degraded watersheds, soil erosion, river siltation, and loss of wildlife habitat, among other damages.[105] These costs are estimated through an ecosystem analysis to be worth Can\$673 million (range Can\$332 million to Can\$1.7 billion) per year.[106] This further factor reduces the industry's benefits by 22–70 percent.

In sum, then, there is a total subsidy to British Columbia's forestry—including both formal and indirect subsidies—of Can\$2.0 billion to Can\$5.9 billion per year, with an intermediate figure of Can\$4.0 billion.[107] This is much more than the other estimates presented earlier, but it is accepted for the purposes of this chapter because of its tightly argued case backed by detailed documentation. Let us conclude, then, with an estimate of at least Can\$4.0 billion, or U.S.\$2.5 billion, per year for British Columbia. Subsidies in other provinces, such as Alberta, Ontario, and Quebec, are not nearly so great, but they are considered large enough to warrant a total estimate for Canada of U.S.\$3.0 billion per year.

By 1991, even government foresters agreed that the allowable annual cut was too high, though there were no reductions until 1996.[108] Harvests may have to decline along British Columbia's coast by as much as 40 percent to make logging sustainable and without environmental damage of numerous sorts.[109]

Despite many financial handouts, British Columbia's forestry sector lost 27,000 jobs during the period 1981–1991 and was the only industrial sector to register a decline. Because of these economic problems and general rundown of a potentially renewable resource, plus the environmental problems cited, all subsidies in this sector are considered to be perverse.

Fortunately, there are some initial signs of a shift in emphasis. First, the province's government has increased stumpage fees somewhat, and it has introduced a Forest Practices Code. Second, three leading timber companies, MacMillan Bloedel Ltd., Western Forest Products Ltd., and International Forest Products Ltd., have pledged to phase out clear-cutting and pursue a stewardship strategy focused on retaining old-growth forests. These three companies control more than half of the province's coastal forests. They say they plan to replace clear-cutting with selective cutting, in which some trees are left to reduce water runoff and soil erosion, to provide wildlife habitat, and to help regenerate the forest. Regrettably, their intentions have yet to show much substance on the ground. Moreover, "selective logging" has now been replaced with "variable retention logging," with a minimum of only 10 percent retention, and "clear-cuts with minimal reserves."[110]

Russia

An equally regrettable situation is occurring in Russia, where the boreal zone contains the largest unbroken tracts of forest in the world. Stretching from the Ural Mountains to the Pacific Ocean and located primarily in Siberia, these boreal forests include half of the world's coniferous forests and 0.2 percent of the planet's forest expanse. Encompassing 4 million square kilometers, they are almost twice as large as Brazil's Amazonian forest.[111]

The Russian government has long supplied exceptionally large subsidies for timber transportation, notably from Siberia. Logs have been shipped by train either to ports in eastern Russia or to Europe, with very little charge to logging concerns for this substantial service.[112] While no statistical details are available on these subsidies, it appears they have been sharply reduced in the past few years.[113] Logging in Siberia (often clear-cut logging), together with fires, has been destroying 40,000 square kilometers of forests per year, while another 65,000 square kilometers have been depleted through the factors listed plus industrial pollution.[114] The joint amount is twice as much as recent annual deforestation in Brazilian Amazonia and four times as much as the area logged each year in the boreal forests of Canada.[115]

Despite the gross lack of detailed and up-to-date information, it is plain that much of the problem reflects subsidies of various shapes and sizes. The going price for a logging permit allows companies to make 65 percent profits.[116] Overall, the government collects a maximum of 20 percent of potential revenues from stumpage fees, sometimes as little as 3 percent. As a result, it forgoes $3–$5 billion in annual income.[117] A median figure of $4 billion is taken here to represent the subsidies' total, though it reflects only loss of stumpage fees and ignores many other subsidies, such as those for rail transportation. Because they are economically inefficient and environmentally destructive, all of these subsidies are considered to be perverse.

In Australia too, subsidies abound. Victoria's state government spends Austral$2.25 on logging subsidies to obtain Austral$1 in timber royalties, for a total net outlay of Austral$170 million (U.S.$100 million) per year.[118] In the Thomson River catchment, the main water supply for Melbourne, subsidies promote the logging of old-growth forests to the detriment of the watershed, even though the water supplies are worth ten times more than the timber harvested and the water yield loss is estimated at Austral$65 million (U.S.$38 million) per year.[119] Total environmental externalities of logging in Victoria are estimated to be on the order of Austral$160 million (U.S.$94 million) per year.[120] This instance is cited for illustrative purposes only, the sum being too small to be considered further.

Subsidies Worldwide

This short review shows that subsidies are a frequent feature of forestry in all three main forest zones, namely, tropical, temperate, and boreal. They are characteristic of developed and developing countries alike. They exert a sizeable influence on the nature and scope of forestry operations, and they contribute markedly to overexploitation and other forms of forest misuse. In fact, were these subsidies to be phased out, that measure alone would probably do more to slow deforestation in many countries than any other single initiative. Of course, subsidies can theoretically contribute to rational forest management too, through, for example, provision of funds to stimulate plantation forestry or to safeguard watersheds with tree cover. But these seem to be so rare and of such small scale in the countries considered that they make only a marginal difference at most in the overall picture. So all forestry subsidies treated in the foregoing discussion are considered perverse on the grounds of their deleterious impacts, both economic and environmental.

What is the overall scale of these perverse subsidies? In the absence of up-to-date data, it is difficult to say in more than exploratory terms. The assessment here postulates some $4 billion per year in those tropical countries reviewed, plus $3 billion in the United States, $3 billion in Canada, and $4 billion in Russia, for a total of $14 billion per year (Table 8.1)—again, a sum considered to be 100 percent perverse. This chapter does not present economic documentation of subsidies in a number of other leading forestry countries, such as Sweden, Germany, Japan, India, Thailand, Papua New Guinea, the Philippines, Ivory Coast, Nigeria, Guyana, and Suriname. So far as can be discerned, many of the same perverse subsidies should obtain in these countries too, but because of lack of documentation they are not considered further.

To emphasize: this is a very crude estimate—nothing more (and nothing less). It does not reflect, for instance, the costs of reforesting overlogged lands, a cost that would be considerable in the dipterocarp (hardwood) forests of Southeast Asia, where loggers often remove one-quarter of the woody biomass and injure another half beyond recovery—and a cost that is almost always disregarded in evaluation of tropical forestry. If, as is all too possible, the estimate is off target, it is more likely to be on the low side.

Note too that $14 billion is a small sum in relation to the value of commercial timber worldwide, $400 billion per year. In the case of marine fisheries, perverse subsidies amount to 31 percent of the total commercial value, whereas in forestry they are only 3.5 percent. However, as we shall shortly see, environmental externalities are unusually important in the case of forestry, whereas in fisheries that

Table 8.1. Forestry Subsidies Worldwide

Tropical forests	$4 billion
United States	$3 billion
Canada	$3 billion
Russia	$4 billion
TOTAL	$14 billion
Externalities	$78 billion
TOTAL	$92 billion

is far from the case (except as regards the depletion of major fish stocks, together with destruction of coral reefs and mangroves). So extensive and significant are forestry externalities that it is worthwhile to look at these implicit subsidies in some detail. Plainly, as forests disappear, so do their environmental goods and services. The external costs of deforestation are borne by present communities and future generations who are thus deprived of forests' benefits—meaning that the external costs are effectively subsidies to deforestation.

Environmental Externalities

Forests supply many goods and services apart from commercial timber and potential agricultural lands. The decline of forests entrains a decline of these goods and services. Herewith is an illustrative selection of forestry values at stake in order to demonstrate the scope and scale of the externalities of deforestation.

Material Goods

Tropical forests provide fuelwood for the 3 billion people in developing countries, who use the wood as their main, if not sole, source of household energy. A proxy indication of how they evaluate their fuelwood may be gained by noting that at least 500 million of them spend between one and two hours a day roaming far and wide to find adequate supplies.[121] Suppose the average length of time spent is one and a half hours per day, or 547 hours per year. Suppose too that their time opportunity cost is $0.10 per hour, reflecting what they could gain by spending the same time on cultivating farm fields. Thus, the shadow cost per person per year is $55. This means that the total value of forests as sources of fuelwood is $28 billion per year. This is to be compared with the cost of establishing enough plantations to take care of all fuelwood needs: $10–$20 billion as a once-and-for-all outlay, plus perhaps $1 billion per year to maintain them.

Then there is a host of nonwood products from tropical forests, including wild fruits, latexes, essential oils, exudates, waxes, tannins, dyes, and medicinals.[122] In India, nonwood products are worth $4.3 billion per year, equivalent to 26 percent of wood products.[123] All in all, the value of nonwood forest products worldwide may now have reached as much as $90 billion a year, including subsistence items and unmarketed items.[124]

Even more abundant are wild species and other forms of biodiversity. While covering only 6 percent of the Earth's land surface, tropical forests are estimated to contain at least 50 percent, possibly 70 percent and conceivably 90 percent, of the Earth's species. Half a square kilometer of Malaysia's forests can feature as many tree and shrub species as the whole of the United States and Canada, while a single bush in Peruvian Amazonia has revealed more ant species than are found in the British Isles.[125] As the forests disappear, so do their species, at a rate of some 50–150 per day, or 18,000–55,000 per year.[126]

Apart from scientific, aesthetic, and ethical values of biodiversity, these losses affect the immediate material welfare of people throughout the world. When we visit our neighborhood pharmacy, there is one chance in four that our purchase, whether a drug, medicinal, or pharmaceutical, owes its manufacture to materials derived from tropical-forest plants.[127] These products include antibiotics, antivirals, analgesics, tranquilizers, diuretics, laxatives, and contraceptive pills, among many other items. Commercial sales are worth $40 billion a year in the developed world, while their economic value is several times larger.[128] The forests are reckoned to contain at least one dozen plant species with the capacity to generate superstar drugs against cancer, provided the plants can be identified before they rank among the five species eliminated each day.[129] Three promising leads against AIDS come from tropical-forest plants. Potential future drugs awaiting discovery in tropical forests could have a theoretical value ranging from $147 billion[130] to $420 billion[131] to $900 billion.[132] Suppose we take a midrange figure of $500 billion, and suppose we accept that only one-tenth of the value is made up of materials from the plants. Then the worth is $50 billion—a point to ponder when we hear that five plant species are being eliminated every day through tropical deforestation.

There are material benefits too from subspecies and populations of wild plants. In the early 1970s, Asia's rice crop was hit by a grassy stunt virus that threatened to devastate 300,000 square kilometers of rice fields. Fortunately, a single gene from a wild rice in an Indian forest offered resistance against the virus. Then, in 1976, another virus, responsible for what is known as ragged stunt disease, emerged, and again, the most potent source of resistance proved to be a wild forest rice. In India alone, the introduction of wild rice strains (plus primitive cultivars) has increased yields by at least $75 million a year.[133]

Environmental Services

Environmental services provided by forests are still more bountiful and valuable than the material goods they supply. Forests stabilize landscapes.[134] They protect soils, helping them to retain their moisture and to store and cycle nutrients.[135] They serve as buffers against the spread of pests and diseases.[136] By preserving watershed functions, they regulate water flows in terms of both quantity and quality,[137] thereby helping to prevent flood-and-drought regimes in downstream territories.[138] They are critical to the Earth's energy balance.[139] They modulate climate at local and regional levels through regulation of rainfall regimes and the albedo effect.[140] They help to reduce global warming through their carbon stocks.[141] Let us take a quick look at certain of these services.

WATERSHED FUNCTIONS

While tropical forests cover only around 5 percent of the Earth's land surface, they receive almost half of the Earth's rainfall on land, often in heavy downpours. Deforestation of upland catchments, with loss of the forests' "sponge" effect, often leads to disruption of watershed systems, causing year-round water flows in downstream areas to give way to flood-and-drought regimes. As many as 40 percent of developing-world farmers depend upon regular water flows from forested watersheds to irrigate their croplands.[142] In several parts of the humid tropics, the greatest limitation on increased food production stems not from lack of agricultural land but from shortages of irrigation water during dry seasons. This is especially the case in Southern Asia and Southeast Asia, where many forests are located above rich alluvial valley lands, several of which support some of the world's highest-density agricultural communities, where farming is carried out primarily through irrigation. Indeed, two-thirds of farmers in southern Asia and Southeast Asia live in such valley lands, and deforestation is more advanced in this region than in virtually any other sector of the tropical-forest biome. Decline of watershed services is already affecting the valley lands of the Ganges, Brahmaputra, Irrawaddy, Salween, Chao Phraya, and Mekong Rivers.[143] In India, the value of forest services in regulating river flows and containing floods has been assessed at roughly $72 billion a year.[144]

Deforestation of watersheds also leads to washing off of topsoil. Siltation of hydropower and irrigation-system reservoirs worldwide, derived in major measure from watershed deforestation in the humid Tropics, was estimated in the mid-1980s to levy a cost of at least $6 billion a year.[145] On just the island of Java, the size of New York State, deforestation-derived siltation of reservoirs, irrigation systems, and harbors levied damage costs worth $58 million in 1987, plus additional damages to coastal fisheries and water supplies for urban communities.[146] Conversely, consider the value of an intact watershed: Canaima National Park in Venezuela, with its 30,000 square kilometers of undisturbed forest, supplies hydroelectricity equivalent to 144 million barrels of oil per year,[147] worth about $2.5 billion in 1983 prices.

The watershed service supplied by forests has been graphically illustrated by recent experience in the Yangtze River basin in China. In mid-1998, there were several weeks of near-record flooding in the river basin, affecting 240 million people and causing $30 billion worth of damage.[148] The Chinese government acknowledged that the disaster was severely exacerbated by deforestation in the upper reaches of the watershed. The government ordained a halt to tree cutting in the areas at issue, as well as conversion of a good many state timber firms into tree-planting firms. The official government view today is that trees are worth three times as much standing as they are cut, simply because of the water-storage and flood-prevention capacity of forests.

Similar flooding disasters have occurred in other parts of the world, notably Honduras, where Hurricane Mitch and its deforestation damage in 1998 caused $5 billion worth of losses.

REGULATION OF RAINFALL REGIMES

Deforestation in the Tropics can result in reduced rainfall.[149] This is especially significant for agriculture. In the states of Penang and Kedah of the northwestern Peninsular Malaysia, which have lost almost all their forests, it was found fifteen years ago that disruption of rainfall regimes had led to 20,000 hectares of paddy rice fields being abandoned and another 72,000 hectares registering a marked production drop-off in this "rice bowl" of the Peninsula.[150] Similar deforestation-associated changes in rainfall have been documented in the Philippines, southwestern India, montane Tanzania, southwestern Ivory Coast, northwestern Costa Rica, and the Panama Canal Zone.[151] Deforestation can also affect rainfall regimes at much wider levels, for example, in the entire Amazonia basin.[152]

CLIMATE REGULATION AND GLOBAL WARMING

Still more important is the climate linkage at the global level, through the carbon sinks of forests worldwide and hence their association with global warming.[153] Forests account for two-thirds of net plant growth and carbon fixation on land.[154] Their plants and soils currently hold 1,200 gigatonnes (billion tonnes) of carbon, out of 2,000 gigatonnes contained in all terrestrial plants and soils (by contrast with 750 gigatonnes in the atmosphere).[155] Around half of the forests' carbon is located in boreal forests, more than one-third is in tropical forests, and one-seventh is in temperate forests.[156] Boreal forests, which constitute the Earth's largest terrestrial biome, probably contain more carbon than do all proven fossil fuel reserves. They thus possess the scope for both the greatest change in the global carbon cycle and the greatest potential feedbacks on climate systems.[157]

When forests are burned—as is the case with cattle ranching and small-scale agriculture in the humid Tropics and with fires both wild and human-made in the Tropics and the boreal zone—they release their carbon. Of the roughly 7.6 gigatonnes of carbon that is emitted each year into the global atmosphere and that contributes around half of greenhouse-effect processes, 1.6 gigatonnes (plus or minus 0.4 gigatonne) come from forest burning in the Tropics;[158] almost all the rest stems from combustion of fossil fuels.[159] Allowing for some sequestration of carbon by temperate and boreal forests, there has generally been a net flux into the atmosphere of 0.9 gigatonne (plus or minus 0.4 gigatonne) of carbon.[160] This amount increased markedly in 1997, when more forests were burned worldwide than in any single year of the recorded past.

Furthermore, global warming itself will cause increased die-off and decomposition of forest biomass, in turn triggering a further release of carbon dioxide.[161] As much as one-third of the world's forests could be threatened in this manner.[162] This will likely apply especially to boreal forests, which, being located in northern high latitudes, where temperatures will rise the most in a greenhouse-affected world, could soon start to undergo marked desiccation and die-off.[163] Were boreal forests to be progressively depleted along these lines, their expanse could decline by at least 40 percent and conceivably 60 percent within the next three to five decades. This would release between 1.5 gigatonnes and 3.0 gigatonnes of carbon per year over the period, probably more than is being emitted annually from tropical deforestation today and equivalent to 20–40 percent of all current anthropogenic (human-caused) emissions of carbon dioxide.[164]

As a conservative estimate, we can use a central value of $20 of eventual global-warming damage for every tonne of carbon released.[165] Conversion of open forests in the Tropics into agricultural land or pastureland would result in a cost of roughly $600–$1,000 per hectare; conversion of closed secondary forest, $2,000–$3,000 per hectare; and conversion of primary forest, $4,000–$4,400 per hectare.[166] The carbon-sink attribute offers a far higher rate of return than does any alternative form of current land use in tropical forests. Alternatively reckoned, to replace the carbon-storage function of tropical forests (never mind temperate and boreal forests) could cost $3.7 trillion[167]—though this figure could be on the high side, given that an alternative analysis postulates only $46 billion for just Brazilian Amazonia.[168]

OVERALL ECONOMIC VALUES

Remarkably, in light of what is at stake overall, there have been scant attempts to come up with aggregate evaluations of forest outputs. Fortunately, there have been some exploratory efforts for a few tropical-forest countries.[169] The analytic methodologies span direct-use values such as production of timber, nonwood forest products, and medicinal plants and opportunities for hunting and fishing, recreation and tourism, and education; indirect-use values include soil conservation, nutrient cycling, watershed protection, flood control, microclimatic effects, and carbon sequestration. In addition, there is existence value, the value conferred in ensuring the survival of a resource. On top of all these, and perhaps the most important in the indefinite long run, are option values, including potential values of future use. Using this conceptual construct, the environmental values of Mexico's forests amount to some $4 billion per year.[170] The total economic value of Costa Rica's 13,000 square kilometers of wildlands, the great majority of them tropical forests, is between $1.7 billion and $3.7 billion annually. Only one-third of the value accrues to Costa Rica, with the rest going to the global community.[171]

An alternative reckoning has recently been provided by ecological economist Robert Costanza and colleagues.[172] They looked at all benefits derived from forests worldwide, principally provision of raw materials, nutrient cycling, erosion control, and climate regulation, plus another ten categories. They came up with an overall value averaging almost $1,000 per hectare per year for the 49 million square kilometers of forests, or a total of $4.7 trillion per year (three examples: climate regulation, $685 billion; erosion control, $466 billion; nutrient cycling, $1.8 trillion). If we are losing just 1 percent of these benefits through loss of 1 percent of forests each year (the deforestation amount is hotly disputed, though most experts agree it is at least 1 percent), then that amounts to $47 billion. Of course, a loss of 1 percent of forests does not mean a loss of 1 percent of forests' environmental values; the second will often be less than the first. We have no way of determining the proportion accurately, so let us accept a rough-and-ready estimate of $50 billion. The true total could conceivably be less but is probably more, if not much more.

Another, though far more limited, way to assess the situation is to recall the 1997 and 1998 fires that eliminated 20,000 square kilometers of forests, or an area at least as large as New Jersey and probably much more (conceivably 97,000 square kilometers),[173] in Kalimantan and other parts of Indonesia (the original government calculation underestimated the area burned by a factor of ten). Almost four-fifths of these fires were set by big forestry and plantation firms in clearing land. This gross mismanagement of forests led to myriad costs. These included not only loss of commercial timber and nonwood products but also health damages: 20 million people suffered smoke-related respiratory troubles with an estimated health cost of $1.4 billion, and more than 1,000 people died.[174] Additional consequences were a decline in crop yields as haze kept the region in daylong twilight; repeated closures of airports and other communications systems (in Malaysia as well as Indonesia); an airplane crash; a ship collision; grand-scale decline of amenity; and loss of much tourism, both in Indonesia and farther afield. Finally, the fires released as much carbon into the atmosphere as did all fossil-fuel emissions in Europe during the same period. Not allowing for this last item and several other incommensurables, the total eventual cost was estimated to be at least $10 billion,[175] possibly twice as much.[176] Just the first figure would have been worth over 5 percent of Indonesia's GDP.

Also in 1998, there were widespread fires in Brazilian Amazonia, emitting their own stocks of carbon dioxide. All in all, more forests were burned in 1997 than ever before.

All these externality calculations are preliminary and exploratory. They need to be firmed up with due dispatch.[177] Then, and only then, shall we be in a position to compute what is at stake as forests decline, and thus to calculate the implicit environmental subsidies involved in deforestation. As the foregoing discussion demonstrates, the externalities are large indeed, surely in the tens of billions of dollars and possibly in the hundreds of billions of dollars per year. In addition, there are significant social externalities, which remain almost entirely undocumented and unquantified economically.

These externalities, were we able to pin them all down, should be counted as additional perverse subsidies. As estimated earlier, they surely total $50 billion per year, possibly many times as much. Even more important, the total looks likely to be formidably expanded as global warming starts to bite. The point is not pursued further here because of lack of documentation and substantive analysis. This is all the more regrettable in that the forestry sector with its many externalities could eventually prove to feature more perverse subsidies than any of the other sectors.

In conclusion, subsidies for forestry are estimated to be $14 billion per year in formal and conventional supports, all of them counted as perverse. Externality costs are estimated to total at least $78 billion per year, all of them perverse. The two sets make a total of $92 billion.

Chapter 9

OVERVIEW ASSESSMENT

At last! We can now consider all subsidies in the six sectors combined and hence all their perverse subsidies. The collective findings are set out in Table 9.1, showing that perverse subsidies now amount to around $2 trillion per year worldwide. This is not to suggest that virtually all subsidies are perverse, though 78 percent qualify as such. This large proportion results from the fact that many activities feature many externalities, usually environmental. While these do not rank as subsidies in any formal or conventional sense, they are increasingly recognized by economists as subsidies insofar as they represent uncompensated costs imposed by a sector on society at large; hence, they are effectively subsidies, and perverse ones too. Indeed, if we were to document all externalities—not just environmental but social externalities as well—we would find that the total would be all the greater, probably much greater, again. As an American analyst[1] has demonstrated, the uncompensated societywide costs of American business (unsafe vehicles, tobacco, and a host of other harmful products, plus pollution and other disruptive effects) total at least $2.6 trillion per year, or five times more than their private profits.

Table 9.1. Subsidies Worldwide

Sector	Conventional Subsidies[a] ($ billion)	Externalities Documented/ Quantified[b] ($ billion)	Total Subsidies ($ billion)	Perverse Subsidies ($ billion)
Agriculture	385	250	635	510
Fossil fuels, nuclear energy	131	200	331	300
Road transportation	800	380	1,180	780
Water	67	180	247	230
Fisheries	25	n/a	25	25
Forestry	14	78	92	92
TOTAL (rounded)	1,420	1,090	2,510	1,950

[a]Established and readily recognized subsidies, including both direct financial transfers and indirect supports such as tax credits. Perverse subsidies as a proportion of conventional subsidies are 66 percent for agriculture; 75 percent for fossil fuels/nuclear energy, and water; 50 percent for roads; and 100 percent for fisheries and forests.

[b]These are 100 percent perverse.

Conventional subsidies as documented in the six sectoral chapters of this book amount to 4 percent of the $35 trillion global economy, and the perverse subsidies amount to 5.6 percent. Were we to include other sectors on top of the six assessed in this report, the two totals and percentages would be that much higher.

These findings are to be compared with the findings of two other recent studies. David Roodman postulates that a selection of subsidies add up to more than $650 billion per year and suggests that a good proportion of them can be categorized as perverse subsidies, though he does not offer an estimate of their share.[2] André de Moor,[3] who covers four of the sectors examined in this report but does not deal with fisheries or forestry, has come up with a subsidy total of well over $700 billion per year (range $707–$887 billion) and suggests a perverse subsidy total somewhere between $250 billion and $550 billion. This book's two totals are larger than those of the other studies primarily because the book considers many more implicit subsidies in the form of environmental externalities. The two in the agriculture sector (soil erosion and pesticides) amount to $250 billion, and the three in the water sector (water-related diseases, time costs of fetching water, and water benefits) amount to $180 billion, making $430 billion together. For reasons explained in Chapter 1, these are all considered to be perverse subsidies. The five instances alone constitute 39 percent of all environmental externalities and 22 percent of all perverse subsidies.

To reiterate a pivotal point, many environmental externalities—including what could ultimately prove to be as big as all the rest put together, global warming—are either underestimated or omitted from the final calculation through sheer lack of documentation of the economic costs entailed.

There are further reasons to think that the total estimated for perverse subsidies, $2 trillion per year, is not unduly high. Environmentally damaging subsidies in just one developed country, Britain, were estimated to be on the order of $33 billion per year in the early 1990s, or 2.7 percent of the country's economy.[4] Environmental costs in just one developing country, China, are estimated to be at least $90 billion per year (possibly twice as much), or 8.5 percent of the country's economy.[5] Total costs worldwide in the road transportation sector alone can be roughly estimated at around $2 trillion per year, possibly more,[6] of which environmental externalities could account for $1 trillion.[7]

The size of both subsidies and perverse subsidies means they exert an exceptionally large influence on the world's economies and environment. The conventional subsidies total is comparable to the GNP of France (which has the world's fourth largest economy), while the perverse subsidies total is almost as big as the GNP of Germany (third largest). The Rio Earth Summit proposed an Agenda 21 budget for sustainable development of $600 billion per year. The world's governments said they could not possibly countenance an annual budget of that size—it was considered fiscally irresponsible as well as completely unrealistic for many other potent reasons. Yet there are three times as many funds in perverse subsidies, these being funds that promote unsustainable development.

Perverse subsidies are large in other senses:

- They are almost three times as large as global military spending per year.
- They are larger than the annual sales of the twenty largest corporations.
- They are four times as much as the annual cash incomes of the 1.3 billion poorest people.
- They are five times as much as the international narcotics industry.
- They are half again as large as the global fossil-fuels industry or the global insurance industry.

In individual sectors too, they are large. Perverse subsidies for road transportation, at $780 billion per year, are greater than the GNPs of all but the top seven countries in the world. Perverse subsidies for agriculture, at $510 billion, are almost half again as large as the GNP of Australia. Perverse subsidies for road transportation in the United States alone, at $430 billion, are almost as large as the GNP of India.

> *Perverse subsidies for road transportation, at $780 billion per year, are greater than the GNPs of all but the top seven countries in the world.*

Perverse Subsidies: The Leaders in Absurdity

Despite some progress in phasing out perverse subsidies, many outsize examples persist. The leaders could well include the following:

- German coal is subsidized to the extent of almost $7 billion per year. It would be more economically efficient (and would reduce coal-related pollution such as acid rain and global warming) for the government to close down all the mines and send the workers home on full pay for the rest of their lives.
- The global ocean fisheries catch—well above sustainable yield—is annually worth $105 billion at dockside, where it is sold for some $80 billion, the shortfall being made up with government subsidies. The result is depletion of many major fisheries to the point of commercial extinction, plus bankruptcy of fishing businesses and sizeable unemployment.
- The Australian government has subsidized some of its most environmentally damaging industries to the tune of Austral$5 billion per year, and the environmental consequences of those industries are expected to cost Australian taxpayers at least Austral$6 billion.[8] The taxpayer ends up paying once to damage the environment and then again to restore it.
- The European Union has subsidized excess food production until there have been milk and wine lakes and butter and beef mountains (not to mention manure mountains). Cereal surpluses of 30 million tonnes in a typical recent year would have been enough to provide an Italian-style diet to 75 million people for one year. Taxpayers footed the bill to supply the subsidies that boosted these crops in the first place; then they paid again to store the excess.
- Japan's government has dedicated nine airports in the northern

part of the country to transporting vegetables and flowers to consumers in the main part of the country. To fly onions to Tokyo costs nearly six times as much as to transport them by road. The airports, paid for entirely by taxpayers, were built ostensibly to integrate isolated farming communities into the Japanese agro-economy. More realistically, they have served as a sop to the farming lobby after it made concessions to the Japanese government's negotiations for the Uruguay Round on world trade.

- In the United States, one government agency heavily subsidizes irrigation for crops that another agency pays farmers not to grow. Note the following comment by an economist critic, Paul Hawken: "The government subsidizes energy costs so that farmers can deplete aquifers to grow alfalfa to feed cows that make milk that is stored in warehouses as surplus cheese that does not feed the hungry."[9]

Also in the United States, gasoline is cheaper than bottled water, thanks to subsidies of many sorts. Despite the view of many Americans that gasoline is expensive, it now costs less in real terms than it did sixty years ago. The same applies to many other aspects of U.S. road transportation, thanks to extensive subsidies. Well might it be said that Detroit and the oil companies are on a kind of welfare. The unpaid costs of road transportation amount to $695 billion per year, equivalent to $2,500 per American. Hidden subsidies for oil serve to create an energy policy by default—a policy that is actually the reverse of the government's stated priorities. Oil subsidies prolong the country's risky dependence on foreign supplies, especially from the Persian Gulf. Moreover, this de facto energy policy discourages private investment in new, cleaner technologies such as hyper-cars and other revolutionary forms of energy efficiency.[10]

All in all, a typical American taxpayer is paying at least $2,000 a year to fund subsidies that undercut both the nation's environment and its economy. The taxpayer then has to pay another $1,000 to repair the environmental damage and to cover higher costs for food and other items.

The Crux: Covert Costs of Perverse Subsidies

Perverse subsidies have several features in common:

- Economically, they push up the costs of government, inducing higher taxes and prices for all. In turn, this means that they aggravate budget deficits.

- They divert government funds from better options for fiscal support, notably health and education.
- They undermine market decisions about investment, and they reduce pressure on businesses to become more efficient.
- They tend to benefit the few at the expense of the many and, worse, the rich at the expense of the poor.
- They often serve to pay the polluter.
- They foster many other forms of environmental degradation, which, apart from their intrinsic harm, act as a further drag on economies.

For all these reasons, perverse subsidies militate against sustainable development. They are a no-no both economically and environmentally.

The Double Dividend

If perverse subsidies were to be greatly reduced (with some subsidies left remaining to placate special interests—the political constraint cannot be ignored, however unpalatable it may be), there would be a double dividend:

1. There would be an end to the formidable obstacles imposed by perverse subsidies on sustainable development.
2. There would be a huge stock of funds available to give a new push to sustainable development—funds on a scale unlikely to become available through any other source. In the case of the United States, for instance, they would amount to more than $520 billion. This is nearly twice as much as the Pentagon's budget.

Compare the prospect to a car. Eliminating perverse subsidies would be like, first, taking off the brakes and moving into high gear. Second, it would be like giving the engine and all the other major mechanisms such a streamlining that the car would start to operate with undreamed-of efficiency.

To grasp the scale of the opportunity, consider the prospect for the United States, with more than $520 billion a year available. This sum could go at least halfway toward taking care of the country's great unmet needs: securing greater funding for capital investment and retirement pensions; strengthening education; boosting scientific and technological advances; rebuilding physical infrastructure; providing health care for 30 million uninsured people; reducing the number of citizens, particularly children, in poverty; slowing environmental decline; and tackling endemic problems such as widespread drug abuse, crime, homelessness, and low foreign aid.[11] To meet even half of these needs would rank among the finest advances in the country's history.

Part III

POLICY

Chapter 10

WHAT SHALL WE DO ABOUT IT ALL?

Finally, the most key question of all: how do we get out of the subsidies mess? This book demonstrates that perverse subsidies are abundant and entrenched. Fortunately, there is better news too: we may have reached a propitious time to tackle them. Many governments are espousing the marketplace economy, with its limited scope for government intervention. Many governments also face fiscal problems that give them further incentive to reduce their intrusions into their economies. So the political climate for reform of subsidies is probably better than it has been in decades. The transition economies in particular face an admirable opportunity thanks to their political and economic liberalization. At the same time, the OECD countries have a special responsibility to set the pace for reform in that they account for well over half of all subsidies.[1]

In addition, there is now a solid track record of countries that have greatly reduced or even abolished some of their subsidies. The following examples should serve as a helpful precedent for other countries:

- New Zealand has eliminated virtually all its agricultural subsidies since the mid-1980s, even though—or perhaps because—its economy is more dependent on agriculture than are those of most OECD countries. There are more farmers in New Zealand today than there were when the subsidy phase-out began. Australia is trying to follow suit, and several Latin American countries, notably Chile and Argentina, have also started to slash their subsidies.
- Russia, Eastern Europe, China, and India have slashed their fossil-fuel subsidies since 1991.
- A long list of countries, headed by Germany, Britain, Sweden, and Denmark, are moving to reduce the vast social costs of the car culture.
- The United States, Mexico, Australia, and South Africa are starting to charge consumers the full cost of water.
- The European Union is reducing subsidies for its fishing fleet, despite sizeable bankruptcies and unemployment in that sector.
- Brazil has halted its subsidies for cattle ranching in Amazonia, a prime source of deforestation.[2]

Other examples are of much smaller scale but show what can be accomplished at the local level. Over the next several years, New York City is to spend $240 million on rebates to customers who replace 6-gallons-per-flush toilets with 1.6-gallons-per-flush models. Cutting the municipal water flows will eliminate the need for an $800 million investment in expansion of wastewater treatment plants.[3]

These various efforts to tackle perverse subsidies in several sectors are laudable indeed, even though they account for only a few percentage points of the perverse subsidies total. They demonstrate that there is a policy push to cut subsidies in countries of the OECD, countries in transition, and developing countries of several sorts and conditions. There are numerous other instances. Some are generalized; for example, many countries are slowly (or, in some instances, rapidly) getting rid of their subsidies as governments loosen control of their economies and open up the marketplace.

Big-Picture Strategies

How shall we set about facing the challenge of eliminating perverse subsidies from the body politic? There are various policy openings available.[4] A leading option is to be opportunistic and to seize on emergent "windows," notably the strong political shift toward marketplace economies. The credo of the marketplace stands opposed to subsidies, let alone perverse subsidies, as a form of government intervention that ipso facto must be distortional and counterproductive (this applies especially to the economies in transition and their switch to market liberalism). Resistance to subsidies in general also stems from the privatization ethos, which is becoming widespread. There can even be opportunity in economic crisis, such as the one that spurred New Zealand's move to drop agricultural subsidies: the public economy was finally overburdened to the breaking point. India's subsidies total over 14 percent of GDP, yet the government seeks to bring down its fiscal deficit to under 4 percent of GDP, thus supplying motivation to cut subsidies drastically.

These formidable opportunities are matched by formidable obstacles, especially in the guise of special-interest groups and their political lobbyists. These groups are often so addicted to their "entitlements" that they suffer severe withdrawal pangs at talk of cutting back any subsidies, let alone perverse subsidies. They find allies in bureaucratic roadblocks and institutional inertia. There are obstacles too in upsets to equity concerns, especially with regard to who no longer gets what. Finally, there is uncertainty about how reduction of perverse subsidies, however rational in principle, will work out in nitty-gritty practice; for instance, will businesses find that it means losing a commercial edge to competitors abroad?

Let us look at the first of these obstacles in a little detail. Subsidies create special-interest groups and political lobbies, leaving the subsidies hard to remove long after they have served their original purpose. All major government centers swarm with lobbyists; Washington, D.C., has 14,000 officially registered practitioners plus numerous consultants and lawyers, all adding up to over 40 for each member of Congress.[5] By definition, these lobbyists are bent on advancing narrow sectoral interests rather than the public good. Moreover, they pack sizeable financial muscle. During the period 1993–1999, 126 "dirty energy" companies donated $39 million to U.S. Congress election campaigns to secure a $7.3 billion stream of taxpayer handouts, making for a 187-fold payoff.[6] During the 1996 national election campaign, oil and gas companies donated almost $12 million to congressional candidates to protect tax breaks worth over $3 billion, for a 250-fold payoff.[7] The American Petroleum Institute spends for public relations and other forms of lobbying almost as much as the total budgets of the top five U.S. environmental groups.[8] All in all, lobbying of the U.S. government by corporations, labor unions, and other special-interest groups runs to at least $100 million a month.[9]

Much the same applies elsewhere. British lobbyists spend $110 million a year on pressuring Parliament. In Brussels, there are 10,000 lobbyists working away at the European Commission.

In the face of subsidy support of this scale and leverage, most efforts to cut back on even the most perverse subsidies amount to spectacular failures. In late 1997, during the run-up to the Kyoto conference on climate change, a coalition of fossil-fuel interests in the United States mounted the Global Climate Information Project, a $13 million advertising campaign for a do-nothing agenda. Worse, the U.S. government helps to perpetuate many subsidies. A recent tax-cut package included $140 million worth of increased tax allowances for the timber industry, tax breaks of at least $600 million for the oil and gas industries, and hundreds of millions of dollars in tax breaks for highways. These latter tax reliefs will exact a double price from American taxpayers: once for the tax breaks themselves and then again for the pollution costs.

There are various ways to overcome these obstacles.[10] One is to formulate alternative policies that target the same subsidies goals in a better fashion while also compensating losers. For example, in the case of the German coal miners, the government could use the saved subsidies to train the unemployed miners for different forms of employment. A related measure is to develop an economic policy context that encourages subsidy removal through, for instance, reducing government controls generally and freeing up markets. This is the new economics ethos in the ascendant in many countries preferring capitalism and unfettered enterprise over centrally planned economies. A further though subsidiary measure is to introduce "sunset" provisions that require surviving subsidies to be rejustified periodically, thus avoiding the entrenchment problem. Many subsidies have a shelf life of only a few years, and few are needed after ten years.

All these measures can be strongly reinforced by promoting transparency about perverse subsidies, especially about their economic and environmental impacts and their costs to both taxpayers and consumers. While discussing the issue, we have found that hardly anyone ever thinks about subsidies, let alone perverse subsidies. Such questions simply do not figure into people's everyday agendas—or into their annual agendas, for that matter. But when they learn that thousands of their tax dollars go down a sinkpit of perversity each year, and that they then have to pay out further thousands of dollars to repair the damage, the issue shoots straight to the top of their agendas: "What can we do to fix such absurdity—and what can we do about it right from tomorrow morning?" The first thing they need to do, of course, is a little homework—to learn the what, how, and where of perverse subsidies. They will find it difficult. Most governments do not want to admit that they engage in what amounts to political (as opposed to financial) corruption on a grand scale. But given the leverage of, for instance, the Freedom of Information Act, obfuscation can be made to give way to transparency, whereupon transparency opens up the road to citizen action.

Perhaps the most important way of all to overcome obstacles is to build support constituencies. Subsidy reform in the United States has made unlikely bedfellows of environmentalists, deficit hawks, and neoconservatives, all of whom agree that Americans should not borrow from the future, whether fiscally or environmentally. Equally important are efforts to mobilize public opinion at large. The more citizens know that many of their tax dollars and consumer payments are going down a rat hole of perverse subsidies, the more they will supply grassroots support for reform. These constituencies—with an interest in the public good rather than in sectoral benefits—can engage in informational campaigns to expose the perversity of many subsidies. Governments cannot deal with perverse subsidies without first learning about their nature and scale. Yet information, especially statistical data, is often incomplete and fragmented across agencies, if it exists at all.[11]

The way ahead is demonstrated by the publisher of the authors' original report on which this book is based, the International Institute for Sustainable Development in Winnipeg, Manitoba, Canada. The Institute has set up a Subsidies Watch list server on the Internet on which it posts monthly accounts of subsidies around the world. To subscribe, visit IISDnet at http://iisd.ca/subsidywatch/default.htm, click on "Subsidy Watch Listserv" in the menu at the left, and be regularly surprised at the many absurdities in this arena—and at the efforts of many nongovernmental organizations (NGOs) as well as a few governments to counter powerful special interests. These NGOs do a cracking good job. Why not join them in their campaign?

Note another success story, this time in the United States. Environmental organizations such as Friends of the Earth, the Sierra Club, and The Wilderness Society have made common cause with economic reform groups such as Citizens for Tax Justice, Taxpayers for Common Sense, and the U.S. Public Interest Research Group (U.S. PIRG). The coalition of more than twenty NGOs, highlights perverse subsidies through periodic reports. A recent report[12] fingered forty-seven government projects on which billions of taxpayer dollars are being wasted, worth $39 billion over a five-year period, with items ranging from subsidies supporting overlogging in Tongass National Forest and price supports for cotton to a royalty holiday for deepwater oil drilling and aid to the Three Gorges Dam in China. These organizations' whistle-blowing has done much to mobilize the social consensus and political will to tackle the (expletive deleted) subsidies.

Supplementary Measures

All of the foregoing measures will help us along the road toward sustainable development as the overarching context that should justify all our economic and environmental endeavors. While removal of perverse subsidies could well do more than any other single initiative, it will need to be backed by supplementary measures.

Regulation

However well the free market eventually works, governments will still need to restrict certain activities. The means available include environmental standards and limits to resource exploitation. While we don't want to aim for zero waste (even saints produce garbage), governments should establish certain minimum levels. Freedom of markets does not mean unlicensed liberty to produce anything at all; there is a huge consumer demand for narcotics, but we decide they are a no-no. Governments can also do more to implement the Polluter Pays Principle, a measure whose rationale is obvious and is agreed upon by international writ. The same applies to the Precautionary Principle, which states that lack of conclusive scientific evidence about, say, the toxic effects of a certain material should not be used as an excuse to roar ahead with its production—a stance of "better safe than sorry."

User Charges

Charges for goods and services—whether as concerns energy, transportation, water, or timber—encourages careful use. Freeway tolls, especially at rush hour, induce automobile drivers to think twice before adding to traffic congestion. These charges should be imposed equitably, with luxury items carrying higher prices. Water to supply private swimming pools or to keep golf courses green should be charged at a higher rate than water for essential purposes, such as household needs.

Tradeable Permits

These offer much potential, yet they remain one of the rarest of all policy measures. Outside the United States there is only a relative handful of instances, while inside the United States there are not nearly so many as there might be. The largest and most successful to date are the permits that control sulfur dioxide emissions and, hence, acid rain. The government decides how much pollution shall be allowed in a certain year, then issues "pollution permits" for, say, one-thousandth of the polluting envisaged. Utilities can then purchase permits for an established fee, whereupon an efficient power station can sell its permits to a more polluting power station, thus profiting the good guys and penalizing the bad guys. When once the government has proclaimed the playing field and its basic rules, the trading process sets up a de facto market with all the efficiencies that entails. Come the next year, the amount of permissible pollution is reduced a bit by the government, thus making the permits that much more scarce and enhancing their value—and thus increasing the incentive for individual polluters to cut back on their emissions. Utilities now trade hundreds of thousands of permits among each other each year. The system has not only reduced sulfur dioxide emissions, but it has saved as much as $3 billion a year as compared with what could have been achieved through a command-and-control system with its inherent inflexibilities.

Green Taxes

These are a prime mode for changing people's behavior toward the environment.[13] At present we mostly tax people for their work and tax business for their profits, both of which are the main supports of our economies—so why penalize them? Why not tax them for downside activities such as pollution, waste, and other environmental sins that undercut our economies? Britain, Sweden, Finland, Denmark, the Netherlands, and Spain have begun to shift the tax burden. Sweden's taxes on acid rain have caused emissions to fall by one-third, while Denmark's taxes on waste have reduced the problem by one-fifth.

It is also efficient for consumers to be rewarded for being environmentally virtuous. Belgium has cut sales taxes on energy-saving materials from 22 to 6 percent and has made drivers of gas guzzlers pay $1,500 more in road tax than owners of fuel-efficient cars.[14] Denmark and Norway impose taxes that reduce the size of vehicles bought.[15] Other countries exempt the smallest and most fuel-efficient vehicles from sales tax while imposing higher taxes on models with poorer fuel economy. Tax shifting does not necessarily change the overall level of taxation and thus does not materially alter a country's competitive position in the world market, which means it can be undertaken unilaterally.[16]

Subsidies to Support the Environment

It can be legitimate in certain circumstances to devise subsidies that promote the environmental cause. The U.S. government is spending $2.2 billion between 1996 and 2002 on agri-environmental measures such as soil conservation and wetlands protection. The European Union is engaged in a suite of similar measures, costing $1.7 billion in 1995 alone. The government of Singapore is supplying a $14 billion subsidy over a twenty-year period to promote public transportation and to help reduce the use of private cars; this is a sizeable subsidy for a government with an annual budget of only some $50 billion.[17]

But there are difficulties with environmental subsidies:[18]

- According to some experts, no subsidy can be a good subsidy. Any subsidy is inherently distortional, and even subsidies in support of the environment confuse market choices. Conversely, subsidies can occasionally help the market to work better—for example, by smoothing the way for new energy technologies. But then, it can be tough to choose among several worthy opportunities, and hence it could be best not to subsidize any at all, leaving the choice to the market.
- Once a new subsidy, however well intentioned, is in place, it can prove difficult to remove at a later time when it has exceeded its shelf life.
- New subsidies are unlikely to achieve their goals in the fast-moving, complex situations of today. In particular, new subsidies are likely to contravene international trade rules.

Perverse Subsidies and the Taxpayer: Some Better News

Finally, consider what else could be achieved for the overburdened taxpayer, as illustrated in a graphic analysis by David Roodman.[19] Of global taxes totaling $7.5 trillion each year, 90 percent constitute a burden on work and investment, thus slowing economic growth. If instead governments were to tax, for instance, pollution more fully, they could raise at least $1 trillion a year worldwide, which could then be used to cut wage and profit taxes by as much as 15 percent. Still more to the point, slashing perverse subsidies would allow governments to cut taxes worldwide by 8 percent or more. In the United States, as in Germany and Japan, where taxes average $6,000–$7,000 a person, there could be a tax cut of around $500 per person—and this is based on a lower figure for perverse subsidies than that postulated in this book.

It is this huge payoff from cutting perverse subsidies that would probably most appeal to the citizen taxpayer, by virtue of its scope for super-sized tax cuts. It would help with the biggest obstacle of all, political palatability. To repeat a pivotal point: however irrational perverse subsidies may seem from economic and environmental standpoints, they are supported by powerful special interests—otherwise, they would not persist. These patrons must be dealt with carefully. Special interests, however invalid, are not to be dismissed as an excrescence on the body politic and hence to be eliminated without further ado. They are to be heeded, and their needs—even if more akin to "needs" (i.e., fake needs)—are to be reckoned with (for instance, retraining for workers thrown out of jobs). To cite the president of France, Jacques Chirac, "Politics is not about the art of the possible; it is about making what is necessary possible." To cite another political supremo, onetime mayor of New York Fiorello La Guardia, "A political leader shouldn't be so far ahead of the band that he can't hear the music." One could also say, "Don't take too long a lead off second base." There can be almost an infinity of distance between a prophet and a politician.

These cautions notwithstanding, the authors trust the reader will have found that this book demonstrates how we can turn a profound problem into a glorious opportunity. There is surely more to play for, in both economic and environmental terms, than in any other sphere of public policy. All we have to do is get on with it. Just think: over $2 trillion awaits us out there.

Notes

Preface

1. P. Hawken, "Natural Capitalism," *Mother Jones* (March–April 1997): 40–54.

Chapter 1. Introduction: What Are Subsidies?

1. T. Panayotou, *Green Markets* (San Francisco: Institute for Contemporary Studies Press, 1993); United Nations Commission on Sustainable Development, *Financial Resources and Mechanisms for Sustainable Development: Overview of Current Issues and Development* (New York: United Nations Commission on Sustainable Development, 1994); see also Wuppertal Institute, "Global Guide to the Subsidies Jungle," *Wuppertal Bulletin of Ecological Tax Reform* 3 (2): 1997.
2. World Commission on Environment and Development, *Our Common Future* (New York: Oxford University Press, 1987).
3. A. P. G. de Moor, *Perverse Incentives: Hundreds of Billions of Dollars in Subsidies Now Harm the Economy, the Environment, Equity, and Trade* (San José, Costa Rica: Earth Council, 1997); D. M. Roodman, *The Natural Wealth of Nations: Harnessing the Market for the Environment* (New York: Norton, 1998).
4. For an earlier treatment of this issue, see N. Myers and J. Kent, *Perverse Subsidies: Tax $s Undercutting Our Economies and Environ-*

ments Alike (Winnipeg, Manitoba, Canada: International Institute for Sustainable Development, 1998).

5. S. Barg, "Eliminating Perverse Subsidies: What's the Problem?" in Organisation for Economic Co-operation and Development (OECD), *Subsidies and Environment: Exploring the Linkages* (Paris: OECD, 1996), 23–41; J. Keppler, *Public Goods, Infrastructure, Externalities, and Subsidies* (Paris: Organisation for Economic Co-operation and Development, 1995); J. Elkington, F. van Dijk, and S. Fennell, *Triple Dividends: A Three-D Tour of the Business Case* (London: Sustain-Ability Limited, 2000); D. Koplow, *Federal Energy Subsidies: Energy, Environmental, and Fiscal Impacts* (Washington, D.C.: Alliance to Save Energy, 1993); OECD, *Subsidies and Environment;* R. P. Steenblik, *Previous Multilateral Efforts to Discipline Subsidies to Natural Resource Based Industries* (Paris: Organisation for Economic Co-operation and Development, 1999); G. Porter, "Natural Resource Subsidies and International Policy," *Journal of Environment and Development* 6 (1997): 276–291.

6. M. Toman, *Analyzing the Environmental Impacts of Subsidies: Issues and Research Directions* (Washington, D.C.: Resources for the Future, 1995); see also Organisation for Economic Co-operation and Development (OECD), *Sustainable Agriculture: Concepts, Issues, and Policies in OECD Countries* (Paris: OECD, 1995); C. P. van Beers and A. P. G. de Moor, *Addicted to Subsidies* (The Hague, Netherlands: Institute for Research on Public Expenditure, 1999).

7. P. Dasgupta, *An Inquiry into Well-Being and Destitution* (Oxford: Clarendon Press, 1994).

8. E. Hope and B. Singh, *Energy Price Increases in Developing Countries: Case Studies of Colombia, Ghana, Indonesia, Malaysia, Turkey, and Zimbabwe* (Washington, D.C.: World Bank, 1995).

9. United Nations Development Programme, *Human Development Report, 1997* (New York: Oxford University Press, 1997).

10. J. Bovard, *The Farm Fia$co* (San Francisco: Institute for Contemporary Studies Press, 1996).

11. Barg, "Eliminating Perverse Subsidies."

12. National Institute of Public Finance and Policy, *Government Subsidies in India* (New Delhi: National Institute of Public Finance and Policy, 1997).

13. OECD, *Subsidies and Environment.*

14. R. Estes, *The Tyranny of the Bottom Line: Why Corporations Make Good People Do Bad Things* (San Francisco: Berrett-Koehler, 1996); see also P. Hawken, A. Lovins, and L. H. Lovins, *Natural Capitalism: Creating the Next Industrial Revolution* (Boston: Little, Brown, 1999).

15. C. A. Meyer, M. C. Cruz, R. Repetto, and R. Woodward, *Population Growth, Poverty, and Environmental Stress: Frontier Migration in the Philippines and Costa Rica* (Washington, D.C.: World Resources Institute, 1992).

16. P. Hawken, "Natural Capitalism," *Mother Jones* (March–April 1997): 40–54.

17. C. Cobb, T. Halstead, and J. Rowe, "If the Economy Is Way Up, Why Is America Down?" *Atlantic Monthly* (October 1995): 3–15.

18. C. Cobb, G. S. Goodman, and M. Wackernagel, *Why Bigger Isn't Better: The Genuine Progress Indicator—1999 Update* (San Francisco: Redefining Progress, 1999); A. MacGillivray and S. Zadek, *Accounting for Change* (London: New Economics Foundation, 1996); New Economics Foundation and Friends of the Earth, *More Isn't Always Better: The Quality of Life Briefing* (London: New Economics Foundation and Friends of the Earth, 1997).

19. C. Caccia, *Keeping a Promise: Towards a Sustainable Budget* (Ottawa, Ontario, Canada: Standing Committee on Environment and Sustainable Development, 1996).

Chapter 2. When Do Subsidies Become Perverse?

1. J. MacNeill, *Changing Land Tenure and Sustainable Development* (Ottawa, Ontario, Canada: MacNeill and Associates, 1994).

2. For further treatment of these generic issues, see A. P. G. de Moor, *Perverse Incentives: Hundreds of Billions of Dollars in Subsidies Now Harm the Economy, the Environment, Equity, and Trade* (San José, Costa Rica: Earth Council, 1997); R. J. P. Gale and S. R. Barg, "The Greening of Budgets: The Choice of Governing Instrument," in R. J. P. Gale, S. R. Barg, and A. Gillis, eds., *Green Budget Reform: An International Casebook of Leading Practices* (London: Earthscan, 1995), 1–29; Organisation for Economic Co-operation and Development (OECD), *Subsidies and Environment: Exploring the Linkages* (Paris: OECD, 1996); D. M. Roodman, *Getting the Signals Right: Tax Reform to Protect the Environment and the Economy* (Washington, D.C.: Worldwatch Institute, 1997); D. M. Roodman, *The Natural Wealth of Nations: Harnessing the Market for the Environment* (New York: Norton, 1998); I. Serageldin, "Beating the Water Crisis," *Our Planet* 8, no. 3 (1996): 4–7.

3. D. Koplow, *Energy Subsidies and the Environment* (Cambridge, Mass.: Industrial Economics Inc., 1995).

4. D. Pimentel and M. Pimentel, eds., *Food, Energy, and Society*, rev. ed. (Boulder: University Press of Colorado, 1996).

5. MacNeill, *Changing Land Tenure.*

6. R. Reynolds et al., *Impacts on the Environment of Reduced Agricultural Subsidies: A Case Study of New Zealand* (Wellington: New Zealand Ministry of Agriculture and Fisheries, 1993); A. A. Shepherd, *New Zealand: The Environmental Effects of Removing Agricultural Subsidies* (Paris: Organisation for Economic Co-operation and Development, 1996).

7. J. MacNeill, P. Winsemius, and T. Yakushiji, *Beyond Interdependence:*

The Meshing of the World's Economy and the Earth's Ecology (New York: Oxford University Press, 1997); N. Myers, "The World's Forests and Their Ecosystem Services," in G. C. Daily, ed., *Nature's Services: Societal Dependence on Natural Ecosystems* (Washington, D.C.: Island Press, 1997), 215–235.

8. J. C. Rylander, "Accounting for Nature: A Look at Attempts to Fashion a 'Green GDP,'" *Renewable Resources Journal* (summer 1996): 19–23.

9. Australia Department of the Environment, Sport and Territories, *Subsidies to the Use of Natural Resources* (Canberra: Australia Department of the Environment, Sport and Territories, 1996).

10. D. W. Pearce and G. Atkinson, *Are National Economies Sustainable? Measuring Sustainable Development* (London: University College London, Centre for Social and Economic Research on the Global Environment, 1992).

11. V. Smil and M. Yushi, *The Economic Costs of China's Environmental Degradation* (Boston: American Academy of Arts and Sciences, 1998).

12. MacNeill, *Changing Land Tenure.*

13. D. W. Pearce, *Economic Values and the Natural World* (London: Earthscan, 1993).

14. N. Myers, "The World's Forests: Need for a Policy Appraisal," *Science* 268 (1995): 823–824.

15. D. L. Umali, *Irrigation Induced Salinity* (Washington, D.C.: World Bank, 1993).

16. M. H. Glantz, ed., *Drought Follows the Plow: Cultivating Marginal Areas* (Cambridge, England: Cambridge University Press, 1994).

17. D. Pimentel et al., "Environmental and Economic Costs of Soil Erosion and Conservation Benefits," *Science* 267 (1995): 1117–1122.

18. Pimentel et al., "Environmental and Economic Costs."

19. P. Principe, "Monetizing the Pharmacological Benefits of Plants," in M. J. Balick, W. Elisabetsky, and S. Laird, eds., *Tropical Forest Medical Resources and the Conservation of Biodiversity* (New York: Columbia University Press, 1996), 191–218; see also R. Mendelsohn and M. J. Balick, "The Value of Undiscovered Pharmaceuticals in Tropical Forests," *Economic Botany* 49 (1995): 223–228.

20. Mendelsohn and Balick, "Value of Undiscovered Pharmaceuticals."

21. D. Pearce and S. Puroshothaman, *Protecting Biological Diversity: The Economic Value of Pharmaceutical Plants* (London: University College London, Centre for Social and Economic Research on the Global Environment, 1993).

22. A. Gentry, "Tropical Forest Biodiversity and the Potential for New Medicinal Plants," in A. D. Kinghorn and M. F. Balandrin, eds., *Human Medicinal Agents from Plants* (Washington, D.C.: American Chemical Society, 1993), 13–24.

23. Principe, "Monetizing."

24. D. Pimentel et al., "Economic and Environmental Benefits of Biodiversity," *BioScience* 47 (1997): 747–757.

25. K. Chopra, "The Value of Non-Timber Forest Products: An Estimation for Tropical Deciduous Forests in India," *Economic Botany* 47 (1993): 251–257.

26. T. Panayotou and P. S. Ashton, *Not by Timber Alone: Economics and Ecology for Sustaining Tropical Forests* (Washington, D.C.: Island Press, 1992).

27. K. A. Crews and C. L. Stouffer, *World Population and the Environment* (Washington, D.C.: Population Reference Bureau, 1997).

28. N. Myers, "Tropical Deforestation: Rates and Patterns," in K. Brown and D. W. Pearce, eds., *The Causes of Tropical Deforestation* (London: University College London Press, 1994), 27–40.

29. K. Brown and D. W. Pearce, "The Economic Value of Non-Marketed Benefits of Tropical Forests: Carbon Storage," in J. Weiss, ed., *The Economics of Project Appraisal and the Environment* (London: Edward Elgar, 1994), 102–123.

30. Panayotou and Ashton, *Not by Timber Alone.*

31. S. Postel and S. Carpenter, "Freshwater Ecosystem Services," in G. C. Daily, ed., *Nature's Services: Societal Dependence on Natural Ecosystems* (Washington, D.C.: Island Press, 1997), 195–214.

32. Pimentel et al., "Economic and Environmental Benefits."

33. D. Pimentel, *Handbook of Pest Management in Agriculture,* 2nd ed. (Boca Raton, Fla.: CRC Press, 1991); J. H. Myers, C. Higgins, and E. Kovacs, "How Many Insect Species Are Necessary for the Biological Control of Insects?" *Environmental Entomology* 18 (1989): 541–547.

34. R. L. Naylor and P. R. Ehrlich, "The Value of Natural Pest Control Services in Agriculture," in Daily, *Nature's Services,* 151–174.

35. R. Costanza et al., "The Value of the World's Ecosystem Services and Natural Capital," *Nature* 387 (1997): 253–260.

36. D. Pimentel et al., "Conserving Biological Diversity in Agricultural/ Forestry Systems," *BioScience* 42 (1992): 354–362; see also S. L. Buchmann and G. P. Nabhan, *The Forgotten Pollinators* (Washington, D.C.: Island Press, 1996).

37. Costanza et al., "Value of the World's Ecosystem Services."

38. Pimentel et al., "Economic and Environmental Benefits."

39. Costanza et al., "Value of the World's Ecosystem Services."

40. R. Repetto and J. Lash, "Planetary Roulette: Gambling with the Climate," *Foreign Policy* 108 (1997): 84–98; see also T. E. Downing, "Confidence in Climate Change: Impact Assessment and Economic Evaluation," in H. Audus, ed., *The Assessment of Climate Change Damages,* Report no. IEAGHG/SR6, 81–90 (Cheltenham, England: IEA Greenhouse Gas R&D Programme, 1998); T. E. Downing, A. A. Olsthoorn, and R. S. J. Tol, eds., *Climate Change and Risk* (Andover, England: Routledge, 1998).

41. Downing, Olsthoorn, and Tol, *Climate Change and Risk;* Downing, "Confidence in Climate Change"; S. Fankhauser, *Valuing Climate Change: The Economics of the Greenhouse* (London: Earthscan, 1995); W. D. Nordhaus, *Managing the Global Commons: The Economics of Climate Change* (Cambridge, Mass.: MIT Press, 1994); D. W. Pearce et al., "The Social Costs of Climate Change: Greenhouse Damage and the Benefits of Control," in J. T. Houghton et al., *The Science of Climate Change: The Second Assessment Report of the Intergovernmental Panel on Climate Change,* vol. 3 (Cambridge, England: Cambridge University Press, 1996), 183–189; R. Repetto and D. Austin, *The Costs of Climate Protection: A Guide for the Perplexed* (Washington, D.C.: World Resources Institute, 1997); R. S. J. Tol, "The Damage Costs of Climate Change: Towards More Comprehensive Calculations," *Environmental and Resource Economics* 5 (1995): 353–374.

42. G. C. Daily, P. R. Ehrlich, H. A. Mooney, and A. H. Ehrlich, "Greenhouse Economics: Learn before You Leap," *Ecological Economics* 4 (1991): 1–10; ; G. M. Woodwell and F. T. Mackenzie, eds., *Biotic Feedbacks in the Global Climatic System* (New York: Oxford University Press, 1995).

43. For further recent analysis along these lines, see C. Flavin, "Storm Warnings: Climate Change Hits the Insurance Industry," *World Watch* 7 (1994): 10–20; J. Leggett, *Climate Change and the Financial Sector: The Emerging Threat and the Solar Solution* (Munich: Gerling Akademie Verlag, 1996); M. Tucker, "Climate Change and the Insurance Industry: The Cost of Increased Risk and the Impetus for Action," *Ecological Economics* 22 (1997): 85–96.

44. L. R. Brown et al., *Vital Signs 2000: The Environmental Trends That Are Shaping Our Future* (New York: Norton, 2000); United Nations Environment Programme, *Global Environment Outlook, 2000* (London: Earthscan, 1999).

45. Munich Re, *Weather-Related Natural Disasters, 1998* (Munich: Munich Re, 1998); L. R. Brown et al., *Vital Signs 2000.*

46. Downing, Olsthoorn, and Tol, *Climate Change and Risk;* Downing, "Confidence in Climate Change."

47. Downing, "Confidence in Climate Change."

48. D. Maddison et al., *Blueprint 5: The True Costs of Road Transport* (London: Earthscan, 1996).

49. A. B. Lovins and L. H. Lovins, *Climate: Making Sense and Making Money* (Snowmass, Colo.: Rocky Mountain Institute, 1997); see also P. Hawken, A. Lovins, and L. H. Lovins, *Natural Capitalism: Creating the Next Industrial Revolution* (Boston: Little, Brown, 1999); S. H. Schneider, *Laboratory Earth: The Planetary Gamble We Can't Afford to Lose* (New York: Basic Books, 1997).

50. Lovins and Lovins, *Climate.*

51. Roodman, *Natural Wealth of Nations.*
52. de Moor, *Perverse Incentives.*

Chapter 3. Agriculture

1. This chapter is based primarily on S. S. Batie, *Environmental Benefits Resulting from Agricultural Activities: The Case of Non-European OECD Countries* (East Lansing: Michigan State University, Department of Agricultural Economics, 1996); D. W. Bromley, *The Environmental Implications of Agriculture* (Madison: University of Wisconsin, Department of Agricultural Economics, 1996); A. P. G. de Moor, *Perverse Incentives: Hundreds of Billions of Dollars in Subsidies Now Harm the Economy, the Environment, Equity, and Trade* (San José, Costa Rica: Earth Council, 1997); P. Faeth, *Growing Green: Enhancing the Economic and Environmental Performance of U.S. Agriculture* (Washington, D.C.: World Resources Institute, 1995); G. Gardner, *Shrinking Fields: Cropland Loss in a World of Eight Billion* (Washington, D.C.: Worldwatch Institute, 1996); Organisation for Economic Co-operation and Development (OECD), *Agricultural Policies in OECD Countries: Monitoring and Evaluation, 1999* (Paris: OECD, 1999); D. M. Roodman, *The Natural Wealth of Nations: Harnessing the Market for the Environment* (New York: Norton, 1998); C. F. Runge, "The Environmental Effects of Trade on the Agricultural Sector," in *The Environmental Effects of Trade* (Paris: Organisation for Economic Co-operation and Development, 1994), 19–54; W. N. Thurman, *Assessing the Environmental Impact of Farm Policies* (Washington, D.C.: American Enterprise Institute for Public Policy Research, 1995).
2. OECD, *Agricultural Policies in OECD Countries.*
3. OECD, *Agricultural Policies in OECD Countries;* see also W. Legg, "Agricultural Subsidies and the Environment," in Organisation for Economic Co-operation and Development (OECD), *Subsidies and Environment: Exploring the Linkages* (Paris: OECD, 1996), 117–121.
4. C. Ritson and D. Harvey, eds., *The CAP and the World Economy* (Wallingford, England: CAB International, 1995).
5. Wuppertal Institute, *Road Transport of Goods and the Effects on the Spatial Environment* (Wuppertal, Germany: Wuppertal Institute, 1993).
6. V. Hird and A. Paxton, *The Food Miles Report: The Dangers of Long-Distance Food Transport* (London: SAFE Alliance, 1994).
7. OECD, *Agricultural Policies in OECD Countries.*
8. OECD, *Agricultural Policies in OECD Countries;* see also T. Hepher, *OECD Says Drop in Farm Subsidies May Not Last* (Paris: Organisation for Economic Co-operation and Development, Communications Division, 1997).

9. OECD, *Agricultural Policies in OECD Countries.*
10. Hepher, *OECD Says;* OECD, *Agricultural Policies in OECD Countries;* see also C. Carnel and G. Viatte, "A Fallow Year for Agricultural Reform," *OECD Observer* 182 (1993): 4–6; A. Griffiths and S. Wall, *Applied Economics* (London: Longman, 1993); R. Morgan, *Planet Gauge: The Real Facts of Life* (London: Earthscan, 1994); Roodman, *Natural Wealth of Nations.*
11. Faeth, *Growing Green.*
12. OECD, *Agricultural Policies in OECD Countries.*
13. OECD, *Agricultural Policies in OECD Countries;* see also, and for documentation of other parts of this assessment, Batie, *Environmental Benefits;* Faeth, *Growing Green;* Gardner, *Shrinking Fields;* E. Moos, *Priorities for Agricultural Trade* (Washington, D.C.: U.S. Department of Agriculture, 1996); Rocky Mountain Institute, *Farm Subsidies: Consequences and Alternatives* (Snowmass, Colo.: Rocky Mountain Institute, 1992); C. F. Runge, "Environmental Impacts of Agriculture and Forestry Subsidies," in OECD, *Subsidies and the Environment,* 139–161; D. M. Roodman, *Paying the Piper: Subsidies, Politics, and the Environment* (Washington, D.C.: Worldwatch Institute, 1996); U.S. Department of Agriculture (USDA), *Estimates of Producer and Consumer Subsidy Equivalents: Government Intervention in Agriculture, 1982–1992* (Washington, D.C.: USDA, Economic Research Service, 1994).
14. Cited in A. M. Schlesinger Jr., *The Cycles of American History* (Boston: Houghton Mifflin, 1986); see also Griffiths and Wall, *Applied Economics;* K. Soden, *United States Farm Subsidies* (Snowmass, Colo.: Rocky Mountain Institute, 1988).
15. Faeth, *Growing Green.*
16. Faeth, *Growing Green;* Roodman, *Paying the Piper;* Roodman, *Natural Wealth of Nations.*
17. Faeth, *Growing Green;* Roodman, *Paying the Piper;* Roodman, *Natural Wealth of Nations;* L. Tweeten and C. Zulauf, "Public Policy for Agriculture After Commodity Programs," *Review of Agricultural Economics* 19 (1997): 263–280.
18. E. Gannon, K. A. Cook, and C. Williams, *Faking Takings: Farm Subsidies and Private Property in Perspective* (Washington, D.C.: Environmental Working Group, 1995).
19. R. Paarlberg and D. Orden, "Explaining U.S. Farm Policy in 1996 and Beyond," *American Journal of Agricultural Economics* 78 (1996): 1305–1313; C. Potter, *Against the Grain: Agri-Environmental Reform in the United States and the European Union* (Wallingford, England: CAB International, 1997).
20. K. D. Frederick and P. H. Gleick, *Water and Global Climate Change: Potential Impact on U.S. Water Resources* (Arlington, Va.: Pew Center on Global Climate Change, 1999).
21. B. Bradshaw, *Implications of Reduced Subsidies for Agriculture and*

Agro-Ecosystem Health (Guelph, Ontario, Canada: University of Guelph, Faculty of Environmental Sciences, 1995); P. Faeth et al., *Paying the Farm Bill: U.S. Agricultural Policy and the Transition to Sustainable Agriculture* (Washington, D.C.: World Resources Institute, 1991); W. Legg, "Ecological Agriculture," *OECD Observer*, no. 206 (June 1997): 41–43; R. Steenblik, "When Farmers Fend for the Environment," *OECD Observer* 203 (1997): 16–17; J. Tolman, *Federal Agricultural Policy: A Harvest of Environmental Abuse* (Washington, D.C.: Competitive Enterprise Institute, 1996).

22. D. Pimentel et al., "Environmental and Economic Costs of Soil Erosion and Conservation Benefits," *Science* 267 (1995): 1117–1122.

23. D. H. Meadows, *Home, Home, on the Underpriced, Overgrazed Range* (Hanover, N.H.: Dartmouth College, Department of Environmental Studies, 1995); see also B. D. Gardener, "Some Implications of Federal Grazing, Timber, Irrigation, and Recreation Subsidies," *Choices* 12, no. 3 (1997): 9–14; T. Oppenheimer, "The Rancher Subsidy," *Atlantic Monthly* (January 1996): 26–28, 36–38.

24. For a sound discussion of the equity factor, see Potter, *Against the Grain*.

25. G. Gardner and B. Halweil, *Underfed and Overfed: The Global Epidemic of Malnutrition* (Washington, D.C.: Worldwatch Institute, 2000).

26. Gardner and Halweil, *Underfed and Overfed*; J. Rowe and J. Silverstein, *The GDP Myth: Why "Growth" Isn't Always a Good Thing* (San Francisco: Redefining Progress, 1999).

27. P. Hawken, "Natural Capitalism," *Mother Jones* (March–April 1997): 40–54.

28. OECD, *Agricultural Policies in OECD Countries*; see also C. P. van Beers and A. P. G. de Moor, *Addicted to Subsidies* (The Hague, Netherlands: Institute for Research on Public Expenditure, 1999).

29. S. Gupta, K. Miranda, and I. Parry, "Public Expenditure Policy and the Environment: A Review and Synthesis," *World Development* 23 (1995): 515–528; S. Pagiola et al., "Mainstreaming Biodiversity in Agricultural Development: Toward Good Practice," cited in World Bank, *Expanding the Measure of Wealth: Indicators of Environmentally Sustainable Development* (Washington, D.C.: World Bank, 1997).

30. J. Praveen, "The Short-Run Trade-Off Between Food Subsidies and Agricultural Production Subsidies in Developing Countries," *Journal of Developing Studies* 31 (1994): 265–278; M. Schiff and A. Valdes, *The Plundering of Agriculture in Developing Countries* (Washington, D.C.: World Bank, 1992).

31. P. Kumar, M. Rosegrant, and P. Hazell, *Cereals Prospects in India to 2020: Implications for Policy* (Washington, D.C.: International Food Policy Research Institute, 1995).

32. M. S. Swaminathan, *Sustainable Agriculture: Towards Food Security* (New Delhi: Konark, 1996).

33. J. Staatz, T. Jayne, D. Tschirley, J. Schaffer, J. Dione, J. Oehmke, and M. Weber, "Restructuring Food Systems to Support a Transformation of Agriculture in Sub-Saharan Africa: Experience and Issues," staff paper no. 93-96 (East Lansing: Department of Agricultural Economics, Michigan State University, 1993).

34. A. P. G. de Moor, *Perverse Incentives: Hundreds of Billions of Dollars in Subsidies Now Harm the Economy, the Environment, Equity, and Trade* (San José, Costa Rica: Earth Council, 1997); see also Schiff and Valdes, *Plundering of Agriculture*.

35. B. Dinhem, "Getting Off the Pesticide Treadmill," *Our Planet* 8, no. 4 (1996): 27–28; R. L. Naylor and P. R. Ehrlich, "The Value of Natural Pest Control Services in Agriculture," in G. C. Daily, ed., *Nature's Services: Societal Dependence on Natural Ecosystems* (Washington, D.C.: Island Press, 1997), 151–174; see also G. R. Conway and J. M. Pretty, *Unwelcome Harvest: Agriculture and Pollution* (London: Earthscan, 1991); B. Vorley and D. Keeney, eds., *Bugs in the System: Reinventing the Pesticide Industry for Sustainable Agriculture* (London: Earthscan, 1997).

36. International Institute for Sustainable Development, *Subsidy Watch* 15 (July 2000); see also World Resources Institute, *World Resources Report 1997–1998* (New York: Oxford University Press, 1997).

37. P. R. Ehrlich, A. H. Ehrlich, and G. C. Daily, "Food Security, Population, and Environment," *Population and Development Review* 19, no. 1 (1993): 1–32; D. Pimentel et al., "Impact of Population Growth on Food Supplies and Environment," *Population and Environment* 19 (1997): 9–14; P. Pinstrup-Andersen, *World Food Trends and Future Food Security* (Washington, D.C.: International Food Policy Research Institute, 1994); S. J. Scherr and S. N. Yadav, *Land Degradation in the Developing World: Implications for Food, Agriculture, and the Environment to 2020* (Washington, D.C.: International Food Policy Research Institute, 1996); Swaminathan, *Sustainable Agriculture*.

38. G. Bonnis, "Farmers, Forestry, and the Environment," *OECD Observer* 196 (October–November 1995); J. MacNeill, *Changing Land Tenure and Sustainable Development* (Ottawa, Ontario, Canada: MacNeill and Associates, 1994); L. Maier and R. Steenblik, "Towards Sustainable Agriculture," *OECD Observer* 196 (October–November 1995).

39. L. R. Brown et al., *State of the World, 1993* (New York: Norton, 1993).

40. Pimentel et al., "Environmental and Economic Costs."

41. H. W. Kendall and D. Pimentel, "Constraints on the Expansion of the Global Food Supply," *Ambio* 23, no. 3 (1994): 198–205; L. R. Oldeman, R. T. A. Hakkeling, and W. G. Sombroek, *World Map of the Status of Human-Induced Soil Degradation* (Wageningen, Netherlands: International Soil Reference and Information Centre; Nairobi, Kenya:

United Nations Environment Programme, 1990); World Resources Institute, *World Resources Report, 1998–1999* (New York: Oxford University Press, 1998).

42. Brown et al., *State of the World, 1993;* G. C. Daily, "Restoring Productivity to the World's Degraded Lands," *Science* 269 (1995): 350–354; Pimentel et al., "Environmental and Economic Costs."

43. S. K. Jarnagin and M. A. Smith, *Soil Erosion and Effects on Crop Productivity: Project 2050* (Washington, D.C.: World Resources Institute, 1993); R. Lal and B. A. Stewart, *Soil Degradation* (New York: Springer-Verlag, 1990); see also D. J. Greenland et al., *Soil, Water, and Nutrient Management Research: A New Agenda* (Bangkok: International Board for Soil Research and Management, 1994).

44. Pimentel et al., "Environmental and Economic Costs."

45. V. Smil, "China Shoulders the Cost of Environmental Change," *Environment* 39, no. 6 (1997): 7–9, 33–37; E. van der Voet, R. Kleijn, and U. de Haes, "Nitrogen Pollution in the European Union: Origins and Proposed Solutions," *Environmental Conservation* 23 (1996): 120–132.

46. Smil, "China Shoulders the Cost."

47. A. Dinar, *Policy Reforms for Sustainable Water Resources* (Washington, D.C.: World Bank, 1998).

48. D. Pimentel and A. Grinier, "Environmental and Socio-Economic Costs of Pesticide Use," in D. Pimentel, ed., *Techniques for Reducing Pesticide Use: Economic and Environmental Benefits* (Chichester, England: Wiley, 1997), 51–78; see also Naylor and Ehrlich, "Value of Natural Pest Control Services"; World Resources Institute, *World Resources Report, 1994* (New York: Oxford University Press, 1994).

49. J. Farah, *Pesticide Policies in Developing Countries: Do They Encourage Excessive Use?* (Washington, D.C.: World Bank, 1994); Pimentel, *Techniques for Reducing Pesticide Use;* J. R. Vincent and D. Fairman, *Multilateral Consultations for Promoting Sustainable Development Through Domestic Policy Changes* (Cambridge, Mass.: Harvard Institute for International Development, 1995).

50. Organisation for Economic Co-operation and Development (OECD), *Agricultural Policies, Markets, and Trade: Monitoring and Outlook, 1994* (Paris: OECD, 1994).

51. G. Gardner, "Preserving Agricultural Resources," in L. R. Brown et al., *State of the World 1996* (New York: Norton, 1996), 78–94; Naylor and Ehrlich, "Value of Natural Pest Control Services"; World Health Organization, *Our Planet, Our Health* (Geneva: World Health Organization, 1992).

52. D. Pimentel, *Techniques for Reducing Pesticide Use;* see also Naylor and Ehrlich, "Value of Natural Pest Control Services"; A. Thrupp, *Partnerships for Safe and Sustainable Agriculture* (Washington, D.C.: World Resources Institute, 1996); D. Pimentel et al., "Will Limits of

Earth's Resources Control Human Numbers?" *Environment, Development, and Sustainability* 1 (1999): 19–39.

53. World Health Organization, *Our Planet, Our Health;* see also D. Murray, *Cultivating Crisis: The Human Cost of Pesticides in Latin America* (Austin: University of Texas Press, 1994); National Research Council, *Ecologically Based Pest Management: New Solutions for a New Century* (Washington, D.C.: National Research Council, 1995).

54. Pimentel and Grinier, "Environmental and Socio-Economic Costs"; see also Farah, *Pesticide Policies in Developing Countries;* M. L. Winston, *Nature Wars: People Versus Pests* (Cambridge, Mass.: Harvard University Press, 1997).

55. Pimentel and Grinier, "Environmental and Socio-Economic Costs."

56. W. Legg, "Direct Payments for Farmers?" *OECD Observer* 185 (1993): 26–29.

57. D. W. Pearce, *Blueprint 4: Capturing Global Environmental Values* (London: Earthscan, 1995).

58. See, for example, D. G. Johnson, *World Agriculture in Disarray,* 2nd ed. (London: Macmillan, 1991); Maier and Steenblik, "Towards Sustainable Agriculture"; J. Swinnen and F. A. Van der Zee, "The Political Economy of Agricultural Policies: A Survey," *European Review of Agricultural Economics* 20 (1993): 261–290.

59. K. Watkins, ed., *The Oxfam Poverty Report* (Oxford: Oxfam, 1995).

60. World Resources Institute, *World Resources Report, 1994.*

61. World Resources Institute, *World Resources Report, 1994;* World Bank, *Pollution Control Using Markets* (Washington, D.C.: World Bank, 1995).

62. R. F. Denno and T. J. Perfect, eds., *Plant Hoppers: Their Ecology and Management* (New York: Chapman and Hall, 1994); P. Kenmore, *Indonesia's Integrated Pest Management: A Model for Asia* (Jakarta, Indonesia: Ministry of Agriculture, National IPM Program, 1991); M. Moore, *Redefining Integrated Pest Management: Farmer Empowerment and Pesticide Reduction in the Context of Sustainable Agriculture* (San Francisco: Pesticide Action Network, 1995); L. A. Thrupp, *Institutional and Policy Factors in Pest Management Reforms* (Washington, D.C.: World Resources Institute, 1995); Thrupp, *Partnerships.*

63. United Nations Development Programme, *Human Development Report, 1998* (New York: Oxford University Press, 1998); see also Naylor and Ehrlich, "Value of Natural Pest Control Services."

64. A. Gulati, "Input Subsidies in Indian Agriculture: A Statewise Analysis," *Economic and Political Weekly* (24 June 1989): A57–A65.

65. A. Vaidyanathan, *Second India Series Revisited: Food and Agriculture* (Madras: Madras Institute of Development Studies, for World Resources Institute, Washington D.C., 1993); see also R. Repetto, *The "Second India" Revisited: Population, Poverty, and Environmental Stress over Two Decades* (Washington, D.C.: World Resources Institute, 1994).

66. Gardner, *Shrinking Fields;* for some earlier analysis of reform needs,

see Batie, *Environmental Benefits;* Bradshaw, *Implications of Reduced Subsidies;* Faeth, *Growing Green;* R. Repetto, *Jobs, Competitiveness, and Environmental Regulation: What Are the Real Issues?* (Washington, D.C.: World Resources Institute, 1995); D. A. Sumner, *Agricultural Policy Reform in the United States* (Washington, D.C.: American Enterprise Institute for Public Policy Research, 1995).

67. MacNeill, *Changing Land Tenure;* see also O. Doering, "Federal Policies as Incentives or Disincentives to Ecologically Sustainable Agricultural Systems," *Journal of Sustainable Agriculture* 2 (1992): 21–36; R. E. Just and N. Bockstael, eds., *Commodity and Resource Policies in Agricultural Systems* (New York: Springer-Verlag, 1991); Maier and Steenblik, "Towards Sustainable Agriculture."

68. MacNeill, *Changing Land Tenure.*

69. D. W. Pearce and J. J. Warford, *World Without End: Economics, Environment, and Sustainable Development* (New York: Oxford University Press, 1993); see also E. Lichtenberg and D. Zilberman, "The Welfare Economics of Price Supports in U.S. Agriculture," *American Economic Review* 76 (1986): 1121–1142.

70. L. Maier, "Letting the Land Rest," *OECD Observer* 203 (1997): 12–15.

71. OECD, *Agricultural Policies in OECD Countries;* U.S. Department of Agriculture (USDA), *The 1996 Farm Bill's Conservation Provisions* (Washington, D.C.: USDA, 1996).

72. MacNeill, *Changing Land Tenure;* see also Organisation for Economic Co-operation and Development (OECD), *Sustainable Agriculture: Concepts, Issues, and Policies in OECD Countries* (Paris: OECD, 1995).

73. W. Legg and L. Portugal, "How Agriculture Benefits the Environment," *OECD Observer* 205 (1997): 27–30; K. Parris, "Environmental Indicators for Agriculture," *OECD Observer* 203 (1997): 10–11; Steenblik, "When Farmers Fend for the Environment"; Thrupp, *Partnerships.*

74. Maier and Steenblik, "Towards Sustainable Agriculture"; J. N. Pretty, "Sustainability Works," *Our Planet* 8, no. 4 (1996): 19–22; see also Bradshaw, *Implications of Reduced Subsidies;* Legg, "Ecological Agriculture"; S. Lynch, ed., *Designing Green Support Programs* (Greenbelt, Md.: Henry A. Wallace Institute for Alternative Agriculture, 1994); Repetto, *Jobs, Competitiveness, and Environmental Regulation.*

75. Ritson and Harvey, *CAP and the World Economy.*

76. M. Shah and M. Strong, *Food in the Twenty-First Century: From Science to Sustainable Agriculture* (Washington, D.C.: Consultative Group on International Agricultural Research and World Bank, 1999).

77. R. E. Evanson and M. W. Rosegrant, *Developing Productivity (Non-Price Yield and Area) Projections for Commodity Market Modeling* (Washington, D.C.: International Food Policy Research Institute, 1995); P. Pinstrup-Andersen and R. Pandya-Lorch, *The Future Food and Agricultural Situation in Developing Countries, and the Role of Research and*

Training (Washington, D.C.: International Food Policy Research Institute, 1995).

78. A. F. McCalla, *Agriculture and Food Needs to 2025: Why We Should Be Concerned* (Washington, D.C.: Consultative Group on International Agricultural Research and World Bank, 1994).

Chapter 4. Fossil Fuels and Nuclear Power

1. Union of Concerned Scientists and Tellus Institute, *A Small Price to Pay: U.S. Action to Curb Global Warming Is Possible and Affordable* (Cambridge, Mass.: Union of Concerned Scientists, 1998).
2. P. Hawken, A. Lovins, and L. H. Lovins, *Natural Capitalism: Creating the Next Industrial Revolution* (Boston: Little, Brown, 1999).
3. U.S. Department of Energy, *World Energy Projection* (Washington, D.C.: U.S. Department of Energy, 2000); see also International Energy Agency (IEA), *World Energy Outlook: Looking at Energy Subsidies: Getting the Prices Right* (Paris: IEA, 1999).
4. IEA, *World Energy Outlook*; see also C. Flavin and S. Dunn, *Rising Sun, Gathering Winds: Policies to Stabilize the Climate and Strengthen Economies* (Washington, D.C.: Worldwatch Institute, 1997); R. Gelbspan, *The Heat Is On* (Reading, Mass.: Addison-Wesley, 1997).
5. H. N. Hubbard, "Real Cost of Energy," *Scientific American* 264 (1991): 18–23; D. Koplow, *Energy Subsidies and the Environment* (Cambridge, Mass.: Industrial Economics Inc., 1995); A. B. Lovins, "Negawatts: Twelve Transitions, Eight Improvements, and One Distraction," *Energy Policy* 24.
6. R. Heede, Rocky Mountain Institute, Snowmass, Colo., personal communication (letters of 23 July and 22 August 1997).
7. A. P. G. de Moor, *Perverse Incentives: Hundreds of Billions of Dollars in Subsidies Now Harm the Economy, the Environment, Equity, and Trade* (San José, Costa Rica: Earth Council, 1997); Greenpeace International, *Energy Subsidies in Europe* (Amsterdam: Greenpeace International, 1997).
8. de Moor, *Perverse Incentives*; B. Larsen, *World Fossil Fuel Subsidies and Global Carbon Emissions in a Model with Interfuel Substitution* (Washington, D.C.: World Bank, 1997).
9. Larsen, *World Fossil Fuel Subsidies*; see also IEA, *World Energy Outlook*.
10. World Resources Institute, *World Resources Report, 1998–1999* (New York: Oxford University Press, 1998).
11. World Bank, *World Development Report, 1996* (New York: Oxford University Press, 1996).
12. J. J. Berger, *Charging Ahead: The Business of Renewable Energy and What It Means for America* (New York: Holt, 1997).
13. J. J. MacKenzie, *Climate Protection and the National Interest: The Links Among Climate Change, Air Pollution, and Energy Security* (Washington, D.C.: World Resources Institute, 1997).

14. IEA, *World Energy Outlook;* see also A. Baranzini, J. Goldemberg, and S. Speck, "A Future for Carbon Taxes," *Ecological Economics* 32 (2000): 395–412.

15. de Moor, *Perverse Incentives;* D. Koplow, "Energy Subsidies and the Environment," in Organisation for Economic Co-operation and Development (OECD), *Subsidies and Environment: Exploring the Linkages* (Paris: OECD, 1996), 201–218; Lovins, "Negawatts"; see also D. Koplow and A. Martin, *Fueling Global Warming: Federal Subsidies to Oil in the Untied States* (Washington, D.C.: Greenpeace, 1998); R. J. Shapiro and C. J. Soares, *Cut and Invest to Grow: How to Expand Public Investment While Cutting the Deficit* (Washington, D.C.: Progressive Policy Institute, 1997).

16. de Moor, *Perverse Incentives;* R. Hill, P. O'Keefe, and C. Snape, *The Future of Energy Use* (London: Earthscan, 1995); Koplow, "Energy Subsidies and the Environment"; see also M. A. Shelby et al., *The Climate Implications of Eliminating U.S. Energy and Related Subsidies* (Paris: Organisation for Economic Co-operation and Development, 1994).

17. Greenpeace International, *Energy Subsidies in Europe;* T. B. Johansson et al., *Renewable Energy: Sources for Fuels and Electricity* (Washington, D.C.: Island Press, 1992); Koplow, *Energy Subsidies and the Environment;* Lovins, "Negawatts."

18. de Moor, *Perverse Incentives;* International Energy Agency (IEA), *Energy Policies of IEA Countries, 1994 Review* (Paris: Organisation for Economic Co-operation and Development, 1995); Organisation for Economic Co-operation and Development (OECD), *Reforming Energy and Transport Subsidies: Environmental and Economic Implications* (Paris: OECD, 1997).

19. Greenpeace International, *Energy Subsidies in Europe.*

20. B. Larsen and A. Shah, *Global Climate Change, Economic Policy Instruments, and Developing Countries* (Washington, D.C.: World Bank, 1994).

21. G. K. Ingram and M. Fay, *Valuing Infrastructure Stocks and Gains from Improved Performance* (Washington, D.C.: World Bank, 1994); Larsen and Shah, *Global Climate Change.*

22. World Bank, *Expanding the Measure of Wealth: Indicators of Environmentally Sustainable Development* (Washington, D.C.: World Bank, 1997).

23. E. Gurvich and G. Hughes, *The Environmental Impact of Energy Subsidies: A Case Study of Russia* (Washington, D.C.: World Bank, Pollution Management and Environmental Economics Division, 1996); IEA, *World Energy Outlook;* World Bank, *Expanding the Measure of Wealth;* A. S. Rajkumar, *Energy Subsidies* (Washington, D.C.: World Bank, 1996).

24. IEA, *World Energy Outlook.*

25. World Bank, *Expanding the Measure of Wealth;* see also E. Gurvich et al., "Impacts of Russian Energy Subsidies on Greenhouse Gas Emissions," in OECD, *Reforming Energy and Transport Subsidies;* Rajkumar, *Energy Subsidies.*

26. IEA, *World Energy Outlook.*

27. IEA, *World Energy Outlook;* see also Gurvich et al., "Impacts of Russian Energy Subsidies"; C. P. McPherson, "Policy Reform in Russia's Oil Sector," *Finance and Development* 33, no. 2 (1996): 6–9.

28. IEA, *World Energy Outlook;* World Bank, *Expanding the Measure of Wealth.*

29. Gurvich et al., "Impacts of Russian Energy Subsidies"; see also de Moor, *Perverse Incentives;* D. M. Roodman, *The Natural Wealth of Nations: Harnessing the Market for the Environment* (New York: Norton, 1998).

30. IEA, *World Energy Outlook.*

31. McPherson, "Policy Reform"; Rajkumar, *Energy Subsidies;* Roodman, *Natural Wealth of Nations;* World Bank, *Expanding the Measure of Wealth.*

32. IEA, *World Energy Outlook;* X. Wang, *China's Coal Sector: Moving to a Market Economy* (Washington, D.C.: World Bank, 1996).

33. Flavin and Dunn, *Rising Sun, Gathering Winds;* H. Kane, "Shifting to Sustainable Industries," in L. R. Brown et al., *State of the World, 1996* (New York: Norton, 1996), 152–167.

34. World Resources Institute, *World Resources Report, 1998–1999.*

35. IEA, *World Energy Outlook;* see also McPherson, "Policy Reform"; Rajkumar, *Energy Subsidies;* World Bank, *Expanding the Measure of Wealth.*

36. M. R. Auer and X. Ye, "Reevaluating Energy Efficiency in China," *Environmentalist* 17 (1997): 21–25.

37. World Bank, *Expanding the Measure of Wealth.*

38. IEA, *Energy Policies of IEA Countries;* World Resources Institute, *World Resources Report, 1994* (New York: Oxford University Press, 1994).

39. IEA, *World Energy Outlook;* see also S. Dunn, "King Coal's Weakening Grip on Power," *World Watch* 12, no. 5 (1999): 10–19.

40. IEA, *World Energy Outlook.*

41. Auer and Ye, "Reevaluating Energy Efficiency in China."

42. IEA, *World Energy Outlook;* see also World Resources Institute, *World Resources Report, 1996* (New York: Oxford University Press, 1996).

43. R. Repetto and D. Austin, *The Costs of Climate Protection: A Guide for the Perplexed* (Washington, D.C.: World Resources Institute, 1997); see also Flavin and Dunn, *Rising Sun, Gathering Winds;* World Bank, *Expanding the Measure of Wealth.*

44. IEA, *World Energy Outlook.*

45. IEA, *World Energy Outlook;* see also S. C. Bhattacharyya, "Estimation of Subsidies on Coal in India," *Natural Resources Forum* 19 (1995): 135–142; Rajkumar, *Energy Subsidies.*

46. IEA, *World Energy Outlook.*

47. Larsen and Shah, *Global Climate Change;* de Moor, *Perverse Incentives.*

48. World Bank, *Expanding the Measure of Wealth*; see also Rajkumar, *Energy Subsidies*.
49. World Bank, *Expanding the Measure of Wealth*; see also Flavin and Dunn, *Rising Sun, Gathering Winds*; IEA, *World Energy Outlook*; Rajkumar, *Energy Subsidies*; Roodman, *Natural Wealth of Nations*.
50. IEA, *World Energy Outlook*; World Bank, *Expanding the Measure of Wealth*; Rajkumar, *Energy Subsidies*.
51. Ingram and Fay, *Valuing Infrastructure Stocks*.
52. IEA, *World Energy Outlook*; World Bank, *Expanding the Measure of Wealth*.
53. M. Lennsen and C. Flavin, "Meltdown," *World Watch* 9, no. 3 (1996): 23–31.
54. A. B. Lovins and L. H. Lovins, *Climate: Making Sense and Making Money* (Snowmass, Colo.: Rocky Mountain Institute, 1997); N. Myers, *The Management and Repercussions of Nuclear Power*, Ditchley Foundation Conference Report no. D99/15 (Enstone, England: Ditchley Foundation, 2000).
55. World Resources Institute, *World Resources Report, 1996*; for slightly different figures, see U.S. Department of Energy, Energy Information Administration (EIA), *Annual Energy Review, 1996* (Washington, D.C.: EIA, 1997).
56. de Moor, *Perverse Incentives*.
57. de Moor, *Perverse Incentives*; Myers, *Management and Repercussions of Nuclear Power*.
58. Lovins and Lovins, *Climate*.
59. Larsen and Shah, *Global Climate Change*; see also T. Panayotou, "Win-Win Finance," *Our Planet* 9, no. 1 (1997): 15–18.
60. N. Kunzli, R. Kaiser, S. Medina, G. Studnicka, G. Oberfield, and F. Horack, *Air Pollution Attributable Cases: Health Costs Due to Road Traffic Related Air Pollution* (Geneva: World Health Organization, 1999).
61. Environmental Protection Agency, *The Benefits and Costs of the Clean Air Act, 1970–1990* (Washington, D.C.: Environmental Protection Agency, 1997).
62. ECOTEC, *An Evaluation of the Benefits of Reduced Sulphur Dioxide Emissions* (London: Department of the Environment, Transport and the Regions, 1994).
63. S. Nilsson, "Air Pollution and European Forests," in J. Rose, ed., *Acid Rain: Current Situation and Remedies* (Amsterdam: Gordon and Breach, 1994); United Nations Development Programme, *Human Development Report, 1997* (New York: Oxford University Press, 1997).
64. Editing Board of China Environmental Yearbook (EBCEY), *China Environmental Yearbook* (Beijing: EBCEY, 1997); see also Dunn, "King Coal's Weakening Grip"; World Resources Institute, *How Much Sustainable Development Can We Expect from the Clean*

Development Mechanism? (Washington, D.C.: World Resources Institute, 1999).

65. H. Rodhe, J. Galloway, and D. Zhao, "Acidification in South-East Asia: Prospects for the Coming Decades," *Ambio* 21 (1992): 148–150.

66. United Nations Development Programme, *Human Development Report, 1998* (New York: Oxford University Press, 1998).

67. C. Pope et al., "Particulate Air Pollution as Predictor of Mortality in a Prospective Study of U.S. Adults," *American Journal of Respiratory and Critical Care Medicine* 151 (1995): 669–674.

68. D. S. Shprentz, G. C. Bryner, and J. S. Shprentz, *Breath Taking: Premature Mortality Due to Particle Air Pollution in 239 American Cities* (New York: Natural Resources Defense Council, 1996).

69. R. Wilson and J. Spengler, "Conclusion: Policy Implications: National Dilemma," in R. Wilson and J. Spengler, eds., *Particles in Our Air: Concentrations and Health Effects* (Cambridge, Mass.: Harvard University Press, 1996), 205–216.

70. M. Brower and W. Leon, *The Consumer's Guide to Effective Environmental Choices* (New York: Three Rivers Press, 1999); World Health Organization, *Health and Environment in Sustainable Development: Five Years After the Earth Summit* (Geneva: World Health Organization, 1997).

71. World Resources Institute, *World Resources Report, 1998–1999.*

72. Working Group on Public Health and Fossil-Fuel Combustion, "Short-Term Improvements in Public Health from Global-Climate Policies on Fossil-Fuel Combustion: An Interim Report," *Lancet* (8 November 1997): 350, 1341–1349; see also B. Ostro, *A Methodology for Estimating Air Pollution Health Effects* (Geneva: World Health Organization, 1996); Wilson and Spengler, "Conclusion: Policy Implications."

73. World Bank, *Expanding the Measure of Wealth;* OECD, *Reforming Energy and Transport Subsidies;* see also Working Group on Public Health and Fossil-Fuel Combustion, "Short-Term Improvements in Public Health."

74. J. T. Houghton et al., eds., *The Science of Climate Change: The Second Assessment Report of the Intergovernmental Panel on Climate Change* (New York: Cambridge University Press, 1996).

75. D. Koplow, *Federal Energy Subsidies: Energy, Environmental, and Fiscal Impacts* (Washington, D.C.: Alliance to Save Energy, 1993); D. Koplow and A. Martin, *Federal and Alaskan Subsidies to Oil Exploration, Development, and Transport* (Cambridge, Mass.: Industrial Economics Inc., 1997); Koplow and Martin, *Fueling Global Warming;* see also R. P. Steenblik and P. Coroyannakis, "Reform of Coal Policies in Western and Central Europe: Implication for the Environment," *Energy Policy* 1995: 537–553.

76. de Moor, *Perverse Incentives;* OECD, *Reforming Energy and Transport Subsidies.*

77. de Moor, *Perverse Incentives;* World Bank, *Expanding the Measure of Wealth;* Rajkumar, *Energy Subsidies.*
78. J. Bruce, H. E. Lee, and E. F. Haites, eds., *Climate Change, 1995: Economics and Social Dimensions of Climate Change* (Cambridge, England: Cambridge University Press, 1996); Heede, personal communication.
79. IEA, *World Energy Outlook;* OECD, *Reforming Energy and Transport Subsidies.*
80. Koplow, *Energy Subsidies and the Environment;* see also E. Ruijgrok and F. Oosterhuis, *Energy Subsidies in Western Europe* (Amsterdam: Free University of Amsterdam, Institute for Environmental Studies, for Greenpeace International, Amsterdam, 1997); Steenblik and Coroyannakis, "Reform of Coal Policies."
81. J. S. Gitlitz, *The Relationship Between Primary Aluminum Production and the Damming of World Rivers* (Berkeley, Calif.: International Rivers Network, 1993), cited in Koplow, "Energy Subsidies and the Environment."
82. Koplow, *Federal Energy Subsidies;* Koplow, *Energy Subsidies and the Environment.*
83. R. Heede, R. Morgan, and S. Ridley, *The Hidden Costs of Energy: How Taxpayers Subsidize Energy Development* (Washington, D.C.: Center for Renewable Resources, 1985).
84. Gelbspan, *The Heat Is On.*
85. OECD, *Reforming Energy and Transport Subsidies.*
86. R. Repetto and D. Austin, *The Costs of Climate Protection;* see also Berger, *Charging Ahead.*
87. Greenpeace International, *Energy Subsidies in Europe.*
88. Ruijgrok and Oosterhuis, *Energy Subsidies in Western Europe;* see also Steenblik and Coroyannakis, "Reform of Coal Policies."
89. Repetto and Austin, *The Costs of Climate Protection;* see also M. Grubb, T. Chapuis, and M. Ha Duong, "The Economics of Changing Course: Implications of Adaptability and Inertia for Optimal Climate Policy," *Energy Policy* 23 (1995): 417–432.
90. OECD, *Reforming Energy and Transport Subsidies;* see also M. Shelby et al., *The Climate Change Implications of Eliminating U.S. Energy and Related Subsidies* (Washington, D.C.: Environmental Protection Agency, 1995).
91. Larsen, *World Fossil Fuel Subsidies;* see also Dale W. Jorgenson Associates, *The Elimination of Federal Energy Subsidies: Environmental Gains, Tax Considerations, and Economic Consequences* (Paris: Organisation for Economic Co-operation and Development, 1994).
92. Repetto and Austin, *Costs of Climate Protection.*
93. World Bank, *Monitoring Environmental Progress* (Washington, D.C.: World Bank, 1995); see also B. Larsen and A. Shah, *World Fossil Fuel Subsidies and Global Carbon Emissions* (Washington, D.C.: World Bank, 1992); Shelby et al., *Climate Change Implications.*

94. IEA, *World Energy Outlook.*
95. T. R. Casten, *Turning Off the Heat: Why America Must Double Energy Efficiency to Save Money and Reduce Global Warming* (Washington, D.C.: American Council for an Energy Efficient Economy, 1998); H. Geller and R. N. Elliott, *Industrial Energy Efficiency: Trends, Savings Potential, and Policy Options* (Washington, D.C.: American Council for an Energy-Efficient Economy, 1994); Flavin and Dunn, *Rising Sun, Gathering Winds* (Washington, D.C.: Worldwatch Institute, 1997); D. M. Roodman, *The Natural Wealth of Nations: Harnessing the Market for the Environment* (New York: Norton, 1998).
96. World Energy Council, *New Renewable Energy Resources: A Guide to the Future* (London: Kogan Page, 1994); Lovins, "Negawatts"; E. U. von Weizsacker, A. B. Lovins, and L. H. Lovins, *Factor Four: Doubling Wealth, Halving Resource Use* (London: Earthscan, 1997).
97. Roodman, *Natural Wealth of Nations.*
98. Flavin and Dunn, *Rising Sun, Gathering Winds*; Greenpeace, *The Debate with Industry: The Subsidy Scandal* (Washington, D.C.: Greenpeace, 1997).
99. Hawken, Lovins, and Lovins, *Natural Capitalism.*
100. C. Flavin and S. Dunn, "Responding to the Threat of Climate Change," in L. R. Brown et al., *State of the World, 1998* (New York: Norton, 1998).
101. European Environment Agency, *Europe's Environment: The Second Assessment* (Denmark: European Environment Agency, 1999).
102. Flavin and Dunn, "Responding to the Threat of Climate Change"; Hawken, Lovins, and Lovins, *Natural Capitalism.*
103. Koplow, *Energy Subsidies and the Environment.*
104. Berger, *Charging Ahead.*
105. Wang, *China's Coal Sector.*
106. World Bank, *World Development Report 1994* (Washington, D.C.: World Bank, 1994).
107. D. Wysham, *The World Bank and the G-7: Changing the Earth's Climate for Business* (Washington, D.C.: Institute for Policy Studies, 1997).
108. Gelbspan, *The Heat Is On.*
109. Koplow, "Energy Subsidies and the Environment."
110. World Energy Council, *New Renewable Energy Resources;* see also Berger, *Charging Ahead.*
111. D. M. Roodman and N. Lenssen, *A Building Revolution: How Ecology and Health Concerns Are Transforming Construction* (Washington, D.C.: Worldwatch Institute, 1995).
112. U.S. Department of Energy, Energy Information Administration (EIA), *Annual Energy Review, 1995* (Washington, D.C.: EIA, 1996).
113. Lovins and Lovins, *Climate;* von Weizsacker, Lovins, and Lovins, *Factor Four.*

114. P. Hawken, "Natural Capitalism," *Mother Jones* (March–April 1997): 40–54.

115. Panayotou, "Win-Win Finance."

116. A. Gadgil, A. H. Rosenfeld, and L. Price, *Making the Market Right for Environmentally Sound Energy-Efficient Technology: U.S. Buildings Sector Successes That Must Work in Developing Countries and Eastern Europe,* proceedings of International Symposium on Environmentally Sound Energy Technologies and Their Transfer to Developing Countries and European Economies in Transition, Milan, 21–25 October 1991, cited in Roodman and Lenssen, *A Building Revolution.*

117. Panayotou, "Win-Win Finance."

118. Gadgil, Rosenfeld, and Price, *Making the Market Right.*

119. IEA, *World Energy Outlook;* see also Roodman, *Natural Wealth of Nations.*

120. IEA, *World Energy Outlook;* Keppler, *Public Goods.*

121. Rajkumar, *Energy Subsidies.*

Chapter 5. Road Transportation

1. R. Arnott and K. Small, "The Economics of Traffic Congestion," *American Scientist* 82 (1994): 446–455; see also R. L. Paarlberg, "Caring for the Future: Minimizing Change or Maximizing Choice," in N. R. Goodwin, ed., *As If the Future Mattered* (Ann Arbor: University of Michigan Press, 1996), 186–207.

2. K. J. Button and E. T. Verhoef, eds., *Road Pricing, Traffic Congestion, and the Environment: Issues of Efficiency and Social Feasibility* (Northhampton, Mass.: Edward Elgar, 1998); P. Samwell, "Traffic Congestion: A Solvable Problem," *Issues in Science and Technology* (spring 1999): 30–33.

3. American Automobile Manufacturers Association, *World Motor Vehicle Data, 1998* (Detroit: American Automobile Manufacturers Association, 1998).

4. T. Jones and J. Short, "The Economics of Transport Costs," *OECD Observer* 188 (1994): 11–14; see also Organisation for Economic Co-operation and Development (OECD), *The Economic Costs of Reducing Carbon Dioxide Emissions* (Paris: OECD, 1992).

5. Jones and Short, "Economics of Transport Costs."

6. Organisation for Economic Co-operation and Development (OECD), *Reforming Energy and Transport Subsidies: Environmental and Economic Implications* (Paris: OECD, 1997); National Research Council, *Toward a Sustainable Future: Addressing the Long-Term Effects of Motor Vehicle Transportation on Climate and Ecology* (Washington, D.C.: National Academy Press, 1997).

7. This review is primarily based on M. A. Delucchi, *The Annualized Social Cost of Motor-Vehicle Use in the U.S., 1990–1991: Summary of*

Theory, Data, Methods, and Results (Davis: University of California, Institute of Transportation Studies, 1997); A. P. G. de Moor, *Perverse Incentives: Hundreds of Billions of Dollars in Subsidies Now Harm the Economy, the Environment, Equity, and Trade* (San José, Costa Rica: Earth Council, 1997); H. N. Hubbard, "Real Cost of Energy," *Scientific American* 264 (1991): 18–23; D. Koplow, *Energy Subsidies and the Environment* (Cambridge, Mass.: Industrial Economics Inc., 1995); T. Litman, *Transportation Cost Analysis: Techniques, Estimates, and Implications* (Victoria, British Columbia, Canada: Victoria Transport Policy Institute, 1999); S. Nadis and J. J. MacKenzie, *Car Trouble* (Washington, D.C.: World Resources Institute, 1993); OECD, *Reforming Energy and Transport Subsidies;* D. M. Roodman, *Paying the Piper: Subsidies, Politics, and the Environment* (Washington, D.C.: Worldwatch Institute, 1996); O. Tunali, "A Billion Cars: The Road Ahead," *World Watch* 9, no. 1 (1996): 24–33.

8. U.S. Department of Transportation, *National Transportation Statistics, 1999* (see also *Transportation Statistics Annual Report, 1999*) (Washington, D.C.: U.S. Department of Transportation, Bureau of Transportation Statistics, 1999).

9. Nadis and MacKenzie, *Car Trouble;* U.S. Department of Transportation, *National Transportation Statistics, 1999.*

10. U.S. Department of Transportation, *National Transportation Statistics, 1999.*

11. W. W. Gibbs, "Transportation's Perennial Problems," *Scientific American* 277, no. 4 (1997): 32–35.

12. L. J. Schipper, "Carbon Emissions from Travel in the OECD Countries," in P. C. Stern et al., eds., *Environmentally Significant Consumption* (Washington, D.C.: National Academy Press, 1997), 50–61.

13. U.S. Department of Transportation, *National Transportation Statistics, 1999.*

14. U.S. Department of Transportation, *National Transportation Statistics, 1999;* Zhou Fengqi, *Energy Consumption and Sustainable Development in China* (Beijing: State Planning Commission, Energy Research Institute, Office of the Director-General, 1997).

15. These introductory paragraphs, together with the summary review that follows, derive from Delucchi, *Annualized Social Cost of Motor-Vehicle Use;* D. L. Greene, *Evaluating Energy Subsidies in Transportation: Lessons from Full Social Cost Accounting* (Oak Ridge, Tenn.: Oak Ridge National Laboratory, 1995); S. Haltmaier, "Transport Subsidies: U.S. Case Study," in OECD, *Reforming Energy and Transport Subsidies;* B. Ketcham and C. Komanoff, *Win-Win Transportation: A No-Losers Approach to Financing Transport in New York City and the Region* (Brooklyn: Konheim and Ketcham, 1993); Koplow, *Energy Subsidies and the Environment;* T. Litman, *Reinventing Transportation: Exploring the Paradigm Shift Needed to Reconcile Transportation and Sustainability Objectives* (Victoria, British Colum-

bia, Canada: Victoria Transport Policy Institute, 1999); Nadis and MacKenzie, *Car Trouble;* R. Priddle, *The Meaning of Kyoto* (Paris: International Energy Agency, 1998); M. Shelby et al., *The Climate Change Implications of Eliminating U.S. Energy and Related Subsidies* (Washington, D.C.: Environmental Protection Agency, 1995).

16. C. Morey, *Pollution Line Up: An Environmental Ranking of Automakers* (Cambridge, Mass.: Union of Concerned Scientists, 1999); OECD, *Reforming Energy and Transport Subsidies.*

17. International Center for Technology Assessment, *The Real Price of Gas* (Washington, D.C.: International Center for Technology Assessment, 1998); D. Koplow and A. Martin, *Federal and Alaskan Subsidies to Oil Exploration, Development, and Transport* (Cambridge, Mass.: Industrial Economics Inc., 1997); D. Koplow and A. Martin, *Fueling Global Warming: Federal Subsidies to Oil in the United States* (Washington, D.C.: Greenpeace, 1998); D. Lee, *Full Cost Pricing of Highways* (Cambridge, Mass.: National Transportation Systems Center, 1995).

18. R. Hwang, *Money Down the Pipeline: Uncovering the Hidden Subsidies to the Oil Industry* (Cambridge, Mass.: Union of Concerned Scientists, 1995).

19. Nadis and MacKenzie, *Car Trouble;* Data Resources Inc., *Transportation Sector Subsidies: U.S. Case Study Results* (Paris: Organisation for Economic Co-operation and Development, 1993); D. M. Roodman, *Paying the Piper: Subsidies, Politics, and the Environment* (Washington, D.C.: Worldwatch Institute, 1996).

20. Roodman, *Paying the Piper;* see also C. W. Cobb, *The Roads Aren't Free: Estimating the Full Social Cost of Driving and the Effects of Accurate Pricing* (San Francisco: Redefining Progress, 1998).

21. Lee, *Full Cost Pricing of Highways;* Litman, *Transportation Cost Analysis.*

22. D. C. Shoup, "Cashing Out Employer-Paid Parking: A Precedent for Congestion Pricing," in *Curbing Gridlock: Peak-Period Fees to Relieve Traffic Congestion* (Washington, D.C.: National Research Council, Transportation Research Board, 1994).

23. See D. M. Roodman, *The Natural Wealth of Nations: Harnessing the Market for the Environment* (New York: Norton, 1998).

24. Roodman, *Natural Wealth of Nations;* see also OECD, *Reforming Energy and Transport Subsidies;* DRI/McGraw-Hill, *Transportation Sector Subsidies: U.S. Case Study* (Washington, D.C.: Environmental Protection Agency, Office of Policy, Planning, and Evaluation, 1994); Shelby et al., *Climate Change Implications.*

25. Lee, *Full Cost Pricing of Highways.*

26. Ketcham and Komanoff, *Win-Win Transportation.*

27. Cobb, *Roads Aren't Free.*

28. Delucchi, *Annualized Social Cost of Motor-Vehicle Use.*

29. Arnott and Small, "Economics of Traffic Congestion"; see also Paarl-berg, "Caring for the Future."

30. P. R. Krugman, "The Tax Reform Obsession," *New York Times Magazine* (7 April 1996): 2–3.

31. R. Repetto et al., *Green Fees: How a Tax Shift Can Work for the Environment and the Economy* (Washington, D.C.: World Resources Institute, 1992).

32. D. Shrank and T. Lomax, *Mobility Study: 1982 to 1996* (College Station: Texas Transportation Institute, 1998); see also Litman, *Transportation Cost Analysis*.

33. Delucchi, *Annualized Social Cost of Motor-Vehicle Use.*

34. J. MacKenzie, R. Dower, and D. Chen, *The Going Rate* (Washington, D.C.: World Resources Institute, 1992).

35. Sierra Club, *Sprawl Costs Us All: How Your Taxes Fuel Suburban Sprawl* (Washington, D.C.: Sierra Club, 2000); Texas Transportation Institute, *Urban Roadway Congestion Annual Report, 1998* (College Station: Texas Transportation Institute, 1998); U.S. Department of Transportation, *National Transportation Statistics, 1999.*

36. International Energy Agency (IEA), *Cars and Climate Change* (Paris: IEA, 1993).

37. Roodman, *Natural Wealth of Nations.*

38. Gibbs, "Transportation's Perennial Problems."

39. G. Miller (chairman of committee), *Taking from the Taxpayer: Public Subsidies for Natural Resource Development* (Washington, D.C.: U.S. House of Representatives, Committee on Natural Resources, 1994); see also T. Miller, *The Costs of Highway Crashes* (Washington, D.C.: Federal Highway Administration, 1994); Nadis and MacKenzie, *Car Trouble.*

40. R. Elvik, "The External Costs of Traffic Injury: Definition, Estimation, and Possibilities for Internalization," *Accident Analysis and Prevention* 26 (1995): 719–732.

41. L. Blincoe, *Economic Cost of Motor Vehicle Crashes, 1994* (Washington, D.C.: National Highway Traffic Safety Administration, 1995); see also National Highway Institute, *Estimating the Impacts of Urban Transportation Alternatives*, Report no. FHWA-HI-94-053 (Washington, D.C.: Federal Highway Administration, 1995).

42. MacKenzie, Dower, and Chen, *Going Rate.*

43. MacKenzie, Dower, and Chen, *Going Rate.*

44. Litman, *Transportation Cost Analysis.*

45. L. R. Brown, *OPEC Has the World over a Barrel Again* (Washington, D.C.: Worldwatch Institute, 2000); B. Wallace, "The Multidimensional Nature of Population/Environmental Problems," *Politics and the Life Sciences* 16 (1997): 224–226.

46. U.S. Department of Energy, Energy Information Administration (EIA), *Annual Energy Review, 1995* (Washington, D.C.: EIA, 1996).

47. P. Hawken, "Natural Capitalism," *Mother Jones* (March–April 1997): 40–54.
48. Hwang, *Money Down the Pipeline.*
49. A. Cavallo, "Security of Supply: A Major Neglected Fossil Fuel Subsidy," *Wind Engineering* 20 (1996): 47–52.
50. Koplow and Martin, *Federal and Alaskan Subsidies to Oil;* Koplow and Martin, *Fueling Global Warming.*
51. Hwang, *Money Down the Pipeline;* see also Koplow and Martin, *Federal and Alaskan Subsidies to Oil;* Koplow and Martin, *Fueling Global Warming;* Nadis and MacKenzie, *Car Trouble.*
52. Nadis and MacKenzie, *Car Trouble.*
53. R. Heede, personal communication, 21 January 1998 (Snowmass, Colo.: Rocky Mountain Institute, 1998); National Research Council (Transportation Research Board), *Toward a Sustainable Future Addressing the Long-Term Effects of Motor Vehicle Transportation on Climate and Ecology* (Washington, D.C.: National Academy Press, 1997); see also Haltmaier, "Transport Subsidies"; K. A. Small and C. Kazimi, "On the Costs of Air Pollution from Motor Vehicles," *Journal of Transport Economics and Policy* 29 (1995): 7–32.
54. Koplow and Martin, *Federal and Alaskan Subsidies to Oil;* Koplow and Martin, *Fueling Global Warming;* see also M. A. Delucchi and J. Murphy, *Government Expenditures Related to the Use of Motor Vehicles* (Davis: University of California, Institute of Transportation Studies, 1995).
55. M. A. Delucchi, *Summary of Non-Monetary Externalities of Motor Vehicle Use* (Davis: University of California, Institute of Transportation Studies, 1995); see also J. Hall et al., *Economic Assessment of the Health Benefits from Improvements in Air Quality in the South Coast Air Basin, Los Angeles* (Los Angeles: South Coast Air Quality Management District, 1989); Hwang, *Money Down the Pipeline;* C. Komanoff, *Pollution Taxes for Roadway Transportation* (Brooklyn: Konheim and Ketcham, 1994); Small and Kazimi, "On the Costs of Air Pollution"; Transportation Research Board, National Research Council, *Toward a Sustainable Future.*
56. J. MacKenzie, R. Dower, and D. Chen, *The Going Rate* (Washington, D.C.: World Resources Institute, 1992).
57. National Research Council, *Toward a Sustainable Future;* Haltmaier, "Transport Subsidies."
58. Lee, *Full Cost Pricing of Highways.*
59. Delucchi, *Summary of Non-Monetary Externalities;* Hwang, *Money Down the Pipeline;* see also Cobb, *Roads Aren't Free.*
60. Hall et al., *Economic Assessment.*
61. Gibbs, "Transportation's Perennial Problems."
62. Environmental Protection Agency, *Benefits and Costs of the Clean Air Act Amendments* (1999), available on-line at http://www.epa.gov/oar/sect812.

63. World Health Organization, *Pollution from Cars Kills More People Than Do Car Accidents* (Geneva: World Health Organization, 1999).

64. J. T. Houghton et al., eds., *The Science of Climate Change: The Second Assessment Report of the Intergovernmental Panel on Climate Change* (New York: Cambridge University Press, 1996); R. Repetto and J. Lash, "Planetary Roulette: Gambling with the Climate," *Foreign Policy* 108 (1997): 84–98.

65. S. Fankhauser, *Valuing Climate Change: The Economics of the Greenhouse* (London: Earthscan, 1995); see also Chapter 2.

66. D. Maddison et al., *Blueprint 5: The True Costs of Road Transport* (London: Earthscan, 1996); for further appraisals of environmental externalities, broadly consistent with the foregoing figures, see Hwang, *Money Down the Pipeline;* Ketcham and Komanoff, *Win-Win Transportation;* D. Koplow, *Federal Energy Subsidies: Energy, Environmental, and Fiscal Impacts* (Washington, D.C.: Alliance to Save Energy, 1993); M. D. Lowe, "Reinventing Transport," in L. R. Brown et al., eds., *State of the World, 1994* (New York: Norton, 1994), 81–98; P. Miller and J. Moffet, *The Price of Mobility: Uncovering Hidden Costs of Transportation* (Washington, D.C.: Natural Resources Defense Council, 1993); Roodman, *Natural Wealth of Nations.*

67. OECD, *Reforming Energy and Transport Subsidies.*

68. Cobb, *Roads Aren't Free.*

69. Lee, *Full Cost Pricing of Highways;* see also Litman, *Reinventing Transportation;* Litman, *Transportation Cost Analysis.*

70. J. H. Kay, *Asphalt Nation: How the Automobile Took Over America and How We Can Take It Back* (New York: Crown, 1997).

71. J. DeCicco and M. Thomas, *Green Guide to Cars and Trucks: Model Year 1998* (Washington, D.C.: American Council for an Energy-Efficient Economy, 1998).

72. Delucchi, *Annualized Social Cost of Motor-Vehicle Use.*

73. International Center for Technology Assessment, *Real Price of Gas.*

74. Lee, *Full Cost Pricing of Highways.*

75. Delucchi, *Annualized Social Cost of Motor-Vehicle Use.*

76. International Center for Technology Assessment, *Real Price of Gas;* Hawken, "Natural Capitalism."

77. National Research Council, *Toward a Sustainable Future.*

78. United Nations, *Energy Statistics Yearbook* (New York: United Nations, 1995); National Research Council, *Toward a Sustainable Future.*

79. J.-P. Orfeuil, "Transport Subsidies and the Environment," in Organisation for Economic Co-operation and Development (OECD), *Subsidies and Environment: Exploring the Linkages* (Paris: OECD, 1996), 163–173.

80. Maddison et al., *Blueprint 5;* see also P. Kageson, *Getting the Prices Right: A European Scheme for Making Transport Pay Its True Costs*

(Stockholm: European Federation for Transport and Environment, 1993).

81. W. Rothengatter and S. Mauch, *External Effects of Transport* (Paris: Union Internationale des Chemins de Fer, 1994).

82. Maddison et al., *Blueprint 5;* see also Rothengatter and Mauch, *External Effects of Transport;* EcoPlan, *Damage Costs of Air Pollution: A Survey of Existing Estimates* (Brussels: European Federation for Transport and Environment, 1992); Hubbard, "Real Cost of Energy"; Lowe, "Reinventing Transport"; Roodman, *Natural Wealth of Nations.*

83. H. Morisugi, *Social Costs of Motor Vehicle Use in Japan* (Paris: Organisation for Economic Co-operation and Development, 1997); OECD, *Reforming Energy and Transport Subsidies.*

84. de Moor, *Perverse Incentives.*

85. de Moor, *Perverse Incentives;* see also J. DeCicco and H. Morris, *The Costs of Transport in South-East Wisconsin* (Washington, D.C.: American Council for an Energy Efficient Economy, 1998).

86. F. Bousquet and C. Queiroz, *Russian Road Financing System* (Washington, D.C.: World Bank, 1995); de Moor, *Perverse Incentives;* International Energy Agency (IEA), *World Energy Outlook: Looking at Energy Subsidies: Getting the Prices Right* (Paris: IEA, 1999).

87. C. Zegras and T. Litman, *An Analysis of the Full Costs and Impacts of Transportation in Santiago de Chile* (Washington, D.C., and Santiago, Chile: International Institute for Energy Conservation, 1997).

88. P. DuPont and K. Egan, "Solving Bangkok's Transport Woes: The Need to Ask the Right Questions," *World Transport and Policy Practice* 3, no. 1 (1997): 25–37; C. Poboon et al., *Bangkok: Anatomy of a Traffic Disaster* (Perth, Australia: Murdoch University, Institute for Sustainability and Technology Policy, 1994); A. Shaefer and D. Victor, "The Past and Future of Global Mobility," *Scientific American* 277, no. 4 (1997): 58–63.

89. P. Newman and J. Kenworthy, *Sustainability and Cities: Overcoming Automobile Dependence* (Washington, D.C.: Island Press, 1998); World Health Organization, *Health and Environment in Sustainable Development: Five Years After the Earth Summit* (Geneva: World Health Organization, 1997); see also Gibbs, "Transportation's Perennial Problems"; Zhou Fengqi, *Energy Consumption.*

90. World Health Organization, *Health and Environment in Sustainable Development.*

91. Centre for Science and Environment, *Slow Murder: The Deadly Story of Vehicular Pollution in India* (New Delhi: Centre for Science and Environment, 1996).

92. D. W. Pearce, "Benefit-Cost Analysis, Environment, and Health in the Developed and Developing World," *Environment and Development Economics* 2 (1997): 210–214; D. W. Pearce et al., *The Economic Value of Environmental Benefits in Developing Countries* (London: Edward Elgar, 1997).

93. United Nations Development Programme, *Human Development Report, 1998* (New York: Oxford University Press, 1998).
94. Gibbs, "Transportation's Perennial Problems"; Zegras and Litman, *Analysis of Full Costs and Impacts.*
95. Zhou Fengqi, *Energy Consumption.*
96. I. G. Heggie, *Management and Financing of Roads: An Agenda for Reform* (Washington, D.C.: World Bank, 1995).
97. de Moor, *Perverse Incentives.*
98. K. J. Button, *Transport Economics,* 2nd ed. (Aldershot, England: Edward Elgar, 1993); K. Button, ed., *Internalizing the Social Costs of Transport* (Paris: Organisation for Economic Co-operation and Development, 1994).
99. To cite the graphic phrasing of A. P. G. de Moor and P. Calamai in *Subsidizing Unsustainable Development: Undermining the Earth with Public Funds* (San José, Costa Rica: Earth Council, 1997).
100. OECD, *Reforming Energy and Transport Subsidies.*
101. For the latest extensive survey of this complex and contentious issue, see Delucchi, *Annualized Social Cost of Motor-Vehicle Use;* Lee, *Full Cost Pricing of Highways;* Litman, *Reinventing Transportation;* Litman, *Transportation Cost Analysis;* OECD, *Reforming Energy and Transport Subsidies;* J. J. MacKenzie, *Climate Protection and the National Interest: The Links Among Climate Change, Air Pollution, and Energy Security* (Washington, D.C.: World Resources Institute, 1997); Maddison et al., *Blueprint 5;* World Bank, *Sustainable Transport: Priorities for Policy Reform* (Washington, D.C.: World Bank, 1996).
102. Maddison et al., *Blueprint 5.*
103. Worldwatch Institute, *Briefing on Bicycles and Cities* (Washington, D.C.: Worldwatch Institute, 1998).
104. D. Sperling and S. A. Shaheen, eds., *Transportation and Energy: Strategies for a Sustainable Transportation System* (Washington, D.C.: American Council for an Energy-Efficient Economy, 1995); National Research Council, *Toward a Sustainable Future.*
105. D. Shoup, *Curbing Gridlock: Peak-Period Fees to Relieve Traffic Congestion* (Washington, D.C.: National Research Council, 1994); see also T. Litman, "Policy Implications of Full Social Costing," in *Transport at the Millennium: Annals of the American Academy of Political and Social Science 553* (September 1997): 143–156.
106. M. El-Gasseir, *The Potential Benefits and Workability of Pay-as-You-Drive Automobile Insurance* (San Francisco: Energy Resources, Conservation, and Development Commission, 1990); see also Litman, *Reinventing Transportation.*
107. Button and Verhoef, *Road Pricing, Traffic Congestion, and the Environment;* World Resources Institute, *World Resources Report, 1996* (New York: Oxford University Press, 1996).
108. Samwell, "Traffic Congestion."

109. T. Litman, *Evaluating Carsharing Benefits* and *Evaluating Public Transit Benefits and Costs* (Victoria, British Columbia, Canada: Victoria Transport Policy Institute, 1998).
110. J. Fox-Rubin, *Rethinking Automobility* (Snowmass, Colo.: Rocky Mountain Institute, 1998).
111. U.S. Department of Transportation, *National Transportation Statistics, 1999.*
112. OECD, *Reforming Energy and Transport Subsidies.*
113. H. Harvey, *Using Technology to Solve the Carbon Dilemma* (San Francisco: Energy Foundation, 1998).
114. Harvey, *Using Technology.*
115. J. Rabinovitch and J. Leitman, "Urban Planning in Curitiba," *Scientific American* (March 1996): 30–33.
116. Samwell, "Traffic Congestion"; see also C. Winston and C. Shirley, *Alternate Route: Towards Efficient Urban Transportation* (Washington, D.C.: Brookings Institution, 1998); J. A. Dunn, *Driving Forces: The Automobile, Its Enemies, and the Politics of Mobility* (Washington, D.C.: Brookings Institution, 1998).

Chapter 6. Water

1. H. D. Frederiksen, Harald D. Frederiksen Associates, Eugene, Oreg., personal communication (letter of 28 December 1997).
2. A. Dinar, *Policy Reforms for Sustainable Water Resources* (Washington, D.C.: World Bank, 1998); W. Jones, *The World Bank and Irrigation* (Washington, D.C.: World Bank, 1995). For further general reviews of the water sector, see M. Falkenmark, "Dilemma When Entering Twenty-First Century: Rapid Change but Lack of Sense of Urgency," *Water Policy* 1 (1998): 421–436; M. Falkenmark, "Forward to the Future: A Conceptual Framework for Water Dependence," *Ambio* 28 (1999): 356–361; T. Gardner-Outlaw and R. Engelman, *Sustaining Water, Easing Scarcity: A Second Update* (Washington, D.C.: Population Action International, 1997); P. Gleick, *Water, 2050: Moving Toward a Sustainable Vision for the Earth's Fresh Water* (Oakland, Calif.: Pacific Institute for Studies in Development, Environment, and Security, 1997); P. Gleick, *The World's Water, 2000–2001* (Washington, D.C.: Island Press, 2000); D. Pimentel et al., "Water Resources: Agriculture, the Environment, and Society," *BioScience* 47 (1997): 97–106; S. Postel, "Water for Food Production: Will There Be Enough in 2025?" *BioScience* 48, no. 8 (1998): 629–637; S. Postel, "Redesigning Irrigated Agriculture," in L. R. Brown et al., *State of the World, 2000* (New York: Norton, 2000), 39–57; M. W. Rosegrant, *Water Resources in the Twenty-First Century: Challenges and Implications for Action* (Washington, D.C.: International Food Policy Research Institute, 1997).
3. P. Gleick, *The World's Water, 1998–1999* (Washington, D.C.: Island

Press, 1998); M. Shah and M. Strong, *Food in the Twenty-First Century: From Science to Sustainable Agriculture* (Washington, D.C.: Consultative Group on International Agricultural Research and World Bank, 1999).

4. D. M. Roodman, *Paying the Piper: Subsidies, Politics, and the Environment* (Washington, D.C.: Worldwatch Institute, 1996).

5. S. Postel, *Dividing the Waters: Food Security, Ecosystem Health, and the New Politics of Scarcity* (Washington, D.C.: Worldwatch Institute, 1996); Gleick, *The World's Water, 1998–1999*.

6. D. Pimentel and M. Pimentel, eds., *Food, Energy, and Society* (Boulder: University Press of Colorado, 1996).

7. S. Postel, "Dividing the Waters: Food Security, Ecosystem Health, and the New Politics of Scarcity," (Washington, D.C.: Worldwatch Institute, 1996); see also S. Postel, *Last Oasis,* rev. ed. (New York: Norton, 1997).

8. Postel, *Dividing the Waters;* Postel, "Dividing the Waters"; M. Falkenmark, "Landscape as Life Support Provider: Water-Related Limitations," in F. Graham-Smith, ed., *Population: The Complex Reality* (London: Royal Society; Golden, Colo.: North American Press, 1994), 103–116.

9. Falkenmark, "Landscape as Life Support Provider"; see also P. H. Gleick, "Basic Water Requirements for Human Activities: Meeting Basic Needs," *Water International* 21 (1996): 83–92; Gleick, *Water, 2050;* Postel, *Dividing the Waters.*

10. Gardner-Outlaw and Engelman, *Sustaining Water, Easing Scarcity;* see also Gleick, *Water, 2050.*

11. J. A. Allan, "Water in the Middle East and in Israel-Palestine: Some Local and Global Issues," in M. Haddad and E. Feitelson, eds., *Joint Management of Shared Aquifers* (Jerusalem: Palestine Consultancy Group and Truman Research Institute of the Hebrew University, 1995), 31–44.

12. Postel, "Dividing the Waters"; Postel, "Last Oasis."

13. Pimentel et al., "Water Resources."

14. M. Kreith, *Water Inputs in California Food Production* (Sacramento, Calif.: Water Education Foundation, 1991).

15. H. W. Kendall and D. Pimentel, "Constraints on the Expansion of the Global Food Supply," *Ambio* 23, no. 3 (1994): 198–205; see also G. Bonnis and R. Steenblik, "Water, Agriculture, and the Environment," *OECD Observer* 212 (1998): 1–4.

16. T. E. Downing and M. L. Parry, "Climate Change and World Food Security," *Food Policy* 19 (1994): 99–104.

17. Gleick, *The World's Water, 1998–1999;* Postel, "Redesigning Irrigated Agriculture."

18. D. Rind et al., "Potential Evapotranspiration and the Likelihood of Future Drought," *Journal of Geophysical Research* 95 (1990): 9983–10004.

19. I. Serageldin, *Sustainability and the Wealth of Nations: First Steps in an On-Going Journey* (Washington, D.C.: World Bank, 1995); see also A. P. G. de Moor, *Perverse Incentives: Hundreds of Billions of Dollars in Subsidies Now Harm the Economy, the Environment, Equity, and Trade* (San José, Costa Rica: Earth Council, 1997).

20. Postel, "Redesigning Irrigated Agriculture."

21. Gleick, "Basic Water Requirements"; Postel, *Dividing the Waters*; I. Serageldin, *Water Supply, Sanitation, and Environmental Sustainability: The Financing Challenge* (Washington, D.C.: World Bank, 1994).

22. R. Repetto, *Skimming the Water: Rent Seeking and the Performance of Public Irrigation Systems* (Washington, D.C.: World Resources Institute, 1986).

23. S. Gupta, K. Miranda, and I. Parry, "Public Expenditure Policy and the Environment: A Review and Synthesis," *World Development* 23 (1995): 515–528; R. K. Sampath, "Issues in Irrigation Pricing in Developing Countries," *World Development* 20 (1992): 967–977.

24. A. Dinar and A. Subramanian, *Water Pricing Experiences: An International Perspective* (Washington, D.C.: World Bank, 1997).

25. Repetto, *Skimming the Water.*

26. S. Postel, G. Daily, and P. Ehrlich, "Human Appropriation of Renewable Fresh Water," *Science* 271 (1996): 785–788.

27. Gardner-Outlaw and Engelman, *Sustaining Water, Easing Scarcity*; Postel, "Redesigning Irrigated Agriculture"; see also D. Seckler, D. Molden, and R. Barker, *Water Scarcity in the Twenty-First Century* (Colombo, Sri Lanka: International Irrigation Water Management Institute, 1999); Gleick, "Basic Water Requirements"; M. W. Rosegrant and C. Ringler, *World Water Vision Scenarios: Consequences for Food Supply, Demand, Trade, and Food Security* (Washington, D.C.: International Food Policy Research Institute, 1999).

28. G. C. Gallopin and F. Rijsberman, "Three Global Water Scenarios," *International Journal of Water* 1 (2000): 5–7; D. Seckler, U. Amarasinghe, D. Molden, R. Desilva, and R. Barker, *World Water Demand and Supply, 1990 to 2025: Scenarios and Issues* (Colombo, Sri Lanka: International Water Management Institute, Research Report No. 19, 1998); Seckler et al., *Water Scarcity in the Twenty-first Century.*

29. R. Nicholls, *Climate Change and Its Impacts: A Global Perspective* (Bracknell, England: Middlesex University and U.K. Meteorological Office, 1997); Pimentel et al., "Water Resources"; World Health Organization, *Our Planet, Our Health* (Geneva: World Health Organization, 1992).

30. Pimentel and Pimentel, *Food, Energy, and Society.*

31. Centre for Science and Environment, *Slow Murder: The Deadly Story of Vehicular Pollution in India* (New Delhi: Centre for Science and Environment, 1996).

32. Water Supply and Sanitation Collaborative Council. "Vision 21: A Shared Vision for Water Supply, Sanitation, and Hygiene and a Frame-

work for Action." Paper presented at the Second World Water Forum, The Hague, The Netherlands, 17–22 March 2000. See also D. W. Pearce and J. J. Warford, *World Without End: Economics, Environment, and Sustainable Development* (New York: Oxford University Press, 1993).

33. J. Christmas and C. Rooy, "The Water Decade and Beyond," *Water International* 16 (1991): 127–134.
34. G. Gardner, *Shrinking Fields: Cropland Loss in a World of Eight Billion* (Washington, D.C.: Worldwatch Institute, 1996).
35. Jones, *World Bank and Irrigation.*
36. Repetto, *Skimming the Water.*
37. Dinar, *Policy Reforms;* S. Postel, *Pillar of Sand* (New York: Norton, 1999).
38. F. Ghassemi, A. J. Jakeman, and H. A. Nix, *Salinization of Land and Water Resources: Human Causes, Extent, Management, and Case Studies* (Sydney, Australia: University of New South Wales Press, 1995); see also H. E. Dregne and M. T. Chou, *Global Desertification: Dimensions and Costs* (Lubbock: Texas Tech University Press, 1992); Jones, *World Bank and Irrigation;* World Bank, *World Development Report, 1992* (New York: Oxford University Press, 1992).
39. D. Seckler, *Designing Water Resources Strategies for the Twenty-First Century* (Arlington, Va.: Winrock International, 1993); D. Seckler, "The New Era of Water Resources Management: From 'Dry' to 'Wet' Water Savings," *Issues in Agriculture* 8 (Washington, D.C.: CGIAR/World Bank, 1996); Serageldin, *Sustainability and the Wealth of Nations.*
40. Postel, *Pillar of Sand.*
41. P. H. Gleick et al., *California Water, 2020: A Sustainable Vision* (Oakland, Calif.: Pacific Institute for Studies in Development, Environment, and Security, 1995).
42. Postel, "Redesigning Irrigated Agriculture"; Postel, *Pillar of Sand.*
43. Gardner, *Shrinking Fields.*
44. L. R. Brown and H. Kane, *Full House: Reassessing the Earth's Population Carrying Capacity* (New York: Norton, 1994); Postel, "Redesigning Irrigated Agriculture."
45. Seckler, Molden, and Barker, *Water Scarcity.*
46. L. R. Brown, C. Flavin, and H. French, foreword to Brown et al., *State of the World, 2000.*
47. Postel, "Redesigning Irrigated Agriculture"; Seckler, Molden, and Barker, *Water Scarcity.*
48. Postel, "Redesigning Irrigated Agriculture"; see also Brown, Flavin, and French, foreword to Brown, *State of the World, 2000.*
49. Postel, "Redesigning Irrigated Agriculture"; M. Rosegrant and R. Gazmuri-Schleyer, "Establishing Tradable Water Rights: Implementation of the Mexican Water Law," *Irrigation and Drainage Systems* 10, no. 3 (1996): 263–279.

50. Postel, "Redesigning Irrigated Agriculture."

51. Aral Sea Program Unit, *Aral Sea Program, Phase 1* Washington, D.C.: World Bank, 1994); K.-L. Kiessling, ed., *Alleviating the Consequences of an Ecological Catastrophe: Proceedings of Conference on the Aral Sea* (Stockholm: Royal Swedish Academy of Sciences, 1999).

52. I. Serageldin, "Beating the Water Crisis," *Our Planet* 8, no. 3 (1996): 4–7; N. F. Glazovsky, "The Aral Sea Basin," in J. X. Kasperson, R. E. Kasperson, and B. L. Turner, eds., *Regions at Risk: Comparisons of Threatened Environments* (Tokyo: United Nations University Press, 1995), 92–139.

53. D. Sinclair, "Government Irrigation Subsidies Result in Huge Economic and Environmental Losses Worldwide," *Ambio* 16 (1987): 149–151.

54. R. Costanza et al., "The Value of the World's Ecosystem Services and Natural Capital," *Nature* 387 (1997): 253–260.

55. S. Postel and S. Carpenter, "Freshwater Ecosystem Services," in G. C. Daily, ed., *Nature's Services: Societal Dependence on Natural Ecosystems* (Washington, D.C.: Island Press, 1997), 195–214.

56. P. H. Gleick, ed., *Water in Crisis: A Guide to the World's Freshwater Resources* (New York: Oxford University Press, 1993); Serageldin, *Sustainability and the Wealth of Nations.*

57. N. Myers, "Linking Environment and Security," *Bulletin of the Atomic Scientists* 4, no. 8 (1987): 46–47.

58. J. Briscoe, *Water as an Economic Good: The Idea and What It Means in Practice* (Washington, D.C.: World Bank, 1996); G. Yep, *Reduction of Unaccounted-for Water: The Job Can Be Better Done* (Washington, D.C.: World Bank, 1995).

59. World Bank, *Water Resources Management: World Bank Policy Study* (Washington, D.C.: World Bank, 1993).

60. Rosegrant and Gazmuri-Schleyer, "Establishing Tradable Water Rights."

61. Gleick, *Water in Crisis;* Postel, *Dividing the Waters.*

62. R. Repetto, "Population, Resources, Environment: An Uncertain Future," *Population Bulletin* 42, no. 2 (1987) (booklet); Organization for Economic Cooperation and Development (OECD), *Water Subsidies and the Environment* (Paris: OECD, 1997); U.S. Department of Agriculture (USDA), *Agricultural Resources and Environmental Indicators* (Washington, D.C.: USDA, Economic Research Service, 1994).

63. G. Armstrong, "Australia's Environmental Policy: The Ends and Means," in P. Sheehan, B. Grewal, and M. Kumnick, eds., *Dialogues on Australia's Future* (Melbourne, Australia: Victoria University of Technology, 1996), 257–280; D. Mussared, "Waterworks," *Ecos* 85 (1995): 13–16.

64. M. Falkenmark and R. A. Suprapto, "Population-Landscape Interactions in Development: A Water Perspective to Environmental Sustainability," *Ambio* 11 (1992): 31–36; Gleick, *Water in Crisis;* Pearce and Warford, *World without End;* Postel, "Redesigning Irrigated Agriculture"; Sampath, "Issues in Irrigation Pricing."

65. F. van der Leeden, F. L. Troise, and D. K. Todd, *The Water Encyclopedia*, 2nd ed. (Chelsea, Mich.: Lewis, 1990).

66. Tata Energy Research Institute, *Looking Back to Think Ahead—Green India 2047: Growth with Resource Enhancement of Environment and Nature* (New Delhi: Tata Energy Research Institute, 1998).

67. M. Falkenmark and C. Widstrand, "Population and Water Resources: A Delicate Balance," *Population Bulletin* 47, no. 3 (1992); Serageldin, *Water Supply, Sanitation, and Environmental Sustainability.*

68. Food and Agriculture Organization of the United Nations (FAO), *State of Food and Agriculture, 1994* (Rome: FAO, 1994).

69. van der Leeden, Troise, and Todd, *Water Encyclopedia;* H. J. W. Verplancke, E. B. A. De Strooper, and M. F. L. Boodt, *Water Saving Techniques for Plant Growth* (Dordrecht, Netherlands: Kluwer, 1992).

70. S. Mundle and M. G. Rao, "Volume and Composition of Government Subsidies in India, 1987–1988," *Economic and Political Weekly* (4 May 1991): 1157–1172; T. Shah, *Groundwater Markets and Irrigation Development: Political Economy and Practical Policy* (Bombay: Oxford University Press, 1993).

71. Serageldin, *Water Supply, Sanitation, and Environmental Sustainability.*

72. P. K. Pachauri, *The Energy Scene in India: Last Two Decades* (New Delhi: Tata Energy Research Institute, for World Resources Institute, Washington, D.C., 1994); see also Mundle and Rao, "Volume and Composition of Government Subsidies"; Shah, *Groundwater Markets and Irrigation Development.*

73. Pachauri, *Energy Scene in India;* see also Mundle and Rao, "Volume and Composition of Government Subsidies"; Shah, *Groundwater Markets and Irrigation Development.*

74. P. Faeth, ed., *Agricultural Policy and Sustainability: Case Studies from India, Chile, the Philippines, and the United States* (Washington, D.C.: World Resources Institute, 1993); Tata Energy Research Institute, *Looking Back to Think Ahead.*

75. R. Bahatia and M. Falkenmark, *Water Resource Policies and the Urban Poor: Innovative Approaches and Policy Imperatives* (Washington, D.C.: World Bank, 1993).

76. Postel, *Pillar of Sand.*

77. Postel, *Pillar of Sand.*

78. P. Gleick, *The World's Water, 2000–2001;* Verplancke, De Strooper, and Boodt, *Water Saving Techniques for Plant Growth.*

79. P. Gleick, *The World's Water, 1998–1999;* Postel, "Redesigning Irrigated Agriculture"; S. Postel, *Emerging Water Shortages Threaten Food Supplies, Regional Peace* (Washington, D.C.: Worldwatch Institute, 1999); Postel, *Pillar of Sand;* World Humanity Trust, *Governance for a Sustainable Future: IV, Working with Water* (London: World Humanity Action Trust, 2000.

80. H. A. Cohen and S. Plaut, "Quenching the Levant's Thirst," *Middle East Quarterly* (March 1995): 37–44.

81. H. A. Cohen and S. Plaut, "Quenching the Levant's Thirst," *Middle East Quarterly* (March 1995): 37–44.
82. Cohen and Plaut, "Quenching the Levant's Thirst."
83. P. Pinstrup-Andersen, *World Food Trends and Future Food Security* (Washington, D.C.: International Food Policy Research Institute, 1994).
84. Postel, "Redesigning Irrigated Agriculture"; U.S. Department of Agriculture (USDA), *Production, Supply, and Distribution* (Washington, D.C.: USDA, 1999).
85. K. D. Frederick and P. Gleick, *Water and Global Climate Change: Potential Impacts on U.S. Water Resources* (Arlington, Va.: Pew Center on Global Climate Change, 1999); Gleick et al., *California Water, 2020;* D. Pimentel et al., "Impact of Population Growth on Food Supplies and Environment," *Population and Environment* 19 (1997): 9–14.
86. Repetto, *Skimming the Water.*
87. M. Brower and W. Leon, *The Consumer's Guide to Effective Environmental Choices* (New York: Three Rivers Press, 1999); see also B. D. Gardener, "Some Implications of Federal Grazing, Timber, Irrigation, and Recreation Subsidies," *Choices* 12, no. 3 (1997): 9–14; Gleick et al., *California Water, 2020;* Postel, *Pillar of Sand;* Roodman, *Paying the Piper.*
88. Pimentel et al., "Water Resources"; see also USDA, *Agricultural Resources and Environmental Indicators.*
89. Postel, *Pillar of Sand;* see also P. Gleick, *The World's Water, 2000–2001.*
90. T. L. Anderson, ed., *Water Marketing: The Next Generation* (London: Rowan and Littlefield, 1996); A. Jones and J. Dyer, *The Water Efficiency Revolution* (Snowmass, Colo.: Rocky Mountain Institute, 1995); see also Frederiksen, personal communication; M. Gaffney, "The Taxable Surplus in Water Resources," *Contemporary Policy Issues* 10 (1992): 74–82; Gardener, "Some Implications"; M. Reisner, *Cadillac Desert: The American West and Its Disappearing Water* (New York: Viking, 1996).
91. Gleick et al., *California Water, 2020;* Reisner, *Cadillac Desert;* see also H. D. Frederiksen, "Water Crisis in the Developing World: Misconceptions About Solutions," *Journal of Water Resources Planning and Management* (March–April 1996): 79–87; G. Miller, *Taking from the Taxpayer: Public Subsidies for Natural Resource Development* (Washington, D.C.: Committee on Natural Resources, U.S. House of Representatives, 1994); Postel, *Emerging Water Shortages;* Postel, *Pillar of Sand.*
92. California Department of Water Resources, *California Water Plan Update,* vol. 1 (Sacramento: California Department of Water Resources, 1994); Gaffney, "Taxable Surplus in Water Resources"; Jones and Dyer, *Water Efficiency Revolution;* Reisner, *Cadillac Desert.*
93. World Bank, *Water Resources Management.*

94. Gleick et al., *California Water, 2020.*

95. P. Hawken, A. Lovins, and L. H. Lovins, *Natural Capitalism: Creating the Next Industrial Revolution* (Boston: Little, Brown, 1999).

96. Jones and Dyer, *Water Efficiency Revolution;* see also J. Gladstone, *Water Efficiency for Today and Tomorrow* (Seattle, Wash.: Water Department, 1992).

97. D. M. Tate and D. M. Lacelle, *Municipal Water Rates in Canada: Current Practices and Prices, 1991* (Ottawa, Ontario: Environment Canada, Water and Habitat Conservation Branch, 1995).

98. de Moor, *Perverse Incentives;* see also World Bank, *World Development Report 1994* (Washington, D.C.: World Bank, 1994); Yep, *Reduction of Unaccounted for Water.*

99. World Bank, *World Development Report 1994;* see also de Moor, *Perverse Incentives;* Roodman, *Paying the Piper.*

100. World Bank, *Water Resources Management;* see also Bahatia and Falkenmark, *Water Resource Policies and the Urban Poor;* Yep, *Reduction of Unaccounted-for Water;* J. Briscoe and M. Garn, *Financing Agenda 21: Fresh Water* (Washington, D.C.: World Bank, 1994); R. Tsuar and A. Dinar, *Efficiency and Equity Considerations in Pricing and Allocating Irrigation Water* (Washington, D.C.: World Bank, 1995).

101. J. Xie, *Water Subsidies, Water Use, and the Environment* (Washington, D.C.: World Bank, 1996).

102. Bahatia and Falkenmark, *Water Resource Policies and the Urban Poor.*

103. L. Hongliang, Chinese Research Academy of Environmental Sciences, Beijing, personal communication (letter of 24 December 1997).

104. Rosegrant and Gazmuri-Schleyer, "Establishing Tradable Water Rights."

105. Serageldin, *Sustainability and the Wealth of Nations.*

106. Pearce and Warford, *World Without End.*

107. W. J. Cosgrove and F. R. Rijsberman, "Creating a Vision for Water Life and the Environment," *Water Policy* 1 (1998): 115–122; R. Engelman and P. LeRoy, *Sustaining Water: An Update* (Washington, D.C.: Population Action International, 1995); Falkenmark, "Landscape as Life Support Provider"; Gardner-Outlaw and Engelman, *Sustaining Water, Easing Scarcity;* Postel, "Dividing the Waters"; Postel, *Pillar of Sand;* A. K. N. Reddy, R. H. Williams, and T. B. Johansson, *Energy After Rio: Prospects and Challenges* (New York: United Nations Development Programme, 1997).

108. Costanza et al., "Value of the World's Ecosystem Services."

109. Postel and Carpenter, "Freshwater Ecosystem Services."

110. Bonnis and Steenblik, "Water, Agriculture, and the Environment"; OECD, *Water Subsidies and the Environment;* Organization for Economic Cooperation and Development (OECD), *Agricultural Water Pricing in OECD Countries* and *Industrial Water Pricing in OECD Countries* (Paris: OECD, 1999).

111. Roodman, *Paying the Piper;* see also Gaffney, "Taxable Surplus in Water Resources."
112. Gleick et al., *California Water, 2020.*
113. A. Dinar, M. W. Rosegrant, and R. Meinzen-Dick, *Water Allocation Mechanisms: Principles and Examples* (Washington, D.C.: World Bank, 1998).
114. M. Rosegrant, *Dealing with Water Scarcity in the Next Century* (Washington, D.C.: International Food Policy Research Institute, 1995).
115. E. R. Osann and J. E. Young, *Saving Water, Saving Dollars: Efficient Plumbing Products and the Protection of America's Waters* (Washington, D.C.: American Council for an Energy-Efficient Economy, 1998); Postel, "Water for Food Production."
116. Postel, *Dividing the Waters.*
117. United Nations Development Programme, *Human Development Report, 1998* (New York: Oxford University Press, 1998).
118. Bahatia and Falkenmark, *Water Resource Policies and the Urban Poor;* see also Rosegrant, *Water Resources in the Twenty-First Century;* Serageldin, *Water Supply, Sanitation, and Environmental Sustainability.*
119. T. L. Anderson, "Water, Water Everywhere but Not a Drop to Sell," in J. L. Simon, ed., *The State of Humanity* (Oxford, England: Blackwell, 1995), 425–433; de Moor, *Perverse Incentives;* H. D. Frederiksen and C. Perry, *Needs and Priorities in Water-Related Research* (Colombo, Sri Lanka: International Irrigation Management Institute, 1995); Postel, *Dividing the Waters;* Postel, *Last Oasis;* Roodman, *Paying the Piper.*
120. T. L. Anderson and P. Snyder, *Water Markets: Priming the Invisible Pump* (Washington, D.C.: Cato Institute, 1997); Cohen and Plaut, "Quenching the Levant's Thirst"; A. Keller, J. Keller, and D. Seckler, *Integrated Water Resource Systems: Theory and Policy Implications* (Colombo, Sri Lanka: International Irrigation Management Institute, 1995); Rosegrant and Gazmuri-Schleyer, "Establishing Tradable Water Rights"; Seckler, *Designing Water Resources Strategies;* Seckler, *New Era of Water Resources Management.*
121. Anderson, *Water Marketing;* Frederiksen and Perry, *Needs and Priorities;* Dinar, Rosegrant, and Meinzen-Dick, *Water Allocation Mechanisms;* M. Rosegrant, R. Gazmuri-Schleyer, and. S. Yadav, "Water Policy for Efficient Agricultural Diversification: Market-Based Approaches," *Food Policy* 20 (1995): 203–223; Seckler, "New Era of Water Resources Management."
122. Dinar, *Policy Reforms;* A. Keller and J. Keller, *Effective Efficiency: A Water Use Efficiency Concept for Allocating Freshwater Resources* (Arlington, Va.: Winrock International, 1995); R. Pinkham and S. Chaplin, *Water 2010: Four Scenarios for Twenty-First-Century Water Systems* (Snowmass, Colo.: Rocky Mountain Institute, 1996); Postel, *Dividing the Waters.*

123. Anderson and Snyder, *Water Markets*; M. W. Rosegrant, C. Ringler, and R. V. Gerpacio, *Water and Land Resources and Global Food Supply* (Washington, D.C.: International Food Policy Research Institute, 1997).

124. Gleick, *Water in Crisis.*

125. Postel, "Redesigning Irrigated Agriculture."

126. F. Cairncross, *Green Inc.: A Guide to Business and the Environment* (London: Earthscan, 1995).

127. C. W. Howe, "Sharing Water Fairly," *Our Planet* 8, no. 3 (1996): 15–17.

128. D. M. Roodman, *Getting the Signals Right: Tax Reform to Protect the Environment and the Economy* (Washington, D.C.: Worldwatch Institute, 1997).

129. R. G. Schleyer and M. W. Rosegrant, "Chilean Water Policy: The Role of Water Rights, Institutions, and Markets," in M. W. Rosegrant and R. G. Scheleyer, *Tradeable Water Rights: Experiences in Reforming Water Allocation Policy* (Washington, D.C.: IFPRI, 1994); Postel, *Pillar of Sand.*

130. C. M. Goriz, A. Subramanian, and J. Simas, *Irrigation Management Transfer in Mexico* (Washington, D.C.: World Bank, 1995); Postel, "Redesigning Irrigated Agriculture"; S. H. Johnson, "Irrigation Management Transfer: Decentralizing Public Irrigation in Mexico," *Water International* 22, no. 3 (1997): 159–167; Organisation for Economic Co-operation and Development, *Agricultural Water Policy in OECD Countries* (Paris: OECD, 1998).

131. R. Lamm, ed., *Microirrigation for a Changing World* (St. Joseph, Minn.: American Society of Agricultural Engineers, 1995); Postel, *Emerging Water Shortages.*

132. A. K. Wong et al., *Sustainable Use of Water: California Success Stories* (Oakland, Calif.: Pacific Institute for Studies in Development, Environment, and Security, 1999).

133. Gardner, *Shrinking Fields.*

134. Frederiksen, personal communication.

135. G. Chichilnisky and G. Heal, *Securitizing the Biosphere* (New York: Columbia University, Graduate School of Business, 1998).

136. Chichilnisky and Heal, *Securitizing the Biosphere.*

137. Chichilnisky and Heal, *Securitizing the Biosphere.*

Chapter 7. Fisheries

1. S. Iudicello, M. Weber, and R. Wieland, *Fish, Markets, and Fishermen: The Economics of Overfishing* (Washington, D.C.: Island Press, 1999); see also W. E. Schrank, "The Newfoundland Fishery: Past, Present, and Future," in *Subsidies and Depletion of World Fisheries* (Godalming, England: WWF International, 1997), 35–70.

2. C. Safina, *Song for the Blue Ocean* (New York: Henry Holt, 1998); C. Safina, "Scorched-Earth Fishing," *Issues in Science and Technology* 14, no. 3 (1998): 33–36; Schrank, "Newfoundland Fishery"; M. P. Sis-

senwine and A. A. Rosenberg, "Marine Fisheries at a Critical Juncture," *Fisheries* 18, no. 10 (1993): 6–14.

3. C. Safina, "The World's Imperiled Fish," *Scientific American* 273, no. 5 (1995): 30–37; Safina, *Song for the Blue Ocean.*

4. R. J. R. Grainger and S. M. Garcia, *Chronicles of Marine Fishery Landings (1950–1994): Trend Analysis and Fisheries Potential* (Rome: Food and Agriculture Organization of the United Nations, 1996); A. P. McGinn, *Rocking the Boat: Conserving Fisheries and Protecting Jobs* and *Scaling Back to Promote Sustainable Fisheries* (Washington, D.C.: Worldwatch Institute, 1998); J. R. McGoodwin, *Crisis in the World's Fisheries: People, Problems, and Policies* (Stanford, Calif.: Stanford University Press, 1995); M. Milazzo, *Subsidies in World Fisheries* (Washington, D.C.: World Bank, 1998); D. Pauly et al., "Fishing Down Marine Food Webs," *Science* 279 (1998): 860–863; M. L. Weber and J. A. Gradwohl, *The Wealth of Oceans: Environment and Development on Our Ocean Planet* (New York: Norton, 1995).

5. L. W. Botsford, J. C. Castilla, and C. H. Peterson, "The Management of Fisheries and Marine Ecosystems," *Science* 277 (1997): 509–515.

6. For documentation of these data, see Botsford, Castilla, and Peterson, "Management of Fisheries"; Food and Agriculture Organization of the United Nations (FAO), *The State of World Fisheries and Aquaculture, 1998* (Rome: FAO, 1999); A. P. McGinn, *Safeguarding the Health of the Oceans* (Washington, D.C.: Worldwatch Institute, 1999); G. Porter, *Fishing Subsidies, Overfishing, and Trade* (Nairobi, Kenya: United Nations Environment Programme, 1998); G. Porter, *Estimating Overcapacity in the Global Fishing Fleet* (Washington, D.C.: World Wildlife Fund–US, 1998); Safina, *Song for the Blue Ocean;* Safina, "Scorched-Earth Fishing"; J. Thorpe, J. Lannan, G. A. E. Gall, C. E. Nash, *Conservation of Fish and Shellfish Resources* (London, Academic Press, 1995); M. L. Weber, *A Global Assessment of Major Fisheries at Risk, Relevant Management Regimes, and Non-Governmental Organizations* (Philadelphia, Pa.: Pew Charitable Trusts, 1998).

7. Botsford, Castilla, and Peterson, "Management of Fisheries"; FAO, *State of World Fisheries and Aquaculture, 1998;* R. Grainger, *Recent Trends in Global Fishery Production* (Rome: Food and Agriculture Organization of the United Nations, 1999).

8. C. Safina, "Where Have All the Fishes Gone?" *Issues in Science and Technology* 10, no. 3 (1994): 37–43; P. Weber, *Net Loss: Fish, Jobs, and the Marine Environment* (Washington, D.C.: Worldwatch Institute, 1994).

9. FAO, *State of World Fisheries and Aquaculture, 1998.*

10. Botsford, Castilla, and Peterson, "Management of Fisheries"; M. Holden, *The Common Fisheries Policy: Origin, Evaluation, and Future* (Oxford, England: Blackwell Science, 1994); McGinn, *Safeguarding the Health of the Oceans;* Safina, "The World's Imperiled Fish," *Scientific American* 273, no. 5 (1995): 30–37.

11. Food and Agriculture Organization, *The Ocean's Most Valuable Commercial Species Are Fished to Capacity* (Rome: Food and Agriculture Organization, 1994); McGinn, *Rocking the Boat;* McGinn, *Scaling Back.*

12. Botsford, Castilla, and Peterson, "Management of Fisheries"; E. A. Norse, ed., *Global Marine Biological Diversity: A Strategy for Building Conservation into Decision Making* (Washington, D.C.: Island Press, 1993); S. Northridge, *The Environmental Impacts of Fisheries in the European Community Waters* (Brussels: Marine Resources Assessment Group, 1991); D. Pauly et al., eds., *The Footprint of Distant Water Fleets on World Fisheries* (Godalming, England: WWF International, 1999), 144–172.

13. S. M. Garcia and C. Newton, *Current Situation, Trends, and Prospects in World Capture Fisheries* (Rome: Food and Agriculture Organization of the United Nations, 1995); Grainger and Garcia, *Chronicles of Marine Fishery Landings;* Milazzo, *Subsidies in World Fisheries;* P. Weber, *Protecting Oceanic Fisheries and Jobs,* in L. R. Brown et al., *State of the World, 1995* (New York: Norton, 1995); World Resources Institute, "Fish Consumption and Aquatic Ecosystems," in *Critical Consumption Trends and Implications: Degrading Earth's Ecosystems* (Washington, D.C.: World Resources Institute, 1999).

14. Botsford, Castilla, and Peterson, "Management of Fisheries"; Food and Agriculture Organization of the United Nations (FAO), *State of World Fisheries and Aquaculture, 1997* (Rome: FAO, 1997); FAO, *State of World Fisheries and Aquaculture, 1998.*

15. Botsford et al., "Management of Fisheries"; Norse, *Global Marine Biological Diversity;* P. J. Ouster, "Sensible Fishing," *Issues in Science and Technology* 14, no. 4 (1998): 19–20.

16. J. M. Broadus and R. V. Vartanov, eds., *The Oceans and Environmental Security: Shared U.S. and Russian Perspectives* (Washington, D.C.: Island Press, 1994); F. Cairncross, *Green Inc.: A Guide to Business and the Environment* (London: Earthscan, 1995).

17. See P. Weber, *Net Loss: Fish, Jobs, and the Marine Environment* (Washington, D.C.: Worldwatch Institute, 1995); McGinn, *Rocking the Boat.*

18. M. de Alessi, *Fishing for Solutions* (London: Institute of Economic Affairs, 1998); S. S. Hanna, "From Single-Species to Biodiversity: Making the Transition in Fisheries Management," *Biodiversity and Conservation* 8 (1999): 45–54; Porter, *Fishing Subsidies, Overfishing, and Trade;* Iudicello, Weber, and Wieland, *Fish, Markets, and Fishermen;* R. P. Steenblik and G. R. Munro, *International Work on Fishing Subsidies: An Update* (Paris: Organisation for Economic Co-operation and Development, 1999).

19. Hanna, "From Single-Species to Biodiversity"; McGoodwin, *Crisis in the World's Fisheries;* Porter, *Fishing Subsidies, Overfishing, and Trade;* Weber and Gradwohl, *Wealth of Oceans.*

20. T. Matthiasson, "Why Fishing Fleets Tend to Be Too Big," *Marine*

Resource Economics 11 (1996): 173–179; Safina, "World's Imperiled Fish"; see also Steenblik and Munro, *International Work on Fishing Subsidies;* World Trade Organization, *Environmental and Trade Benefits of Removing Subsidies in the Fisheries Sector* (New York: World Trade Organization, 1997).

21. Safina, "World's Imperiled Fish."

22. Food and Agriculture Organization of the United Nations (FAO), *Marine Fisheries and the Law of the Sea: A Decade of Change* (Rome: FAO, 1993).

23. FAO, *Marine Fisheries and the Law of the Sea;* see also R. Engelman and P. LeRoy, *Catching the Limit: Population and the Decline of Fisheries* (Washington, D.C.: Population Action International, 1995); Milazzo, *Subsidies in World Fisheries;* Safina, "Scorched-Earth Fishing"; Safina, *Song for the Blue Ocean;* Thorpe et al., "Conservation of Fish and Shellfish"; Weber, *Net Loss.*

24. McGinn, *Rocking the Boat;* McGinn, *Scaling Back;* Safina, *Song for the Blue Ocean;* Safina, "The World's Imperiled Fish."

25. Milazzo, *Subsidies in World Fisheries;* see also McGinn, *Rocking the Boat;* McGinn, *Scaling Back;* Porter, *Fishing Subsidies, Overfishing, and Trade;* Porter, *Estimating Overcapacity;* D. Schorr, "Towards Rational Disciplines on Subsidies to the Fishery Sector: A Call for New International Rules and Mechanisms," in Pauly et al., *Footprint of Distant Water Fleets,* 144–172.

26. McGinn, *Rocking the Boat;* McGinn, *Scaling Back.*

27. Schorr, "Towards Rational Disciplines."

28. McGinn, *Rocking the Boat;* McGinn, *Scaling Back.*

29. McGinn, *Rocking the Boat;* McGinn, *Scaling Back;* Milazzo, *Subsidies in World Fisheries.*

30. Porter, *Estimating Overcapacity* Safina, "Song for the Blue Ocean," 1997; Safina, "Scorched-Earth Fishing"; see also Garcia and Newton, *Current Situation, Trends, and Prospects*; McGinn, *Rocking the Boat;* McGinn, *Scaling Back;* McGoodwin, *Crisis in the World's Fisheries;* Weber, *Net Loss.*

31. McGinn, *Rocking the Boat;* McGinn, *Scaling Back;* Safina, *Song for the Blue Ocean;* Safina, "Scorched-Earth Fishing"; Steenblik and Munro, *International Work on Fishing Subsidies.*

32. McGinn, *Rocking the Boat;* McGinn, *Scaling Back;* Sissenwine and Rosenberg, "Marine Fisheries at a Critical Juncture."

33. National Fish and Wildlife Foundation, *FY 1996 Fisheries and Wildlife Assessment* (Washington, D.C.: National Fish and Wildlife Foundation, 1995); see also M. L. Weber, *A History of Federal Fisheries Management, 1940–1995* (Washington, D.C.: U.S. Marine Fisheries Service, 1995).

34. E. A. Norse, Marine Conservation Biology Institute, Redmond, Wash., personal communication, 1998.

35. Milazzo, *Subsidies in World Fisheries.*

36. Milazzo, *Subsidies in World Fisheries.*

37. Milazzo, *Subsidies in World Fisheries.*
38. For a fine general discussion of policy options, see Porter, *Fishing Subsidies, Overfishing, and Trade;* Porter, "Estimating Overcapacity"; R. Steenblik and J. Wallis, *The OECD's Program of Work in the Area of Fishery Policies* (Paris: Organisation for Economic Co-operation and Development, 1998).
39. K. L. Gimbel, ed., *Limiting Access to Marine Fisheries: Keeping the Focus on Conservation* (Washington, D.C.: Center for Marine Conservation and World Wildlife Fund–US, 1994); Grainger and Garcia, *Chronicles of Marine Fishery Landings;* McGinn, *Rocking the Boat;* McGinn, *Scaling Back.*
40. McGinn, *Rocking the Boat;* McGinn, *Scaling Back.*
41. McGinn, *Rocking the Boat.*
42. A. Hatcher and K. Robinson, eds., *Overcapacity, Overcapitalization, and Subsidies in European Fisheries* (Portsmouth, England: Centre for the Economics and Management of Aquatic Resources, 1999).
43. Hatcher and Robinson, *Overcapacity, Overcapitalization, and Subsidies;* Weber, *Global Assessment of Major Fisheries at Risk.*
44. J. Gates, D. Holland, and E. Gudmundsson, "Theory and Practice of Fishing Vessel Buyback Programs," in World Wide Fund for Nature International, *Subsidies and Depletion of World Fisheries* (Gland, Switzerland: World Wide Fund for Nature International, 1997), 71–117.
45. Safina, "Scorched-Earth Fishing"; see also Sissenwine and Rosenberg, "Marine Fisheries at a Critical Juncture"; National Fish and Wildlife Foundation, *FY 1996 Fisheries and Wildlife Assessment;* National Marine Fisheries Service, *Our Living Oceans: Second Annual Report on the Status of U.S. Living Marine Resources* (Washington, D.C.: U.S. Department of Commerce, 1992).
46. Safina, *Song for the Blue Ocean.*
47. Milazzo, *Subsidies in World Fisheries.*
48. B. B. Sharp, "From Regulated Access to Transferable Harvesting Rights: Policy Insights from New Zealand," *Marine Policy* 21 (1997): 501–517.
49. R. M. Fujita, D. D. Hopkins, and W. R. Z. Willey, "Creating Incentives to Curb Overfishing," *Forum for Applied Research and Public Policy* 11 (1996): 29–34; R. M. Fujita, J. Philip, and D. D. Hopkins, *The Conservation Benefits of Individual Transferable Quotas* (Oakland, Calif.: Environmental Defense Fund, 1996).

Chapter 8. Forestry

1. E. B. Barbier et al., *The Economics of Tropical Forest Land Use Options: Methodology and Valuation Techniques* (London: London Environmental Economics Centre, 1992); M. Gillis, *Forest Incentive Policies* (Washington, D.C.: World Bank, 1994); R. Repetto, *Macro-*

economic Policies and Deforestation (Tokyo: United Nations University Press; Helsinki: WIDER, 1990).

2. N. Sizer, D. Downes, and D. Kaimowitz, *Tree Trade, Liberalization of International Commerce in Forest Products: Risks and Opportunities* (Washington, D.C.: World Resources Institute, 1999).

3. World Resources Institute, *Critical Consumption Trends and Implications: Degrading Earth's Ecosystems* (Washington, D.C.: World Resources Institute, 1999); see also W. Devall, ed., *Clearcut: The Tragedy of Industrial Forestry* (San Francisco: Sierra Club Books, 1994); N. Dudley, J.-P. Jeanrenaud, and F. Sullivan, *Bad Harvest: The Timber Trade and the Degradation of the World's Forests* (London: Earthscan, 1995); Food and Agriculture Organization, *FAO Provisional Outlook for Global Forest Products Consumption, Production, and Trade to 2010* (Rome: Food and Agriculture Organization, 1997); Sizer et al., "Tree Trade"; J. R. Vincent, "The Tropical Timber Trade and Sustainable Development," *Science* 256 (1992): 1651–1655.

4. Food and Agriculture Organization of the United Nations (FAO), *Forest Resources Assessment, 1990* (Rome: FAO, 1995); see also R. Costanza et al., "The Value of the World's Ecosystem Services and Natural Capital," *Nature* 387 (1997): 253–260.

5. N. Myers, "Tropical Forests: The Policy Challenge," *Environmentalist* 12 (1992): 15–27.

6. S. Nilsson and A. Shvidenko, *The Ukranian Forest Sector in a Global Perspective* (Laxenburg, Austria: International Institute for Applied Systems Analysis, 1999); see also J. N. Abramowitz and A. T. Mattoon, "Reorienting the Forest Products Economy," in L. R. Brown et al., eds., *State of the World, 1999* (New York: Norton, 1999), 60–77.

7. Abramowitz and Mattoon, "Reorienting the Forest Products Economy"; see also W. Ascher, *Why Governments Waste Natural Resources: Policy Failures in Developing Countries* (Baltimore, Md.: Johns Hopkins University Press, 1999); E. B. Barbier and J. C. Burgess, *Timber Trade and Tropical Deforestation: Global Trends and Evidence from Indonesia* (York, England: University of York, Department of Environmental Economics and Environmental Management, 1993); Sizer, Downes, and Kaimowitz, *Trade and Liberalization of International Commerce.*

8. FAO, *Forest Resources Assessment, 1990.*

9. M. Ryan and C. Flavin, "Facing China's Limits," in L. R. Brown et al., *State of the World, 1995* (New York: Norton, 1995), 113–131; J. Spears and E. Ayensu, "Resources, Development, and the New Century: Forestry," in Repetto, ed., *The Global Possible* (New Haven, Conn.: Yale University Press, 1985), 299–336.

10. F. Cairncross, *Green Inc.: A Guide to Business and the Environment* (London: Earthscan, 1995); F. J. Seymour and N. K. Dubash, *The Right Conditions: The World Bank, Structural Adjustment, and Forest Policy Reform* (Washington, D.C.: World Resources Institute, 2000);

P. Wolvekamp, ed., *Forests for the Future: Local Strategies for Forest Protection, Economic Welfare, and Social Justice* (New York: Zed Books, 1999).

11. World Bank, *World Development Report, 1992* (New York: Oxford University Press, 1992).

12. For some overviews of forestry economics and the role of subsidies, see J. von Amsberg, *Economic Parameters of Deforestation* (Washington, D.C.: World Bank, 1994); B. Day, *Economic Distortions and Their Influence on Forests* (London: University College London, Centre for Social and Economic Research on the Global Environment, 1997); M. Gillis, "Tacit Taxes and Sub-Rosa Subsidies Through State-Owned Enterprises," in R. M. Bird, ed., *More Taxing Than Taxes? The Tax-like Effects of Nontax Policies in LDCs* (San Francisco: Institute for Contemporary Studies Press, 1998), 181–235; W. F. Hyde, G. S. Amacher, and W. Magrath, *Deforestation, Scarce Forest Resources, and Forest Land Use: Theory, Empirical Evidence, and Policy Implications* (Washington, D.C.: World Bank, 1993); J. R. Vincent, A. N. A. Ghani, and H. Yusuf, *Economics of Timber Fees and Logging in Tropical Forest Concessions* (Cambridge, Mass.: Harvard Institute for International Development, 1993).

13. M. Gautam et al., *The Challenges of World Bank Involvement in Forests* (Washington, D.C.: World Bank, 2000); see also C. Hamilton, "The Sustainability of Logging in Indonesia's Tropical Forests: A Dynamic Input-Output Analysis," *Ecological Economics* 21 (1997): 183–195.

14. Gautam et al., *Challenges of World Bank Involvement.*

15. Gautam et al., *Challenges of World Bank Involvement;* Sizer, Downes, and Kaimowitz, *Trade and Liberalization of International Commerce;* M. Toha, *Estimated Deforestation Rate for Indonesia* (Jakarta, Indonesia: Ministry of Forestry, 2000); T. Walton, *Is There a Future for Indonesia's Forests?* (Jakarta, Indonesia: World Bank, 2000).

16. Food and Agriculture Organization of the United Nations (FAO) and Government of Indonesia, *Situation and Outlook of the Forestry Sector in Indonesia* (Rome: FAO; Jakarta, Indonesia: Government of Indonesia, 1990).

17. Walton, *Is There a Future for Indonesia's Forests?*

18. See, e.g., Hamilton, "Sustainability of Logging"; Walton, *Is There a Future for Indonesia's Forests?*

19. Gautam et al., *Challenges of World Bank Involvement;* Walton, *Is There a Future for Indonesia's Forests?*

20. C. V. Barber, N. C. Johnson, and E. Hafild, *Breaking the Logjam: Obstacles to Forest Policy Reform in Indonesia and the United States* (Washington, D.C.: World Resources Institute, 1994); M. Gillis, "Forest Concession Management and Revenue Policies," in N. Sharma, ed., *Managing the World's Forests* (Dubuque, Iowa: Kendall/Hunt, 1992); N. Johnson and B. Cabarle, *Surviving the Cut: Natural Forest Man-*

agement in the Humid Tropics (Washington, D.C.: World Resources Institute, 1993).

21. M. Gillis, "Indonesia: Public Policies, Resource Management, and the Tropical Forest," in R. Repetto and M. Gillis, eds., *Public Policies and the Misuse of Forest Resources* (New York: Cambridge University Press, 1988); Gillis, *Forest Incentive Policies;* see also W. Ascher, *Political Economy and Problematic Forestry Policies in Indonesia: Obstacles to Incorporating Sound Economics and Science* (Durham, N.C.: Duke University, Center for International Development Research, 1993); Barbier and Burgess, *Timber Trade and Tropical Deforestation.*

22. World Bank, *Indonesia Forestry Sector Review* (Jakarta, Indonesia: World Bank, 1993); see also J. N. Abramovitz, "Sustaining the World's Forests," in L. R. Brown et al., *State of the World, 1998* (New York: Norton, 1998); Barber, Johnson, and Hafild, *Breaking the Logjam;* R. Broad, "The Political Economy of Natural Resources: Case Studies of the Indonesian and Philippine Forest Sectors," *Journal of Developing Areas* 29 (1995): 317–340; P. Dauvergne, "The Politics of Deforestation in Indonesia," *Pacific Affairs* 66 (1993): 497–518; D. M. Roodman, "Public Money and Human Purpose: The Future of Taxes," *World Watch* 8, no. 5 (1995): 10–19.

23. J. R. Vincent, "Don't Boycott Tropical Timber," *Journal of Forestry* 88, no. 4 (1990): 56; see also J. R. Vincent, "Rent Capture and the Feasibility of Tropical Forest Management," *Land Economics* 66 (1990): 212–223.

24. S. Hammer and S. Shetty, *East Asia's Environment* (Washington, D.C.: World Bank, 1995).

25. Gautam et al., *Challenges of World Bank Involvement;* Sizer, Downes, and Kaimowitz, *Trade and Liberalization of International Commerce;* Walton, *Is There a Future for Indonesia's Forests?* See also D. Brown, *Addicted to Rent: Corporate and Spatial Distribution of Forest Resources Indonesia: Implications for Forest Sustainability and Government Policy* (Jakarta, Indonesia: Indonesia-U.K. Tropical Forest Management Program, 1999); J. R. Vincent, "Timber Trade, Economics, and Tropical Forest Management," in R. B. Primack and T. E. Lovejoy, eds., *Ecology, Conservation, and Management of Southeast Asian Rainforests* (New Haven, Conn.: Yale University Press, 1995), 241–262.

26. Hamilton, "Sustainability of Logging."

27. Barber, Johnson, and Hafild, *Breaking the Logjam.*

28. Gillis, "Indonesia"; E. G. T. Manurung and J. Buongiorno, "Effects of the Ban on Tropical Log Exports on the Forestry Sector of Indonesia," *Journal of World Forest Resource Management* 8 (1997): 21–49.

29. B. Fitzgerald, *An Analysis of Indonesian Trade Policies* (Washington, D.C.: World Bank, 1986); R. Goodland and H. Daly, "If Tropical Log Export Bans Are So Perverse, Why Are There So Many?" *Ecological Economics* 18 (1996): 189–196.

30. Manurung and Buongiorno, "Effects of the Bank."
31. Barber, Johnson, and Hafild, *Breaking the Logjam.*
32. M. Ahmad, *Economic Rent in Indonesia's Timber Production* (East Lansing: Michigan State University Press, 1997); H. Brookfield and Y. Byron, eds., *Southeast Asia's Environmental Future: The Search for Sustainability* (Tokyo: United Nations University Press, 1993); P. Dauvergne, *Shadows in the Forest: Japan and the Political Economy of Deforestation in Southeast Asia* (Cambridge, Mass.: MIT Press, 1997); J. Fox, M. Wasson, and G. Applegate, *Forest Use Policies and Strategies in Indonesia: A Need for Change* (Jakarta, Indonesia: World Bank, 1999); Gautam et al., *Challenges of World Bank Involvement;* Walton, *Is There a Future for Indonesia's Forests?*
33. Fox, Wasson, and Applegate, *Forest Use Policies;* A. I. Fraser, personal communication (letter of 15 May 1997); J. A. Gray and S. Hadi, *Fiscal Policies and Pricing in Indonesia's Forests* (Jakarta: Ministry of Forestry, Government of Indonesia, 1990).
34. Fraser, personal communication.
35. World Bank, *Indonesia: Environment and Development: Challenges for the Future* (Washington, D.C.: World Bank, 1994).
36. See, e.g., Gautam et al., *Challenges of World Bank Involvement;* Sizer, Downes, and Kaimowitz, *Trade and Liberalization of International Commerce;* Walton, *Is There a Future for Indonesia's Forests?* See also Ascher, *Why Governments Waste;* Day, *Economic Distortions;* Gillis, "Tacit Taxes and Sub-Rosa Subsidies."
37. C. Barr et al., *Corporate Debt and the Indonesian Forestry Sector* (Bogor, Indonesia: Center for International Forestry Research, 2000).
38. Repetto and Gillis, *Public Policies;* see also Barber, Johnson, and Hafild, *Breaking the Logjam.*
39. Hamilton, "Sustainability of Logging."
40. J. O. Browder, "Public Policy and Deforestation in the Brazilian Amazon," in Repetto and Gillis, *Public Policies,* 247–298; see also S. B. Hecht, "Logics of Livestock and Deforestation: The Case of Amazonia," in T. Downing et al., eds., *Development or Destruction: The Conversion of Tropical Forests to Pasture in Latin America* (Boulder, Colo.: Westview Press, 1992), 7–25; Repetto, *Macroeconomic Policies;* R. Repetto et al., *The Forests for the Trees: Government Policies and the Misuse of Forest Resources* (World Resources Institute, 1988).
41. Repetto, *The Forest for the Trees;* R. Schneider, *Government and the Economy on the Amazon Frontier* (Washington, D.C.: World Bank, 1995).
42. Browder, "Public Policy and Deforestation"; J. O. Browder, ed., *Fragile Lands of Latin America* (Boulder, Colo.: Westview Press, 1989); see also H. Binswanger, *Brazilian Policies That Encourage Deforestation in the Amazon* (Washington, D.C.: World Bank, 1989); Schneider, *Government and the Economy.*
43. E. Y. Arima and C. Uhl, "Ranching in the Brazilian Amazon in a

National Context: Economics, Policy, and Practice," *Society and Natural Resources* 10, no. 5 (1997): 433–451; J. Heath and H. Binswanger, "Natural Resource Degradation Effects of Poverty and Population Growth Are Largely Policy Induced: The Case of Colombia," *Environment and Development Economics* 1 (1996): 65–84; Schneider, *Government and the Economy;* D. Southgate, ed., *Alternatives to Tropical Deforestation* (New York: Oxford University Press, 1997).

44. R. Repetto, *The Forest for the Trees? Government Policies and the Misuse of Forest Resources* (Washington, D.C.: World Resources Institute, 1988).

45. Gillis, "Forest Concession Management"; see also Browder, "Public Policy and Deforestation"; Hyde, Amacher, and Magrath, *Deforestation;* M. Mattos and C. Uhl, "Economic and Ecological Perspectives on Ranching in the Eastern Amazon," *World Development* 22 (1994): 145–158; R. Schneider, *Brazil: An Analysis of Environmental Problems in the Amazon* (Washington, D.C.: World Bank, 1992); Southgate, *Alternatives to Tropical Deforestation;* J. von Amsberg, *Economic Parameters of Deforestation.*

46. See, for example, D. Southgate, "Economic Progress and Habitat Conservation in Latin America," in T. M. Swanson, ed., *The Economics and Ecology of Biodiversity Decline: The Forces Driving Global Change* (Cambridge, England: Cambridge University Press, 1995), 91–98; Southgate, *Alternatives to Tropical Deforestation;* see also L. E. Andersen, *A Cost-Benefit Analysis of Deforestation in the Brazilian Amazon* (Rio de Janeiro: Institute for Applied Economics Research, 1996); Schneider, *Government and the Economy;* C. Uhl et al., "Natural Resource Management in the Brazilian Amazon: An Integrated Research Approach," *BioScience* 47 (1997): 160–168.

47. Arima and Uhl, "Ranching in the Brazilian Amazon"; Mattos and Uhl, "Economic and Ecological Perspectives."

48. E. Barbier, J. Burgess, and A. Markandya, "The Economics of Tropical Deforestation," *Ambio* 20 (1991): 55–58; Binswanger, *Brazilian Policies;* J. A. Krautkraemer, "Incentives, Development, and Population: A Growth-Theoretic Perspective," in T. M. Swanson, ed., *The Economics and Ecology of Biodiversity Decline* (Cambridge, England: Cambridge University Press, 1995), 13–24; R. Schneider, *Government and the Economy on the Amazon Frontier* (Washington, D.C.: World Bank, 1994); Uhl et al., "Natural Resource Management."

49. Andersen, *Cost-Benefit Analysis;* Barber, Johnson, and Hafild, *Breaking the Logjam;* Uhl et al., "Natural Resource Management."

50. Repetto, *Macroeconomic Policies;* Southgate, *Alternatives to Tropical Deforestation.*

51. N. Sizer and D. Plouvier, *Increased Investment and Trade by Transnational Logging Companies in Africa, the Caribbean, and the Pacific: Implications for the Sustainable Management and Conservation of Tropical Forests* (Washington, D.C.: World Resources Institute, 1999);

Sizer, Downes, and Kaimowitz, *Trade and Liberalization of International Commerce.*

52. E. B. Barbier et al., *The Economics of the Tropical Timber Trade* (London: Earthscan, 1994); Hyde, Amacher, and Magrath, *Deforestation;* Repetto and Gillis, *Public Policies;* Southgate, *Alternatives to Tropical Deforestation;* J. R. Vincent and M. Gillis, "Deforestation and Forest Land Use: A Comment," *World Bank Observer* 13, no. 1 (1998): 133–140; von Amsberg, *Economic Parameters of Deforestation.*

53. Hammer and Shetty, *East Asia's Environment.*

54. Vincent, "Don't Boycott Tropical Timber."

55. Sizer, Downes, and Kaimowitz, *Trade and Liberalization of International Commerce;* World Commission on Forests and Sustainable Development, *Our Forests, Our Future* (Cambridge, England: Cambridge University Press, 1999); see also K. Talbot and M. Brown, "Forest Plunder in Southeast Asia: An Environmental Security Nexus in Burma and Cambodia," *Environment and Security Project Report* (Washington, D.C.: Woodrow Wilson International Center for Scholars, 1998), 53–60.

56. R. Beattie, "Environmental Accounting: Including the Environment in Measures of Well-Being," in J. Sullivan, ed., *Environmental Policies: Implications for Agricultural Trade* (Washington, D.C.: U.S. Department of Agriculture, Economic Research Service, 1994), 6–12; see also N. M. Kishor and L. F. Constantino, *Forest Management and Competing Land Uses: An Economic Analysis for Costa Rica* (Washington, D.C.: World Bank, 1993).

57. T. Heindrichs, *Innovative Financing Instruments in the Forestry and Nature Conservation Sector of Costa Rica* (Eschborn, Germany: GTZ, 1997); see also M. Richards, *Internalising the Externalities of Tropical Forestry: A Review of Innovative Financing and Incentive Mechanisms* (London: Overseas Development Institute, 1999).

58. A. Peuker, *Public Policies and Deforestation: A Case Study of Costa Rica* (Washington, D.C.: World Bank, 1992).

59. R. De Camino et al., *Forest Policy and the Evolution of Land Use: An Evaluation of Costa Rica's Forest Development and World Bank Assistance* (Washington, D.C.: World Bank, 2000); Wolvekamp, *Forests for the Future.*

60. G. Aplet et al., *Defining Sustainable Forestry* (Washington, D.C.: Island Press, 1993); Ascher, *Why Governments Waste;* Dudley, Jeanrenaud, and Sullivan, *Bad Harvest;* Hyde, Amacher, and Magrath, *Deforestation;* Sizer, Downes, and Kaimowitz, *Trade and Liberalization of International Commerce;* Vincent, "Timber Trade, Economics, and Tropical Forest Management"; von Amsberg, *Economic Parameters of Deforestation.*

61. D. Poore et al., *No Timber Without Trees* (London: Earthscan, 1989).

62. M. L. Ross, "The Political Economy of Boom and Bust Logging in Indonesia, the Philippines, and East Malaysia, 1950–1994" (Ph.D.

diss., Princeton University, Department of Political Science, 1996); M.
Ross, "Conditionality and Logging Reforms in the Tropics," in R. O.
Keohane and M. A. Levy, eds., *Institutions for Environmental Aid:
Pitfalls and Promise* (Cambridge, Mass.: MIT Press, 1996), 176–197.

63. R. Repetto and N. Sizer, *Why Finance Sustainable Forestry?* (Washington, D.C.: World Resources Institute, 1996).

64. Cairncross, *Green Inc.*

65. D. M. Roodman, *The Natural Wealth of Nations: Harnessing the Market for the Environment* (New York: Norton, 1998).

66. Gillis, "Indonesia," cited in Ascher, *Why Governments Waste.*

67. D. G. Bryant et al., *The Last Frontier Forests: Ecosystems and Economies on the Edge* (Washington, D.C.: World Resources Institute, 1997).

68. R. W. Gorte and M. L. Corn, *The Forest Service Budget: Trust Funds and Special Accounts* (Washington, D.C.: Congressional Research Service, 1997); The Wilderness Society, *America's National Forests: A Vision for the Future* (Washington, D.C.: Wilderness Society, 1999); see also B. Baker, "Rethinking Roads in the Nation's Forests," *BioScience* 48 (1998): 156.

69. H. J. Cortner and D. L. Schweitzer, "Below-Cost Timber Sales and the Political Marketplace," *Environmental Management* 17 (1993): 7–14; B. D. Gardener, "Some Implications of Federal Grazing, Timber, Irrigation, and Recreation Subsidies," *Choices* 12, no. 3 (1997): 9–14.

70. Abramowitz and Mattoon, "Reorienting the Forest Products Economy"; see also D. W. Floyd, ed., *Forest of Discord: Options for Governing Our National Forests and Federal Public Lands* (Bethesda, Md.: Society of American Foresters, 1999); G. Miller (chairman of committee), *Taking from the Taxpayer: Public Subsidies for Natural Resource Development* (Washington, D.C.: U.S. House of Representatives, Committee on Natural Resources, 1994).

71. R. O'Toole, *Timber Sale Subsidies, but Who Gets Them?* (Oak Grove, Oreg.: Thoreau Institute, 1995); Thoreau Institute and R. O'Toole, *Review of the Proposed 1999 Forest Service Budget* (Oak Grove, Oreg.: Thoreau Institute, 1999); see also C. F. Runge and T. Jones, "Subsidies, Tax Disincentives, and the Environment: An Overview and Synthesis," in Organisation for Economic Co-operation and Development (OECD), *Subsidies and Environment: Exploring the Linkages* (Paris: OECD, 1996), 7–21.

72. Devall, *Clearcut;* O'Toole, *Timber Sale Subsidies.*

73. Thoreau Institute and O'Toole, *Review of Proposed 1999 Forest Service Budget.*

74. Thoreau Institute and O'Toole, *Review of Proposed 1999 Forest Service Budget;* see also C. Alkire, *Returns to the Treasury from National Forest Timber Programs, FY 1992* (Washington, D.C.: Wilderness Society, 1993); R. W. Gorte, *Timber Sales Cost Accounting: The Forest Service and TSPIRS* (Washington, D.C.: Congressional Research

Service, 1993); E. Losos et al., "Taxpayer-Subsidized Resource Extraction Harms Species," *BioScience* 45 (1995): 446–455; D. M. Roodman, *Paying the Piper: Subsidies, Politics, and the Environment* (Washington, D.C.: Worldwatch Institute, 1996).

75. Abramowitz and Mattoon, "Reorienting the Forest Products Economy."

76. Roodman, *Paying the Piper;* see also S. Holmer, *Forest Appropriations Initiative (FY 2000)* (Washington, D.C.: American Lands Alliance, 1999); Thoreau Institute and O'Toole, *Review of Proposed 1999 Forest Service Budget.*

77. For an extended exposition on this theme, see O'Toole, *Timber Sale Subsidies;* Thoreau Institute and O'Toole, *Review of Proposed 1999 Forest Service Budget;* Roodman, *Paying the Piper;* see also Abramowitz and Mattoon, "Reorienting the Forest Products Economy"; Floyd, *Forest of Discord.*

78. K. Durbin, "Sawdust Memories," *Amicus Journal* Fall (1997).

79. P. Pittman, D. Katz, and J. Lancelot, *Clearcutting Virgin Rainforest on the Tongass: $100 Million* (Washington, D.C.: Natural Resources Defense Council and Taxpayers for Common Sense, 1997); Roodman, *Natural Wealth of Nations;* C. Servid and D. Snow, *The Book of the Tongass* (New York: Milkweed, 1999); N. Sizer, *Perverse Habits: The G8 and Subsidies That Harm Forests and Economies* (Washington, D.C.: World Resources Institute, 2000).

80. W. Proxmire, *Japan Gets the Logs and the United States Gets Rolled* (Washington, D.C.: Senate Office Building, Office of Senator William Proxmire, 1997).

81. Pittman, Katz, and Lancelot, *Clearcutting Virgin Rainforest;* P. K. Schoonmaker, B. von Hagen, and E. C. Wolf, eds., *The Rain Forests of Home: Profile of a North American Bioregion* (Washington, D.C.: Island Press, 1996); see also The Wilderness Society, *America's Vanishing Rain Forest: A Report on Federal Timber Management in Southeast Alaska* (Washington, D.C.: Wilderness Society, 1986); Sizer, *Perverse Habits.*

82. Proxmire, *Japan Gets the Logs.*

83. R. O'Toole, Thoreau Institute, Oak Grove, Oreg., personal communication (letter of April 2000); Thoreau Institute and O'Toole, *Review of Proposed 1999 Forest Service Budget;* see also Floyd, *Forest of Discord;* Roodman, *Natural Wealth of Nations;* Wilderness Society, *America's National Forests.*

84. J. Talberth and K. Moskawitz, *The Economic Case Against National Forest Logging* (Santa Fe, N.M.: Forest Conservation Council, 2000).

85. Talberth and Moskawitz, *Economic Case Against National Forest Logging.*

86. Talberth and Moskawitz, *Economic Case Against National Forest Logging.*

87. Floyd, *Forest of Discord;* C. Maser, ed., *Sustainable Forestry: Philoso-*

phy, Science, and Economics (Boca Raton, Fla.: St. Lucie Press, 1994); Roodman, *Natural Wealth of Nations;* Thoreau Institute and O'Toole, *Review of Proposed 1999 Forest Service Budget;* Wilderness Society, *America's National Forests.*
88. Abramowitz and Mattoon, "Reorienting the Forest Products Economy"; U.S. Department of Agriculture (USDA), Committee of Scientists, *Sustaining the People's Lands: Recommendations for Stewardship of the National Forests and Grasslands in the Next Century* (Washington, D.C.: USDA, Committee of Scientists, 1999); see also B. Goodman, "U.S. Forest Service Proposes Ban on Road Construction," *Bioscience* 50, no. 9 (2000): 744.
89. J. E. Williams, C. A. Wood, and M. P. Dombeck, *Watershed Restoration: Principles and Practices* (Bethesda, Md.: American Fisheries Society, 1997).
90. M. Dombeck, *A Natural Resource Agenda for the Twenty-First Century* (Washington, D.C.: U.S. Department of Agriculture, Forest Service, 1998); M. Dombeck, *Conservation for the New Century* (Washington, D.C.: U.S. Department of Agriculture, Forest Service, 1999); U.S. Department of Agriculture (USDA), Forest Service, *Forest Service Limits New Road Construction in Most National Forests* (Washington, D.C.: USDA, Forest Service, 1999).
91. H. M. Anderson, "Reshaping National Forest Policy," *Issues in Science and Technology* 16, no. 1 (1999): 80–87; Abramowitz and Mattoon, "Reorienting the Forest Products Economy."
92. D. Gawthrop, *Vanishing Halo* (Vancouver, British Columbia, Canada: Greystone Books, 1999).
93. Sierra Legal Defence Fund, *Profits or Plunder: Mismanagement of B.C.'s Forests* (Victoria, British Columbia, Canada: Sierra Legal Defence Fund, 1998); Sierra Legal Defence Fund et al., *British Columbia: Forestry Report Card, 1997–1998* (Victoria, British Columbia, Canada: Sierra Legal Defence Fund, 1999).
94. Sizer, Downes, and Kaimowitz, *Trade and Liberalization of International Commerce;* see also Abramowitz and Mattoon, "Reorienting the Forest Products Economy"; Gawthrop, *Vanishing Halo;* Global Forest Watch, *Canada's Forests at a Crossroads: An Assessment in the Year 2000* (Washington, D.C.: World Resources Institute, 2000); Greenpeace Canada, *Broken Promises: The Truth About What's Happening to B.C.'s Forests* (Vancouver, British Columbia, Canada: Greenpeace Canada, 1997); British Columbia Ministry of Environment, Lands and Parks, *Greenpeace Report "Broken Promises": An Analysis* (Vancouver, British Columbia, Canada: British Columbia Ministry of Environment, Lands and Parks, 1997); M. Mascall and B. Campbell, "Public Investment in the B.C. Forests Industry, 1988–1989 to 1995–1996," in Greenpeace Canada, *Broken Promises.*
95. D. Downes and D. Kaimowitz, *Tree Trade: Liberalization of International Commerce in Forest Products: Risks and Opportunities* (Wash-

ington, D.C.: World Resources Institute and Center for International Environmental Law, 1999); B. Parfitt, *Forest Follies: Adventures and Misadventures in the Great Canadian Forest* (Vancouver, British Columbia, Canada: Harbour, 1998); F. Wilson, *Cutting Cost$: The Politics of Trees and Fees in B.C.* (Vancouver, British Columbia: Canadian Centre for Policy Alternatives, 1999).

96. D. J. Schor, *Ecologically Sustainable Forestry and Economic Incentives* (Ottawa, Ontario, Canada: Library of Parliament, 1996).

97. R. Q. Grafton, R. W. Lynch, and H. W. Melson, "British Columbia's Stumpage System: Economic and Trade Policy Implications," *Canadian Public Policy* 24 (1998): S41–S50.

98. Schor, *Ecologically Sustainable Forestry;* see also Downes and Kaimowitz, *Tree Trade;* M. Mascall and B. Campbell, *Public Investment by Governments in the B.C. Forest Industry, 1988–1989 to 1995–1996* (Quathiaski Cove, British Columbia, Canada: Michael Mascall and Associates, 1997).

99. Mascall and Campbell, *Public Investment by Governments.*

100. Sizer, Downes, and Kaimowitz, *Trade and Liberalization of International Commerce.*

101. Wilson, *Cutting Cost$;* see also Parfitt, *Forest Follies.*

102. Sizer, Downes, and Kaimowitz, *Trade and Liberalization of International Commerce;* Downes and Kaimowitz, *Tree Trade;* Mascall and Campbell, *Public Investment by Governments;* Wilson, *Cutting Cost$;* see also Abramowitz and Mattoon, "Reorienting the Forest Products Economy"; Parfitt, *Forest Follies.*

103. R. Gale, F. Gale, and T. Green, *Accounting for the Forests: A Methodological Critique of Pricewaterhouse's Report "The Forest Industry in British Columbia 1997"* (Victoria, British Columbia, Canada: Ecological Economics Inc., 1999).

104. Gale, Gale, and Green, *Accounting for the Forests.*

105. Sierra Legal Defence Fund, *Profits or Plunder.*

106. Gale, Gale, and Green, *Accounting for the Forests.*

107. Gale, Gale, and Green, *Accounting for the Forests.*

108. British Columbia Ministry of Forests, *Providing for the Future: Sustainable Forest Management in British Columbia* (Victoria, British Columbia, Canada: British Columbia Ministry of Forests, 1996).

109. Natural Resources Canada, *The State of Canada's Forests, 1997–1998* (Ottawa, Ontario: Natural Resources Canada, 1999).

110. R. Gale, personal communication, April 2000.

111. Gawthrop, *Vanishing Halo.*

112. T. P. Kolchugina and T. S. Vinson, "Role of Russian Forests in the Global Carbon Balance," *Ambio* 24 (1995): 258–264; A. Z. Shvidenko and S. Nilsson, "What Do We Know About the Siberian Forests?" *Ambio* 23 (1994): 396–404; A. Yablokov, senior environmental adviser to President Boris Yeltsin, personal communication during stay at author's home in Oxford, England, 9 April 1997.

113. Day, *Economic Distortions*.

114. V. Alexeyev, *Human and Natural Impacts on the Health of Russian Forests* (Moscow: USSR Academy of Sciences, Institute of Forest and Timber Research, Siberian Branch, 1991); Kolchugina and Vinson, "Role of Russian Forests"; Shvidenko and Nilsson, "What Do We Know About the Siberian Forests?"

115. J. P. Hall, "Forest Health Monitoring in Canada: How Healthy Is the Boreal Forest?" *Water, Air, and Soil Pollution* 82 (1995): 77–85; W. A. Kurz and M. J. Apps, "An Analysis of Future Carbon Budgets of Canadian Boreal Forests," *Water, Air, and Soil Pollution* 82 (1995): 321–331.

116. N. Shulyakovskaya, "Wood Wars: Corruption Threatens Welfare of Siberia," *St. Petersburg (Russia) Times*, 16 February 2000.

117. Sizer, Downes, and Kaimowitz, *Trade and Liberalization of International Commerce*; World Commission on Forests and Sustainable Development, *Our Forests, Our Future*; Gawthrop, *Vanishing Halo*.

118. A. K. Dragun, *The Subsidization of Logging in Victoria* (Melbourne, Australia: La Trobe University, Department of Economics, 1995).

119. C. Hamilton, "The Economics of Logging High Conservation Value Native Forests," *Economic and Labor Relations Review* 6 (1995): 159–179; Reed Sturgess and Associates, *Economic Evaluation of Wood and Water from the Thomson Catchment* (Melbourne, Australia: Melbourne Water Corporation and Department of Conservation and Natural Resources, 1994).

120. Dragun, *Subsidization of Logging*.

121. K. A. Crews and C. L. Stouffer, *World Population and the Environment* (Washington, D.C.: Population Reference Bureau, 1997); S. K. Kumar and D. Hotchkiss, *Consequences of Deforestation for Women's Time Allocation, Agricultural Production, and Nutrition in Hill Areas of Nepal* (Washington, D.C.: International Food Policy Research Institute, 1988); I. Tinker, "The Real Rural Energy Crisis: Womens' Time," in A. V. DeSai, ed., *Human Energy* (New Delhi: Wiley Eastern, 1990).

122. J. A. Lampietti and J. A. Dixon, *To See the Forest for the Trees: A Guide to Non-Timber Forest Benefits* (Washington, D.C.: World Bank, 1995).

123. K. Chopra, "The Value of Non-Timber Forest Products: An Estimation for Tropical Deciduous Forests in India," *Economic Botany* 47 (1993): 251–257.

124. D. Pimentel et al., "Economic and Environmental Benefits of Biodiversity," *BioScience* 47 (1997): 747–757.

125. E. O. Wilson, *The Diversity of Life* (Cambridge, Mass.: Harvard University Press, 1992).

126. Wilson, *Diversity of Life*.

127. M. J. Balick, W. Elisabetsky, and S. Laird, eds., *Tropical Forest Medical Resources and the Conservation of Biodiversity* (New York: Columbia University Press, 1996).

128. P. Principe, "Monetizing the Pharmacological Benefits of Plants," in Balick, Elisabetsky, and Laird, *Tropical Forest Medical Resources,* 191–218.
129. M. Suffness, D. J. Newman, and K. Snader, "Discovery and Development of Anti-Neoplastic Agents from Natural Sources," *Bioorganic Marine Chemistry* 3 (1989): 131–168.
130. R. Meldelsohn and M. J. Balick, "The Value of Undiscovered Pharmaceuticals in Tropical Forests," *Economic Botany* 49 (1995): 223–228.
131. D. Pearce and S. Puroshothaman, *Protecting Biological Diversity: The Economic Value of Pharmaceutical Plants* (London: University College London, Centre for Social and Economic Research on the Global Environment, 1993).
132. A. Gentry, "Tropical Forest Biodiversity and the Potential for New Medicinal Plants," in A. D. Kinghorn and M. F. Balandrin, eds., *Human Medicinal Agents from Plants* (Washington, D.C.: American Chemical Society, 1993), 13–24.
133. R. E. Evanson, "Genetic Resources: Assessing Economic Value," in J. R. Vincent, E. W. Crawford, and J. Hoehn, eds., *Valuing Environmental Benefits in Developing Economies* (East Lansing: Michigan State University Press, 1991), 169–181.
134. G. M. Woodwell, "Forests: What in the World Are They For?" in G. M. Woodwell and K. Ramakrishna, eds., *World Forests for the Future: Their Use and Conservation* (New Haven, Conn.: Yale University Press, 1993), 1–20.
135. C. F. Jordan, *Nutrient Cycling in Tropical Forest Ecosystems* (Chichester, England: Wiley, 1985).
136. G. M. Woodwell, "Biotic Feedbacks from the Warming of the Earth," in G. M. Woodwell and F. T. Mackenzie, eds., *Biotic Feedbacks in the Global Climatic System* (New York: Oxford University Press, 1995), 3–21.
137. L. Bruinzeel, *Hydrology of Moist Tropical Forests and Effects of Conservation: A State of Knowledge Review* (Paris: UNESCO, International Hydrological Programme, 1990).
138. S. Sfeir-Younis, *Soil Conservation in Developing Countries: A Background Report* (Washington, D.C.: World Bank, 1986).
139. Woodwell, "Forests."
140. E. Salati and C. A. Nobre, "Possible Climatic Impacts of Tropical Deforestation," in N. Myers, ed., *Tropical Forests and Climate* (Dordrecht, Netherlands: Kluwer, 1992), 177–196.
141. Woodwell and Mackenzie, *Biotic Feedbacks.*
142. World Commission on Forests and Sustainable Development, *Our Forests, Our Future.*
143. A. T. Durning, "Redesigning the Forest Economy," in L. R. Brown et al., eds., *State of the World, 1994* (New York: Norton, 1994), 22–40; N. Myers, *Deforestation Rates in Tropical Forests and Their Climatic Implications* (London: Friends of the Earth, 1989).

144. T. Panayotou and P. S. Ashton, *Not by Timber Alone: Economics and Ecology for Sustaining Tropical Forests* (Washington, D.C.: Island Press, 1992); see also Chopra, "Value of Non-Timber Forest Products"; J. V. S. Murty, *Watershed Management in India* (New Delhi: Wiley Eastern, 1994).

145. K. Mahmood, *Reservoir Sedimentation: Impact, Extent, and Mitigation* (Washington, D.C.: World Bank, 1987).

146. W. Magrath and P. Arens, *The Costs of Soil Erosion on Java: A Natural Resource Accounting Approach* (Washington, D.C.: World Bank, 1989).

147. J. R. Garcia, "Waterfalls, Hydropower, and Water for Industry: Contributions from Canaima National Park, Venezuela," in J. A. McNeely and K. R. Miller, eds., *National Parks, Conservation, and Development: The Role of Protected Areas in Sustaining Society* (Washington, D.C.: Smithsonian Institution Press, 1984), 588–591.

148. United Nations Environment Programme (UNEP), *Global Environment Outlook 2000* (London: Earthscan, 1999); L. R. Brown et al., *Vital Signs 1998* (New York: Norton, 1998).

149. Salati and Nobre, "Possible Climatic Impacts"; N. Myers, "Tropical Deforestation and Climatic Change," *Environmental Conservation* 15, no. 4 (1988): 293–298; J. Shukla, C. Nobre, and P. Sellers, "Amazon Deforestation and Climate Change," *Science* 247 (1990): 1322–1325.

150. N. W. Chan, "Drought Trends in Northwestern Peninsular Malaysia," *Wallaceana* 44 (1986): 8–9.

151. V. M. Meher-Homji, "Probable Impact of Deforestation on Hydrological Processes," in Myers, *Tropical Forests and Climate*, 163–174.

152. Salati and Nobre, "Possible Climatic Impacts."

153. M. Apps and D. Price, eds., *Forest Ecosystems, Forest Management, and the Global Carbon Cycle* (New York: Springer-Verlag, 1996); P. Ciais et al., "A Large Northern Hemisphere Terrestrial CO_2 Sink," *Science* 269 (1995): 1098–1102; Woodwell and MacKenzie, *Biotic Feedbacks*.

154. D. Zak, "Response of Terrestrial Ecosystems to Carbon Dioxide Fertilization," in S. J. Hassol and J. Katzenberger, eds., *Elements of Change, 1994* (Aspen, Colo.: Aspen Global Change Institute, 1995), 202–204.

155. J. T. Houghton, G. J. Jenkins, and J. J. Ephramus, eds., *Climate Change: The IPCC Scientific Assessment (Final Report of Working Group 1)* (New York: Cambridge University Press, 1990); Woodwell, "Forests."

156. R. K. Dixon et al., "Carbon Pools and Flux of Global Forest Ecosystems," *Science* 263 (1994): 185–190; M. Apps et al., "Boreal Forests and Tundra," *Water, Air, and Soil Pollution* 70 (1993): 39–53.

157. S. Nilsson, "Air Pollution and European Forests," in J. Rose, ed., *Acid Rain: Current Situation and Remedies* (Amsterdam: Gordon and Breach, 1994); see also, N. Myers ed., *Tropical Forests and Climate* (Dordrecht, Netherlands: Kluwer, 1992).

158. R. A. Houghton, "Roles of Forests in Global Warming," in K. Rama-krishna and G. M. Woodwell, eds., *World Forests for the Future: Their Use and Conservation* (New Haven, Conn.: Yale University Press, 1993), 21–58.

159. Dixon et al., "Carbon Pools."

160. Dixon et al., "Carbon Pools."

161. Apps and Price, *Forest Ecosystems;* M. Hulme and D. Viner, *A Climate Change Scenario for Assessing the Impact of Climate Change on Tropical Rain Forests* (Washington, D.C.: World Wildlife Fund–US, 1995).

162. J. T. Houghton et al., eds., *The Science of Climate Change: The Second Assessment Report of the Intergovernmental Panel on Climate Change* (New York: Cambridge University Press, 1996); see also Hulme and Viner, *Climate Change Scenario.*

163. M. Apps, ed., "Boreal Forests and Global Climate," *Water, Air, and Soil Pollution* 82 (1995), special issue; Dixon et al., "Carbon Pools."

164. K. Jardine, *The Carbon Bomb: Climate Change and the Fate of the Northern Boreal Forests* (Amsterdam: Stichting Greenpeace Council, 1994); Houghton et al., *Science of Climate Change.*

165. K. Brown and D. W. Pearce, "The Economic Value of Non-Marketed Benefits of Tropical Forests: Carbon Storage," in J. Weiss, ed., *The Economics of Project Appraisal and the Environment* (London: Edward Elgar, 1994), 102–123; S. Fankhauser, "The Social Costs of Greenhouse Gas Emissions: An Expected Value Approach," *Energy Journal* 15 (1994): 157–184.

166. Brown and Pearce, "Economic Value of Non-Marketed Benefits."

167. Panayotou and Ashton, *Not by Timber Alone.*

168. B. Guitierez and D. W. Pearce, *Estimating the Environmental Benefits of the Amazon Forest: An Intertemporal Valuation Exercise* (London: CSERGE/University College, 1992); see also K. Brown and W. N. Adger, "Economic and Political Feasibility of International Carbon Offsets," *Forest Ecology and Management* 68 (1994): 217–229.

169. H. Gregersen et al., *Measuring and Capturing Forest Values: Issues for the Decision Maker* (St. Paul: University of Minnesota, College of Natural Resources, 1997); Brown and Pearce, "Economic Value of Non-Marketed Benefits"; see also Richards, *Internalising the Externalities of Tropical Forestry.*

170. W. N. Adger et al., "Total Economic Value of Forests in Mexico," *Ambio* 24 (1995): 286–296.

171. R. Castro, *The Economic Opportunity Costs of Wildlands Conservation Areas: The Case of Costa Rica* (Cambridge, Mass.: Harvard University, Department of Economics, 1994); L. Constantino and N. Kishor, *Forest Management and Competing Land Uses: An Economic Analysis for Costa Rica* (Washington, D.C.: World Bank, 1993); D. Pimentel et al., "The Value of Forests to World Food Security," *Human Ecology* 25 (1997): 91–120.

172. Costanza et al., "Value of the World's Ecosystem Services."

173. BAPPENAS (National Development Planning Agency), *Causes, Extent, Impact, and Costs of 1997–1998 Fires and Drought* (Jakarta, Indonesia: Asian Development Bank, 1999); R. Dennis and A. Hoffmann, *Large-Scale, Catastrophic Fires and Secondary Forests in Western Indonesia* (Bogor, Indonesia: Center for International Forestry Research, 2000).
174. UNEP, *Global Environment Outlook 2000.*
175. J. N. Abramowitz, "Sustaining the World's Forests," in Brown et al., *State of the World, 1998,* 20–41.
176. N. Dudley, *The Year the World Caught Fire* (Gland, Switzerland: World Wide Fund for Nature International, 1997); see also BAPPENAS and Asian Development Bank, *Extent and Costs of the 1997–1998 Fires and Drought in Indonesia* (Jakarta, Indonesia: BAPPENAS; Manila: Asian Development Bank, 2000); C. V. Barber and J. Schweithelm, *Trial by Fire: Forest Fires and Forest Policy in Indonesia's Era of Crisis and Reform* (Washington, D.C.: World Resources Institute, 1999); Walton, *Is There a Future for Indonesia's Forests?*
177. Richards, *Internalising the Externalities of Tropical Forestry;* Seymour and Dubash, *The Right Conditions.*

Chapter 9. Overview Assessment

1. R. Estes, *The Tyranny of the Bottom Line: Why Corporations Make Good People Do Bad Things* (San Francisco: Berrett-Koehler, 1996).
2. D. M. Roodman, *The Natural Wealth of Nations: Harnessing the Market for the Environment* (New York: Norton, 1998).
3. A. P. G. de Moor, *Perverse Incentives: Hundreds of Billions of Dollars in Subsidies Now Harm the Economy, the Environment, Equity, and Trade* (San José, Costa Rica: Earth Council, 1997).
4. D. Maddison et al., *Blueprint 5: The True Costs of Road Transport* (London: Earthscan, 1996).
5. V. Smil and M. Yushi, *The Economic Costs of China's Environmental Degradation* (Boston: American Academy of Arts and Sciences, 1998).
6. M. A. Delucchi, *The Annualized Social Cost of Motor-Vehicle Use in the U.S., 1990–1991: Summary of Theory, Data, Methods, and Results* (Davis: University of California, Institute of Transportation Studies, 1997); T. Litman, *Transportation Cost Analysis: Techniques, Estimates, and Implications* (Victoria, British Columbia, Canada: Victoria Transport Policy Institute, 1996).
7. E. U. von Weizsacker, A. B. Lovins, and L. H. Lovins, *Factor Four: Doubling Wealth, Halving Resource Use* (London: Earthscan, 1997).
8. Australia Department of the Environment, Sport and Territories, *Subsidies to the Use of Natural Resources* (Canberra: Australia Department of the Environment, Sport and Territories, 1996).
9. P. Hawken, "Natural Capitalism," *Mother Jones* (March–April 1997): 40–54.

10. R. Heede, Rocky Mountain Institute, Snowmass, Colo., personal communication (letters of 23 July and 22 August 1997); A. B. Lovins, "Negawatts: Twelve Transitions, Eight Improvements, and One Distraction," *Energy Policy* (Snowmass, Colo.: Rocky Mountain Institute, April 1996).
11. R. S. McNamara, "A Vision for Our Nation and the World in the Twenty-First Century," in N. R. Goodwin, F. Ackerman, and D. Kiron, eds., *The Consumer Society* (London: Earthscan, 1997).

Chapter 10. What Shall We Do About It All?

1. Organisation for Economic Co-operation and Development (OECD), *Improving the Environment Through Reducing Subsidies, Part I: Summary and Policy Conclusions* (Paris: OECD, 1998); D. Pearce and D. von Finckenstein, *Advancing Subsidy Reforms: Towards a Viable Policy Package* (London: University College London, Centre for Social and Economic Research on the Global Environment, 1999); D. M. Roodman, *The Natural Wealth of Nations: Harnessing the Market for the Environment* (New York: Norton, 1998); C. van Beers and A. de Moor, *Scanning Subsidies and Policy Trends in Europe and Central Asia*, Environmental Information and Assessment Technical Report no. 2 (Nairobi, Kenya: United Nations Environment Programme, 1998); C. van Beers and J. C. J. M. van den Bergh, *Perseverance of Perverse Subsidies and Their Impact on Trade and the Environment* (Delft, Netherlands: Delft University of Technology, 2000).
2. J. O. Browder and B. J. Godfrey, *Rainforest Cities: Urbanization, Development, and Globalization of the Brazilian Amazon* (New York: Columbia University Press, 1997).
3. G. Chicilnisky and G. Heal, *Securitizing the Biosphere* (New York: Columbia University, Graduate School of Business, 1998); R. Pinkham, A. B. Lovins, and L. H. Lovins, *Let's Tap Water Efficiency Before Spending on Treatment* (Snowmass, Colo.: Rocky Mountain Institute, 1994).
4. R. J. P. Gale, S. R. Barg, and A. Gillis, eds., *Green Budget Reform: An International Casebook of Leading Practices* (London: Earthscan, 1995); International Institute for Sustainable Development (IISD), *Making Budgets Green: Leading Practices in Taxation and Subsidy Reform* (Winnipeg, Manitoba, Canada: IISD, 1994).
5. E. Drew, *The Corruption of American Politics: What Went Wrong and Why* (Secaucus, N.J.: Birch Lane Press, 1999).
6. Greenpeace, *Oiling the Machine: Fossil Fuel Dollars Funneled into the U.S. Political Process* (Washington, D.C.: Greenpeace, 1999); see also Friends of the Earth, *Dirty Little Secrets: Update 1998* (Washington, D.C.: Friends of the Earth, 1998); Friends of the Earth, Taxpayers for Common Sense, and U.S. Public Interest Research Group Education

Fund, *Paying for Pollution: How Taxpayers Subsidize Dangerous and Polluting Energy Programs (A Green Scissors Report)* (Washington, D.C.: Friends of the Earth, 2000).

7. Roodman, *Natural Wealth of Nations*.

8. R. Gelbspan, *The Heat Is On* (Reading, Mass.: Addison-Wesley, 1997).

9. Center for Responsive Politics, *Ten Myths About Money in Politics* (Washington, D.C.: Center for Responsive Politics, 1995); Shuldiner and T. Raymond, *Who's in the Lobby?* (Washington, D.C.: Center for Responsive Politics, 1998).

10. C. P. van Beers and A. P. G. de Moor, *Addicted to Subsidies* (The Hague, Netherlands: Institute for Research on Public Expenditure, 1999); Roodman, *Natural Wealth of Nations;* see also Gale, Barg, and Gillis, *Green Budget Reform;* IISD, *Making Budgets Green*.

11. S. Barg, "Eliminating Perverse Subsidies: What's the Problem?" in Organization for Economic Cooperation and Development (OECD), *Subsidies and Environment: Exploring the Linkages* (Paris: OECD, 1996), 23–41; see also C. F. Runge and T. Jones, "Subsidies, Tax Disincentives, and the Environment: An Overview and Synthesis," in OECD, *Subsidies and Environment,* 7–21.

12. C. Cuff, R. de Gennaro, and G. Kripke, *The Green Scissors Report: Cutting Wasteful and Environmentally Harmful Spending and Subsidies* (Washington, D.C.: Friends of the Earth and National Taxpayers Union Foundation, 1996); see also D. Erlandson, J. Few, and G. Kripke, *Dirty Little Secrets: Polluters Save While People Pay* (Washington, D.C.: Friends of the Earth, 1995).

13. S. Bernow et al., *Ecological Tax Reform* (Solomons: University of Maryland, Institute for Ecological Economics, 1996); M. J. Hamond et al., *Tax Waste, Not Work: How Changing What We Tax Can Lead to a Stronger Economy and a Cleaner Environment* (San Francisco: Redefining Progress, 1997); K. Schlegelmilch, ed., *Green Budget Reform in Europe: Countries at the Forefront* (Berlin: Springer-Verlag, 1998).

14. W. Sachs, R. Loske, and M. Linz, *Greening the North: A Post-Industrial Blueprint for Ecology and Equity* (London, Zed Books, 1998).

15. L. Schipper and G. Eriksson, "Taxation Policies Affecting Automobile Characteristics and Use in Western Europe, Japan, and the United States, 1970–1990," in D. Sperling and S. A. Shaheen, eds., *Transportation and Energy: Strategies for a Sustainable Transportation System* (Washington, D.C.: American Council for an Energy-Efficient Economy, 1995); see also National Research Council, *Toward a Sustainable Future: Addressing the Long-Term Effects of Motor Vehicle Transportation on Climate and Ecology* (Washington, D.C.: National Academy Press, 1997).

16. D. Fullerton, *A Conceptual Framework to Compare Environmental Tax Shift Policies* (San Francisco: Redefining Progress, 1998); G. E.

Metcalf, *A Distributional Analysis of an Environmental Tax Shift* (San Francisco: Redefining Progress, 1998); M. J. Hamond et al., *Tax Waste, Not Work.*

17. P. Hawken, A. Lovins, and L. H. Lovins, *Natural Capitalism: Creating the Next Industrial Revolution* (Boston: Little, Brown, 1999).
18. Barg, "Eliminating Perverse Subsidies."
19. Roodman, *Natural Wealth of Nations;* see also Erlandson, Few, and Kripke, *Dirty Little Secrets.*

Index

267